Undergraduate Topics in Computer Science

Undergraduate Topics in Computer Science (UTiCS) delivers high-quality instructional content for undergraduates studying in all areas of computing and information science. From core foundational and theoretical material to final-year topics and applications, UTiCS books take fresh, concise, and modern approach and are ideal for self-study or for a one- or two-semester course. The texts are all authored by established experts in their fields, reviewed by an international advisory board, and contain numerous examples and problems. Many include fully worked solutions.

For further volumes:
http://www.springer.com/series/7592

Kent D. Lee

Python
Programming
Fundamentals

 Springer

Dr. Kent D. Lee
Dept. Computer Science
Luther College
College Drive 700
52101 Decorah, IA
USA
kentdlee@luther.edu

ISSN 1863-7310
ISBN 978-1-84996-536-1   e-ISBN 978-1-84996-537-8
DOI 10.1007/978-1-84996-537-8
Springer London Dordrecht Heidelberg New York

British Library Cataloguing in Publication Data
A catalogue record for this book is available from the British Library

Library of Congress Control Number: 2010937477

Springer is part of Springer Science+Business Media (www.springer.com)

Preface

Computer Science is a creative, challenging, and rewarding discipline. Computer programmers, sometimes called software engineers, solve problems involving data: computing, moving, and handling large quantities of data are all tasks made easier or possible by computer programs. Money magazine ranked software engineer as the number one job in America in terms of flexibility, creativity, low stress levels, ease of entry, compensation, and job growth within the field [4].

Learning to program a computer is a skill that can bring you great enjoyment because of the creativity involved in designing and implementing a solution to a problem. Python is a good first language to learn because there is very little overhead in learning to write simple programs. Python also has many libraries available that make it easy to write some very interesting programs including programs in the areas of Computer Graphics and Graphical User Interfaces: two topics that are covered in this text.

In this text, students are taught to program by giving them many examples and practice exercises with solutions that they can work on in an interactive classroom environment. The interaction can be accomplished using a computer or using pen and paper. By making the classroom experience active, students reflect on and apply what they have read and heard in the classroom. By using a skill or concept right away, students quickly discover if they need more reinforcement of the concept, while teachers also get immediate feedback. There is a big difference between seeing a concept demonstrated and using it yourself and this text encourages applying concepts immediately to test understanding. This is vital in Computer Science since new skills and concepts build on what we have already learned.

In several places within this book there are examples presented that highlight patterns of programming. These patterns appear over and over in programs we write. In this text, patterns like the *Accumulator Pattern* and the *Guess and Check Pattern* are presented and exercises reinforce the recognition and application of these and other abstract patterns used in problem-solving. Learning a language is certainly one important goal of an introductory text, but acquiring the necessary problem-solving skills is even more important. Students learn to solve problems on their own by recognizing when certain patterns are relevant and then applying these patterns in their own programs.

Recent studies in Computer Science Education indicate the use of a debugger can greatly enhance a student's understanding of programming [1]. A debugger is a tool that lets the programmer inspect the state of a program at any point while it is executing. There is something about actually seeing what is happening as a program is executed that helps make an abstract concept more concrete. This text introduces students to the use of a debugger and includes exercises and examples that show students how to use a debugger to discover how programs work.

There are additional resources available for instructors teaching from this text. They include lecture slides and a sample schedule of lectures for a semester long course. Solutions to all programming exercises are also available upon request. Visit http://cs.luther.edu/~leekent/CS1 for more information.

Python is a good language for teaching introductory Computer Science because it is very accessible and can be incrementally taught so students can start to write programs before having to learn the whole language. However, at the same time, Python is also a developing language. Python 3.1 was recently released to the public. This release of Python included many performance enhancements which were very good additions to the language. There were also some language issues with version 2.6 and earlier that were cleaned up at the same time that were not backwards compatible. The result is that not all Python 2 programs are compatible with Python 3 and vice versa. Because both Python 2 and Python 3 are in use today, this text will point out the differences between the two versions where appropriate. These differences will be described by inset boxes titled **Python 2 ⤳ 3** within the text where the differences are first encountered.

It is recommended that students reading this text use Python 3.1 or later for writing and running their programs. All Python programs presented in the text are Python 3 programs. The libraries used in this text all work with Python 3. However, there may be some libraries that have not been ported to Python 3 that a particular instructor would like to use. In terms of what is covered in this text, the differences between Python 2 and 3 are pretty minor and either language implementation will work to use with the text.

Acknowledgments

I'd like to thank David Ranum, who encouraged me to write a text on introductory programming that included some of the projects I've developed, and Brad Miller, who suggested we try Python as an introductory language. It's wonderful to work with colleagues that care as much as I do about teaching students a rewarding and creative discipline. But most importantly, I would like to thank the students who have taken classes from me. Teaching has given me back much more than the many hours I have invested in it and seeing a student grow in his or her programming skills is its own reward.

I would especially like to thank Nathaniel Lee, who not only let his dad teach him, but was a great sounding board and test subject for this text. Thank you, Nathan, for all your valuable feedback and for your willingness to learn.

Credits

At times in this text Microsoft Windows is referred to when installing software. Windows is a registered trademark of Microsoft Corporation in the United States and other countries. Mac OS X is referred to at times within this text. Mac and Mac OS are trademarks of Apple Inc., registered in the U.S. and other countries. The Garmin Forerunner and Garmin Training Center are referred to in Chap. 4. Garmin is a registered trademark, and Forerunner and Training Center are trademarks of Garmin Ltd. or its subsidiaries in the United States and other countries.

This book also introduces readers to Wing IDE 101, which is used in examples throughout the text. Wing IDE 101 is a free simplified edition of Wing IDE Professional, a full-featured integrated development environment designed specifically for Python. For more information on Wing IDE, see www.wingware.com. Wingware and Wing IDE are trademarks or registered trademarks of Wingware in the United States and other countries.

Suggestions

I welcome suggestions for future printings of this text. If you like this text and have suggestions for future printings, please write up your suggestion(s) and email them to me. The more complete your write up, the more likely I will be to consider your suggestion. If I select your suggestion for a future printing I'll be sure to include your name in the preface as a contributor to the text. Suggestions can be emailed to kentdlee@luther.edu or kentdlee@gmail.com.

Contents

Introduction

1

The intent of this text is to introduce you to computer programming using the Python programming language. Learning to program is a bit like learning to play piano, although quite a bit easier since we won't have to program while keeping time according to a time signature. Programming is a creative process so we'll be working on developing some creative skills. At the same time, there are certain patterns that can be used over and over again in this creative process. The goal of this text and the course you are taking is to get you familiar with these patterns and show you how they can be used in programs. After working through this text and studying and practicing you will be able to identify which of these patterns are needed to implement a program for a particular task and you will be able to apply these patterns to solve new and interesting problems.

As human beings our intelligent behavior hinges on our ability to match patterns. We are pattern-matchers from the moment we are born. We watch and listen to our parents and siblings to learn how to react to situations. Babies watch us to learn to talk, walk, eat, and even to smile. All these behaviors are learned through pattern matching. Computer Science is no different. Many of the programs we create in Computer Science are based on just a few patterns that we learn early in our education as programmers. Once we've learned the patterns we become effective programmers by learning to apply the patterns to new situations. As babies we are wired to learn quickly with a little practice. As we grow older we can learn to use patterns that are more abstract. That is what Computer Science is all about: the application of abstract patterns to solve new and interesting problems.

PRACTICE is important. There is a huge difference between reading something in this text or understanding what is said during a lecture and being able to do it yourself. At times this may be frustrating, but with practice you will get better at it. As you read the text make sure you take time to do the practice exercises. Practice exercises are clearly labeled with a gray background color. These exercises are your chance to use a concept that you have just learned. Answers to practice exercises are included at the end of each chapter so you can check your answers.

Fig. 1.1 The Python interpreter

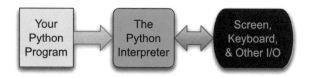

1.1
The Python Programming Language

Python is the programming language this text uses to introduce computer programming. To run a Python program you need an interpreter. The Python interpreter is a program that reads a Python program and then executes the statements found in it as depicted in Fig. 1.1. While studying this text you will write many Python programs. Once your program is written and you are ready to try it you will tell the Python interpreter to execute your Python program so you can see what it does.

For this process to work you must first have Python installed on your computer. Python is free and available for download from the internet. The next section of this chapter will take you through downloading and installing Python. Within the last few years there were some changes to the Python programming language between Python 2 and Python 3. The text will describe differences between the two versions of Python as they come up. In terms of learning to program, the differences between the two versions of Python are pretty minor.

To write Python programs you need an editor to type in the program. It is convenient to have an editor that is designed for writing Python programs. An editor that is specifically designed for writing programs is called an IDE or Integrated Development Environment. An IDE is more than just an editor. It provides highlighting and indentation that can help as you write a program. It also provides a way to run your program straight from the editor. Since you will typically run your program many times as you write it, having a way to run it quickly is handy. This text uses the Wing IDE 101 in many of its examples. This IDE is simple to install and is free for educational use. Wing IDE 101 is available for Mac OS X, Microsoft Windows, and Linux.

When learning to program and even as a seasoned professional, it can be advantageous to run your program using a tool called a debugger. A debugger allows you to run your program, stop it at any point, and inspect the state of the program to help you better understand what is happening as your program executes. The Wing IDE includes an integrated debugger for that purpose. There are certainly other IDEs that might be used and nothing presented in this text precludes you from using something else. Some examples of IDEs for Python development include Netbeans, Eclipse, Eric, and IDLE. Eric's debugger is really quite nice and could serve as an alternative to Wing should Wing IDE 101 not be an option for some reason.

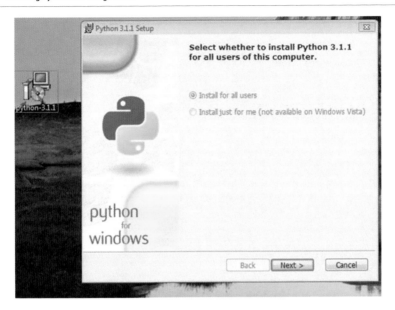

Fig. 1.2 Installing Python on Windows

1.2
Installing Python and Wing IDE 101

To begin writing Python programs on your own computer, you need to have Python in-stalled. There were some significant changes between Python 2.6 and Python 3 which in-cluded a few changes that make programs written for version 3 incompatible with programs written for version 2.6 and vice versa. If you are using this book as part of an introductory course, your instructor may prefer you install one version or the other. Example programs in this text are written using Python 3 syntax but the differences between Python 2 and 3 are few enough that it is possible to use either Python 2 or 3 when writing programs for the exercises in this text. Inset boxes titled **Python 2 ⤳ 3** will highlight the differences when they are first encountered in the text.

    If you are running Windows you will likely have to install Python yourself. You can get the installation package from http://python.org. Click the *DOWNLOAD* link on the page. Then pick the appropriate installer package. Most will want to download the *Python 3.1 (or newer) Windows x86 MSI Installer* package. Once you have downloaded it, double-click the package and take all the defaults to install it as pictured in Fig. 1.2.

    If you have a Mac, then Python is already installed and may be the version you want to use, depending on how new your Mac is. You can find out which version of Python you have by opening a terminal window. Go to the Applications folder and look in the Utilities sub-folder for the Terminal application. Start a terminal and in the window type *python*.

You should see something like this:

```
Kent's Mac> python
Python 3.1.1 (r311:74543, Aug 24 2009, 18:44:04)
[GCC 4.0.1 (Apple Inc. build 5493)] on darwin
Type "help", "copyright", "credits" or "license" for more info.
>>>
```

You can press and hold the control key (i.e. the ctrl key) and press 'd' to exit Python or just close the terminal window. If you do not have version 3.1 or newer installed on your Mac you may wish to download the *Python 3.1 (or newer) MacOS Installer Disk Image* from the http://python.org web site. Once the file is downloaded you can double-click the disk image file and then look for the *Python.mpkg* file and double-click it as pictured in Fig. 1.3. You will need an administrator password to install it which in most cases is just your own password.

If you have a Mac you will also need the X11 Server installed. The X11 Server, called the XQuartz project, is needed to run Wing IDE 101 on a Mac. Directions for installing the X11 Server can be found at http://wingware.com/doc/howtos/osx. The server is provided by Apple and the XQuartz developers and is freely distributed. The X11 server has shipped with Mac OS X since version 10.5.

While you don't need an IDE like Wing to write and run Python programs, the debugger support that an IDE like Wing provides will help you understand how Python programs work. It is also convenient to write your programs in an IDE so you can run them quickly and easily. To install Wing IDE 101 you need to go to the http://wingware.com web site.

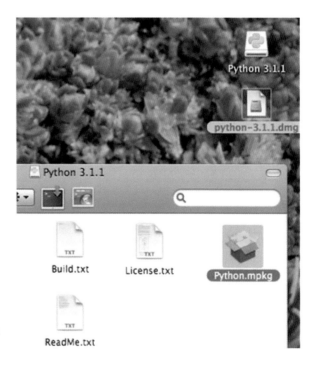

Fig. 1.3 Installing Python on Mac OS X

Fig. 1.4   Installing Wing IDE 101 on Windows

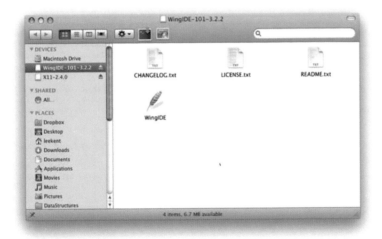

Fig. 1.5   Installing Wing IDE 101 on a Mac

Find the *Download* link at the top of the web page and select *Wing IDE 101* to download the installation package. If you are installing on a Mac, pick the Mac version. If you are installing on Windows, pick the Windows version. Download and run the installation package if you are using Windows. Running the Windows installer should display an installer window like that pictured in Fig. 1.4. Take all the defaults to install it.

Fig. 1.6 Configuring Wing's
Python interpreter

If you are installing Wing IDE 101 on a Mac then you need to mount the disk image. To do this you must double-click a file that looks like *wingide-101-3.2.2-1-i386.dmg*. After double-clicking that file you will have a mounted disk image of the same name, minus the .dmg extension). If you open a Finder window for that disk image you will see a window that looks like Fig. 1.5. Drag the Wing IDE icon to your Applications folder and you can add it to your dock if you like.

Configuring Wing

If you look at Fig. 1.8 you will see that the Python interpreter shows up as *Python 3.1.1.* When you install Wing, you should open it and take a look at your *Python Shell* tab. If you see the wrong version of Python then you need to configure Wing to use the correct Python Shell. To do this you must open Wing and go to the Edit menu. Under the Edit menu, select *Configure Python. . .* and type in the appropriate interpreter. If you are using a Mac and wish to use version 3.1 then you would type *python3.1*. Figure 1.6 shows you what this dialog box looks like and what you would type in on a Mac. In Windows, you should click the browse button and find python.exe. This will be in a directory like *C:\Python31* if you chose the defaults when installing.

There is one more configuration change that should be made. The logical flow of a Python program depends on the program's indentation. Since indentation is so important, Wing can provide a visual cue to the indentation in your program called an *indent guide*. These indent guides will not show up in this chapter, but they will in subsequent chapters. Go to the Edit menu again and select *Preferences*. Then click on the *Indentation* selection in the dialog box as shown in Fig. 1.7. Select the checkbox that says *Show Indent Guides*.

Fig. 1.7 Configuring indent guides

Fig. 1.8 The Wing IDE

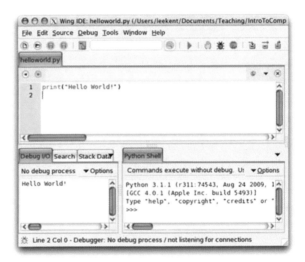

That's it! Whether you are a Mac or Windows user if you've followed the directions in this section you should have Python and Wing IDE 101 installed and ready to use. The next section shows you how to write your first program so you can test your installation of Wing IDE 101 and Python.

1.3
Writing Your First Program

To try out the installation of your IDE and Python you should write a program and run it. The traditional first program is the *Hello World* program. This program simply prints "*Hello World*!" to the screen when it is run. This can be done with one statement in Python.

Open your IDE if you have not already done so. If you are using Windows you can select it by going to the Start menu in the bottom left hand corner and selecting *All Programs*. Look for *Wing IDE 101* under the Start menu and select it. If you are using a Mac, go to the Applications folder and double-click the Wing IDE icon or click on it in your dock if you installed the icon on your dock. Once you've done this you will have a window that looks like Fig. 1.8.

In the IDE window you go to the *File* menu and select *New* to get a new edit tab within the IDE. You then enter one statement, the print statement shown in Fig. 1.8 to print *Hello World!* to the screen. After entering the one line program you can run it by clicking the green debug button (i.e. that button that looks like a bug) at the top of the window. You will be prompted to save the file. Click the *Save Selected Files* button and save it as *helloworld.py*. You should then see *Hello World!* printed at the bottom of the IDE window in the *Debug I/O* tab.

The print statement that you see in this program prints the string "Hello World!" to standard output. Text printed to standard output appears in the *Debug I/O* tab in the Wing IDE. That should do it. If it doesn't you'll need to re-read the installation instructions either here or on the websites you downloaded Python and Wing IDE from or you can find someone to help you install them properly. An IDE is used in examples and practice exercises throughout this text so you'll need a working installation of an IDE and Python to make full use of this text.

Python 2 ⤳ 3

Prior to Python version 3 print statements were different than many other statements in Python because they lacked parentheses[8]. Parentheses were added to print statement in Python 3. So,

```
print "Hello World!"
```

became

```
print("Hello World!")
```

in Python 3 and later. A print statement prints its data and then moves to a new line unless the newline character is suppressed. Before Python 3 the newline was suppressed by adding a comma to the end of the print statement.

```
print "Hello",
print " World!"
```

In Python 3 the same can be done by specifying an empty line end.

```
print("Hello",end="")
print(" World!")
```

1.4
What is a Computer?

So you've written your first program and you've been *using* a computer all your life. But, what is a computer, really? A computer is composed of a Central Processing Unit (abbreviated CPU), memory, and Input/Output (abbreviated I/O) devices. A screen is an output device. A mouse is an input device. A hard drive is an I/O device.

The CPU is the brain of the computer. It is able to store values in memory, retrieve values from memory, add/subtract two numbers, compare two numbers and do one of two

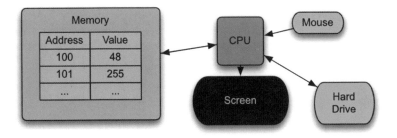

Fig. 1.9 Conceptual view of a computer

things depending on the outcome of that comparison. The CPU can also control which instruction it will execute next. Normally there are a list of instructions, one after another, that the CPU executes. Sometimes the CPU may jump to a different location within that list of instructions depending on the outcome of some comparison.

That's it. A CPU can't do much more than what was described in the previous paragraph. CPU's aren't intelligent by any leap of the imagination. In fact, given such limited power, it's amazing how much we are able to do with a computer. Everything we use a computer for is built on the work of many, many people who have built layers and layers of programs that make our life easier.

The memory of a computer is a place where values can be stored and retrieved. It is a relatively fast storage device, but it loses its contents as soon as the computer is turned off. It is called volatile store. The memory of a computer is divided into different locations. Each location within memory has an address and can hold a value. Figure 1.9 shows the contents of memory location 100 containing the number 48.

The hard drive is non-volatile storage or sometimes called persistent storage. Values can be stored and retrieved from the hard drive, but it is relatively slow compared to the memory and CPU. However, it retains its contents even when the power is off.

In a computer, everything is stored as a sequence of 0's and 1's. For instance, the string 01010011 can be interpreted as the decimal number 83. It can also represent the capital letter 'S'. How we interpret these strings of 0's and 1's is up to us. We can tell the CPU how to interpret a location in memory by which instruction we tell the CPU to execute. Some instructions treat 01010011 as the number 83. Other instructions treat it as the letter 'S'.

One digit in a binary number is called a *bit*. Eight bits grouped together are called a *byte*. Four bytes grouped together are called a *word*. 2^{10} bytes are called a *kilobyte* (i.e. KB). 2^{10} kilobytes are called a *megabyte* (i.e. MB). 2^{10} megabytes are called a *gigabyte* (i.e. GB). 2^{10} gigabytes are called a *terabyte* (i.e. TB). Currently memories on computers are usually in the one to eight GB range. Hard Drives on computers are usually in the 500 GB to two TB range.

Binary	Dec	Char	Binary	Dec	Char	Binary	Dec	Char
0100000	32	␣	1000000	64	@	1100000	96	`
0100001	33	!	1000001	65	A	1100001	97	a
0100010	34	"	1000010	66	B	1100010	98	b
0100011	35	#	1000011	67	C	1100011	99	c
0100100	36	$	1000100	68	D	1100100	100	d
0100101	37	%	1000101	69	E	1100101	101	e
0100110	38	&	1000110	70	F	1100110	102	f
0100111	39	'	1000111	71	G	1100111	103	g
0101000	40	(	1001000	72	H	1101000	104	h
0101001	41	)	1001001	73	I	1101001	105	i
0101010	42	*	1001010	74	J	1101010	106	j
0101011	43	+	1001011	75	K	1101011	107	k
0101100	44	,	1001100	76	L	1101100	108	l
0101101	45	-	1001101	77	M	1101101	109	m
0101110	46	.	1001110	78	N	1101110	110	n
0101111	47	/	1001111	79	O	1101111	111	o
0110000	48	0	1010000	80	P	1110000	112	p
0110001	49	1	1010001	81	Q	1110001	113	q
0110010	50	2	1010010	82	R	1110010	114	r
0110011	51	3	1010011	83	S	1110011	115	s
0110100	52	4	1010100	84	T	1110100	116	t
0110101	53	5	1010101	85	U	1110101	117	u
0110110	54	6	1010110	86	V	1110110	118	v
0110111	55	7	1010111	87	W	1110111	119	w
0111000	56	8	1011000	88	X	1111000	120	x
0111001	57	9	1011001	89	Y	1111001	121	y
0111010	58	:	1011010	90	Z	1111010	122	z
0111011	59	;	1011011	91	[	1111011	123	{
0111100	60	<	1011100	92	\	1111100	124		
0111101	61	=	1011101	93	]	1111101	125	}
0111110	62	>	1011110	94	^	1111110	126	~
0111111	63	?	1011111	95	_	1111111	127	DEL

Fig. 1.10   The ASCII table

1.5
Binary Number Representation

Each digit in a decimal number represents a power of 10. The right-most digit is the number of ones, the next digit is the number of 10's, and so on. To interpret integers as binary numbers we use powers of 2 just as we use powers of 10 when interpreting integers as decimal numbers. The right-most digit of a binary number represents the number of times $2^0 = 1$ is needed in the representation of the integer. Our choices are only 0 or 1 (i.e. we can use one 2^0 if the number is odd), because 0 and 1 are the only choices for digits in a binary number. The next right-most is $2^1 = 2$ and so on. So 01010011 is $0 * 2^7 + 1 * 2^6 + 0 * 2^5 + 1 * 2^4 + 0 * 2^3 + 0 * 2^2 + 1 * 2^1 + 1 * 2^0 = 83$. Any binary number can be converted to its decimal representation by following the steps given above. Any decimal number can be converted to its binary representation by subtracting the largest power of two that is less than the number, marking that digit as a 1 in the binary number and then repeating the process with the remainder after subtracting that power of two from the number.

Practice 1.1 What is the decimal equivalent of the binary number 01010101_2?

Example 1.1 There is an elegant algorithm for converting a decimal number to a binary number. You need to carry out long division by 2 to use this algorithm. If we want to convert 83_{10} to binary then we can repeatedly perform long division by 2 on the quotient of each result until the quotient is zero. Then, the string of the remainders that were accumulated while dividing make up the binary number. For example,

$$83/2 = 41 \quad \textit{remainder 1}$$
$$41/2 = 20 \quad \textit{remainder 1}$$
$$20/2 = 10 \quad \textit{remainder 0}$$
$$10/2 = 5 \quad \textit{remainder 0}$$
$$5/2 = 2 \quad \textit{remainder 1}$$
$$2/2 = 1 \quad \textit{remainder 0}$$
$$1/2 = 0 \quad \textit{remainder 1}$$

The remainders from last to first are 1010011_2 which is 83_{10}. This set of steps is called an algorithm. An algorithm is like a recipe for doing a computation. We can use this algorithm any time we want to convert a number from decimal to binary.

Practice 1.2 Use the conversion algorithm to find the binary representation of 58_{10}.

To add two numbers in binary we perform addition just the way we would in base 10 format. So, for instance, $0011_2 + 0101_2 = 1000_2$. In decimal format this is $3 + 5 = 8$. In binary format, any time we add two 1's, the result is 0 and 1 is carried.

To represent negative numbers in a computer we would like to pick a format so that when a binary number and its opposite are added together we get zero as the result. For this to work we must have a specific number of bits that we are willing to work with.

Typically thirty-two or sixty-four bit addition is used. To keep things simple we'll do some eight bit addition in this text. Consider $00000011_2 = 3_{10}$.

It turns out that the 2's complement of a number is the negative of that number in binary. For example, the numbers $3_{10} = 00000011_2$ and $-3_{10} = 11111101_2$. 11111101_2 is the 2's complement of 00000011. It can be found by reversing all the 1's and 0's (which is called the 1's complement) and then adding 1 to the result.

Example 1.2 Adding 00000011 and 11111101 together gives us

$$\begin{array}{r} 00000011 \\ +11111101 \\ \hline = 100000000 \end{array}$$

This only works if we limit ourselves to 8 bit addition. The carried 1 is in the ninth digit and is thrown away. The result is 0.

Practice 1.3 If $01010011_2 = 83_{10}$, then what does -83_{10} look like in binary? HINT: Take the 2's complement of 83 or figure out what to add to 01010011_2 to get 0.

If binary $11111101_2 = -3_{10}$ does that mean that 253 can't be represented? The answer is yes and no. It turns out that 11111101_2 can represent -3_{10} or it can represent 253_{10} depending on whether we want to represent both negative and positive values or just positive values. The CPU instructions we choose to operate on these values determine what types of values they are. We can choose to use signed integers in our programs or unsigned integers. The type of value is determined by us when we write the program.

Typically, 4 bytes, or one word, are used to represent an integer. This means that 2^{32} different signed integers can be represented from -2^{31} to $2^{31} - 1$. In fact, Python can handle more integers than this but it switches to a different representation to handle integers outside this range. If we chose to use unsigned integers we could represent numbers from 0 to $2^{32} - 1$ using one word of memory.

Not only can 01010011_2 represent 83_{10}, it can also represent a character in the alphabet. If 01010011_2 is to be interpreted as a character almost all computers use a convention called ASCII which stands for the American Standard Code for Information Interchange [12]. This standard equates numbers from 0 to 127 to characters. In fact, numbers from 128 to 255 also define extended ASCII codes which are used for some character graphics. Each ASCII character is contained in one byte. Figure 1.10 shows the characters and their equivalent integer representations.

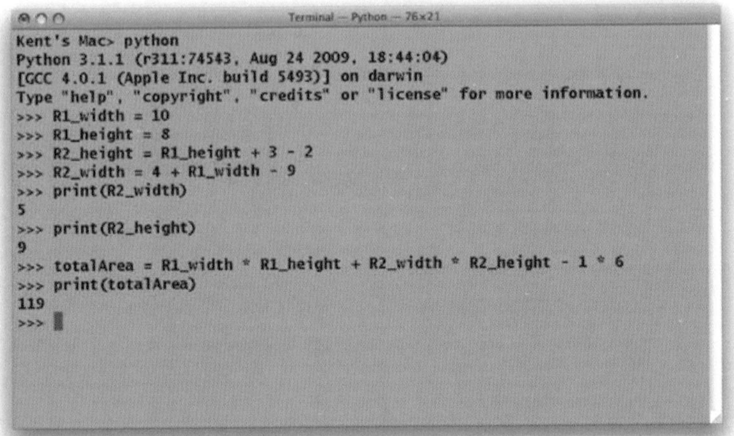

```
●○○                    Terminal — Python — 76×21
Kent's Mac> python
Python 3.1.1 (r311:74543, Aug 24 2009, 18:44:04)
[GCC 4.0.1 (Apple Inc. build 5493)] on darwin
Type "help", "copyright", "credits" or "license" for more information.
>>> R1_width = 10
>>> R1_height = 8
>>> R2_height = R1_height + 3 - 2
>>> R2_width = 4 + R1_width - 9
>>> print(R2_width)
5
>>> print(R2_height)
9
>>> totalArea = R1_width * R1_height + R2_width * R2_height - 1 * 6
>>> print(totalArea)
119
>>>
```

Fig. 1.11 The Python shell

Practice 1.4 What is the binary and decimal equivalent of the space character?

Practice 1.5 What determines how the bytes in memory are interpreted? In other words, what makes 4 bytes an integer as opposed to four ASCII characters?

1.6
What is a Programming Language?

If we were to have to write programs as sequences of numbers we wouldn't get very far. It would be so tedious to program that no one would want to be a programmer. In the spring of 2006 Money Magazine ranked Software Engineer [4] as the number one job in America in terms of overall satisfaction which included things like compensation, growth, and stress-levels. So it must not be all that tedious.

A programming language is really a set of tools that allow us to program at a much higher level than the 0's and 1's that exist at the lowest levels of the computer. Python and the Wing IDE provides us with a couple of tools. The lower right corner of the Wing

Fig. 1.12 Overlapping
rectangles

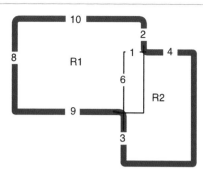

IDE has a tab labeled *Python Shell*. The shell allows programmers to interact with the
Python interpreter. The interpreter is a program that interprets the programs we write. If
you have a Mac or Linux computer you can also start the Python interpreter by opening
up a terminal window. If you use Windows you can start a Command Prompt by looking
under the Accessories program group. Typing *python* at a command prompt starts a Python
interpreter as shown in Fig. 1.11.

Consider computing the area of a shape constructed of overlapping regular polygons.
In Fig. 1.12 all angles are right angles and all distances are in meters. Our job is to
figure out the area in square meters. The lighter lines in the middle help us figure out
how to compute the area. We can compute the area of the two rectangles and then subtract one of the overlapping parts since otherwise the overlapping part would be counted
twice.

This can be computed on your calculator of course. The Python Shell is like a calculator
and Fig. 1.11 shows how it can be used to compute the area of the shape. The first line
sets a variable called *R1_width* to the value of 10. Then *R1_height* is set to 8. We can
store a value in memory and give it a name. This is called an *assignment statement*. Your
calculator can store values. So can Python. In Python these values can be given names that
mean something in our program. *R1_height* is the name we gave to the height of the R1
rectangle. Anytime we want to retrieve that value we can just write *R1_height* and Python
will retrieve its value for us.

Practice 1.6 Open up the Wing IDE or a command prompt and try out the assignment and print statements shown in Fig. 1.11. Make sure to type the statements into
the python shell. You DO NOT type the >>>. That is the Python shell prompt and
is printed by Python. Notice that you can't fix a line once you have pressed enter.
This will be remedied soon.

Practice 1.7 Take a moment and answer these questions from the material you just read.

1. What is an assignment statement?
2. How do we retrieve a value from memory?
3. Can we retrieve a value before it has been stored? What happens when we try to do that?

Interacting directly with the Python shell is a good way to quickly see how something works. However, it is also painful because mistakes can't be undone. In the next section we'll go back to writing programs in an editor so they can be changed and run as many times as we like. In fact, this is how most Python programming is done. Write a little, then test it by running it. Then write a little more and run it again. This is called prototyping and is an effective way to write programs. You should write all your programs using prototyping while reading this text. Write a little, then try it. That's an effective way to program and takes less time than writing a lot and then trying to figure out what went wrong.

1.7
Hexadecimal and Octal Representation

Most programmers do not have to work with binary number representations. Programming languages let programmers write numbers in base 10 and they do the conversion for us. However, once in a while a programmer must be concerned about the binary representation of a number. As we've seen, converting between binary and decimal isn't hard, but it is somewhat tedious. The difficulty arises because 10 is not a power of 2. Converting between base 10 and base 2 would be a lot easier if 10 were a power of 2. When computer programmers have to work with binary numbers they don't want to have to write out all the zeroes and ones. This would obviously be tedious as well. Instead of converting numbers to base 10 or writing all numbers in binary, computer programmers have adopted two other representations for binary numbers, base 16 (called hexadecimal) and base 8 (called octal).

In hexadecimal each digit of a number can represent sixteen different binary numbers. The sixteen hexadecimal digits are 0–9, and A–F. Since 16 is a power of 2, there are exactly 4 binary digits that make up each hexadecimal digit. So, 0000_2 is 0_{16} and 1111_2 is F_{16}. So, the binary number 10101110 is AE in hexadecimal notation and 256 in octal notation. If we wish to convert either of these two numbers to binary format the conversion is just as easy. 1010_2 is A_{16} for instance. Again, these conversions can be done quickly because there are four binary digits in each hexadecimal digit and three binary digits in each octal digit.

Example 1.3 To convert the binary number 01010011_2 to hexadecimal we have only to break the number into two four digit binary numbers 0101_2 and 0011_2. $0101_2 = 5_{16}$ and $0011_2 = 3_{16}$. So the hexadecimal representation of 01010011_2 is 53_{16}.

Python has built-in support of hexadecimal numbers. If you want to express a number in hexadecimal form you preface it with a $0x$ to signify that it is a hexadecimal number. For instance, here is how Python responds to $0x53$ being entered into the Python shell.

```
Kent's Mac> python
Python 3.1.1 (r311:74543, Aug 24 2009, 18:44:04)
[GCC 4.0.1 (Apple Inc. build 5493)] on darwin
Type "help", "copyright", "credits" or "license" for more info.
>>> 0x53
83
>>> 0o123
83
>>>
```

Since $8 = 2^3$, each digit of an octal number represents three binary digits. The octal digits are 0–7. The number $01010011_2 = 123_8$. When converting a binary number to octal or hexadecimal we must be sure to start with the right-most bits. Since there are only 8 bits in 01010011 the left-most octal digit corresponds to the left-most two binary digits. The other two octal digits each have three binary digits. Again, Python has built-in support for representing octal digits. Writing a number with a leading zero and the letter o means that it is in octal format. So $0o123$ is the Python representation of 123_8 and it is equal to 83_{10}.

Python 2 ↝ 3

Originally, octal numbers were written with a leading zero (i.e. 0123). In Python 3, octal numbers must be preceded with a zero and the letter o (i.e. 0o123).[8]

Practice 1.8 Convert the number 58_{10} to binary and then to hexadecimal and octal.

1.8
Writing Your Second Program

Writing programs is an error-prone activity. Programmer's almost never write a non-trivial program perfectly the first time. As programmers we need a tool like an Integrated Development Environment (i.e. IDE) that helps us find and fix our mistakes. Going to the *File* menu of the Wing IDE window and selecting *New* opens a new edit pane. An edit pane can be used to write a program but it won't execute each line as you press enter. When writing

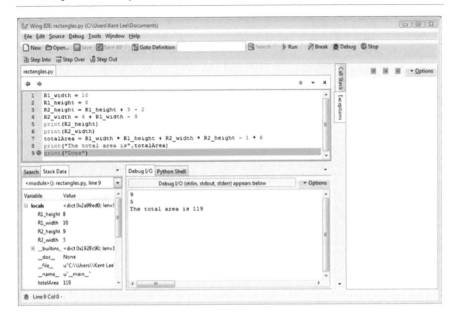

Fig. 1.13 The Wing IDE

a program we can write a little bit and then execute it in the Python interpreter by pressing *F5* on the keyboard or by clicking the debug button.

When we write a program we will almost certainly have to debug it. *Debugging* is the word we use when we have to find errors in our program. Errors are very common and typically you will find a lot of them before the program works perfectly. Debugging refers to removing bugs from a program. Bugs are another name for errors. The use of the words *bug* and *debugging* in Computer Science dates back to at least 1952 and probably much earlier. Wikipedia has an interesting discussion of the word *debugging* if you want to know more. While you can use the Python Shell for some limited debugging, a *debugger* is a program that assists you in debugging your program. Figure 1.13 has a picture of the Wing IDE with the program we've been working on typed into the editor part of the IDE. To use the debugger we can click the mouse in the area where the red circle appears next to the numbers. This is called setting a breakpoint. A breakpoint tells Python to stop running when Python reaches that statement in the program. The program is not finished when it reaches that step, but it stops so you can inspect the state of the program.

The state of the program is contained in the bottom left corner of the IDE. This shows you the *Stack Data* which is just another name for the program's state. You can see that the variables that were defined in the program are all located here along with their values at the present time.

Practice 1.9 Create an edit pane within the Wing IDE and write the program as it appears in Fig. 1.13. Write a few lines, then run it by pressing *F5* on the keyboard or clicking on the *Debug* button. The first time you press *F5* you will be prompted to save the program. Make sure you save your program where you can find it later.

Try setting a break point by clicking where the circle appears next to the numbers in Fig. 1.13. You should see a red circle appear if you did it right. Then run the program again to see that it stops at the breakpoint as it appears in Fig. 1.13. You can stop a program at any point by setting a breakpoint on that line. When the debugger stops at a breakpoint it stops before the statement is executed. You must click the *Debug* button, not the *Run* button to get it to stop at breakpoints.

Look at the Stack Data to inspect the state of the program just before the word *Done* is printed. Make sure it matches what you see here. Then continue the execution by clicking the Debug button or pressing *F5* again to see that *Done* is printed.

1.9
Syntax Errors

Not every error is found using a debugger. Sometimes errors are syntax errors. A syntax error occurs when we write something that is not part of the Python language. Many times a syntax error can occur if we forget to write something. For instance, if we forget a parenthesis or a double quote is left out it will not be a correct Python program. Syntax errors are typically easier to find than bugs in our program because Python can flag them right away for us. These errors are usually highlighted right away by the IDE or interpreter. Syntax errors are those errors that are reported before the program starts executing. You can tell its a syntax error in Wing because there will not be any *Stack Data*. Since a syntax error shows up before the program runs, the program is not currently executing and therefore there is not state information in the stack data. When a syntax error is reported the editor or Python will typically indicate the location of the error *after* it actually occurs so the best way to find syntax errors is to look backwards from where the error is first reported.

Example 1.4 Forgetting a parenthesis is a common syntax error.

```
print(R2_height
```

This is not valid syntax in Python since the right parenthesis is missing. If we were to try to run a Python program that contains this line, the Python interpreter complains that this is not valid syntax. Figure 1.14 shows how the Wing IDE tells us about this syntax error. Notice that the Wing IDE announces that the syntax error occurs on the line after where it actually occurred.

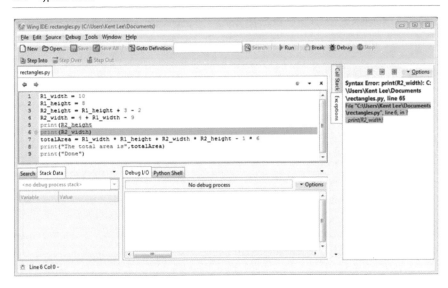

```
Wing IDE: rectangles.py (C:\Users\Kent Lee\Documents)
File  Edit  Source  Debug  Tools  Window  Help
New   Open...   Save   Save All     Goto Definition                    Search   Run   Break   Debug   Stop
Step Into   Step Over   Step Out

rectangles.py                                                          Call Stack         Options
                                                                   Syntax Error: print(R2_width): C:
     1   R1_width = 10                                             \Users\Kent Lee\Documents
     2   R1_height = 5                                             \rectangles.py, line 65
     3   R2_height = R1_height + 3 - 2                             File "C:\Users\Kent Lee\Documents
     4   R2_width = 4 + R1_width - 9                               \rectangles.py", line 6, in ?
     5   print(R2_height                                            print(R2_width)
     6   print(R2_width)
     7   totalArea = R1_width * R1_height + R2_width * R2_height - 1 * 6
     8   print("The total area is",totalArea)
     9   print("Done")

Search  Stack Data                    Debug I/O   Python Shell
<no debug process stack>                          No debug process            Options
Variable        Value

Line 6 Col 0 -
```

Fig. 1.14 A syntax error

There are other types of errors we can have in our programs. Syntax errors are perhaps the easiest errors to find. All other errors can be grouped into the category of *run-time errors*. Syntax errors are detected before the program runs. Run-time errors are detected while the program is running. Unfortunately, run-time errors are sometimes much harder to find than syntax errors. Many run-time errors are caused by the use of invalid operations being applied to values in our programs. It is important to understand what types of values we can use in our programs and what operations are valid for each of these types. That's the topic of the next section.

1.10
Types of Values

Earlier in this chapter we found that bytes in memory can be interpreted in different ways. The way bytes in memory are interpreted is determined by the *type* of the value or object and the operations we apply to these values. Each value in Python is called an object. Each object is of a particular type. There are several data types in Python. These include integer (called *int* in Python), *float*, boolean (called *bool* in Python), string (called *str* in Python), *list*, *tuple*, *set*, dictionary (called *dict* in Python), and *None*.

In the next chapters we'll cover each of these types and discuss the operations that apply to them. Each type of data and the operations it supports is covered when it is needed to learn a new programming skill. The sections on each of these types can also serve as a reference for you as you continue working through the text. You may find yourself coming back to the sections describing these types and their operations over and over

Fig. 1.15 A reference

R1_width

again. Reviewing types and their operations is a common practice among programmers as
they design and write new programs.

1.11
The Reference Type and Assignment Statements

There is one type in Python that is typically not seen, but nevertheless is important to
understand. It is called the reference type. A reference is a pointer that points to an object.
A pointer is the address of an object. Each object in memory is stored at a unique address
and a reference is a pointer that points to an object.

An assignment statement makes a reference point to an object. The general form of an
assignment statement is:

```
<identifier> = <expression>
```

An *identifier* is any letters, digits, or underscores written without spaces between them. The
identifier must begin with a letter or underscore. It cannot start with a digit. The *expression*
is any expression that when evaluated results in one of the *types* described in Sect. 1.10.
The left hand side of the equals sign must be an identifier and only one identifier. The right
hand side of the equals sign can contain any expression that may be evaluated.

In Fig. 1.15, the variable *R1_width* (orange in the figure) is a reference that points at the
integer object 10 colored green in the figure. This is what happens in memory in response
to the assignment statement:

```
R1_width = 10
```

The *0x264* is the reference value, written in hexadecimal, which is a pointer (i.e. the address) that points at the integer object 10. However, typically you don't see reference values in Python. Instead, you see what a reference points to. So if you type *R1_width* in
the Python shell after executing the statement above, you won't see *0x264* printed to the
screen, you'll see 10, the value that *R1_width* refers to. When you set a breakpoint and
look at the stack data in the debugger you will also see what the reference refers to, not the
reference itself (see Fig. 1.13).

It is possible, and common, in Python to write statements like this:

```
x = 1
# do something with x
x = x + 1
```

Fig. 1.16 Before
incrementing x

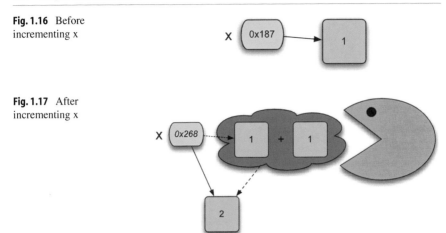

Fig. 1.17 After
incrementing x

According to what we have just seen, Fig. 1.16 depicts the state of memory after executing the first line of code and before executing the second line of code. In the second line of code, writing $x = x + 1$ is not an algebraic statement. It is an assignment statement where one is added to the value that x refers to. The correct way to read an assignment statement is from right to left. The expression on the right hand side of the equals sign is evaluated to produce an object. The equals sign takes the reference to the new value and stores it in the reference named by the identifier on the left hand side of the equals sign. So, to properly understand how an assignment statement works, it must be read from right to left. After executing the second statement (the line beginning with a pound sign is a comment and is not executed), the state of memory looks like Fig. 1.17. The reference called x is updated to point to the new value that results from adding the old value referred to by x and the 1 together.

The space for the two left over objects containing the integers 1 in Fig. 1.17 is reclaimed by the *garbage collector*. You can think of the garbage collector as your favorite arcade game character running around memory looking for unattached objects (objects with no references pointing to them—the stuff in the cloud in Fig. 1.17). When such an object is found the garbage collector reclaims that memory for use later much like the video game character eats dots and fruit as it runs around.

The garbage collector reclaims the space in memory occupied by unreferenced objects so the space can be used later. Not all programming languages include garbage collection but many languages developed recently include it and Python is one of these languages. This is a nice feature of a language because otherwise we would have to be responsible for freeing all of our own memory ourselves.

1.12
Integers and Real Numbers

In most programming languages, including Python, there is a distinction between integers and real numbers. Integers, given the type name *int* in Python, are written as a sequence of

Operation	Operator	Comments
Addition	x + y	*x* and *y* may be floats or ints.
Subtraction	x - y	*x* and *y* may be floats or ints.
Multiplication	x * y	*x* and *y* may be floats or ints.
Division	x / y	*x* and *y* may be floats or ints. The result is always a float.
Floor Division	x // y	*x* and *y* may be floats or ints. The result is the first integer less than or equal to the quotient.
Remainder or Modulo	x % y	*x* and *y* must be ints. This is the remainder of dividing *x* by *y*.
Exponentiation	x ** y	*x* and *y* may be floats or ints. This is the result of raising *x* to the yth power.
Float Conversion	float(x)	Converts the numeric value of *x* to a float.
Integer Conversion	int(x)	Converts the numeric value of *x* to an int. The decimal portion is truncated, not rounded.
Absolute Value	abs(x)	Gives the absolute value of x.
Round	round(x)	Rounds the float, *x*, to the nearest whole number. The result type is always an int.

Fig. 1.18 Numeric operations

digits, like 83 for instance. Real numbers, called *float* in Python, are written with a decimal point as in 83.0. This distinction affects how the numbers are stored in memory and what type of value you will get as a result of some operations.

In Fig. 1.18 the type of the result is a float if either operand is a float unless noted otherwise in the table.

Dividing the integer 83 by 2 yields 41.5 if it is written 81/2. However, if it is written 83//2 then the result is 41. This goes back to long division as we first learned in elementary school. 83//2 is 41 with a remainder of 1. The result of floor division isn't always an *int*. 83//2.0 yields 41.0 so be careful. While floor division returns an integer, it doesn't necessarily return an *int*.

We can insure a number is a float or an integer by writing *float* or *int* in front of the number. So, *float(83)//2* also yields 41.0. Likewise, *int(83.0)//2* yields 41.

There are infinitely many real numbers but only a finite number of floats that can be represented by a computer. For instance, the number *PI* is approximately 3.14159. However,

Python 2 ⤳ 3

In Python 2 the floor division operator was specifically for *floats*. If both operands were *ints* then integer (i.e. floor) division was automatically used by writing the / operator. If you are using Python 2 and want to use integer division then you must insure that both operands are ints. Likewise, if you want to use floating point division you must insure that at least one operand is a float. When using Python 2, to force floating point division of *x/y* you can write:

```
z = float(x) / y
```

It should also be noted that in Python 2 the *round* function returned the same type as its operand. In Python 3 the *round* function returns an *int*.[8]

that number can't be represented in some implementations of Python. Instead, that number is approximated as 3.1415899999999999 in at least one Python implementation. Writing 3.14159 in a Python program is valid, but it is still stored internally as the approximated value. This is not a limitation of Python. It is a limitation of computers in general. Computers can only approximate values when there are infinitely many possibilities because computers are finite machines.

You can use what is called integer conversion to transform a floating point number to its integer portion. In effect, integer conversion truncates the digits after the decimal point in a floating point number to get just the whole number part. To do this you write *int* in front of the floating point number you wish to convert. This does not convert the existing number. It creates a new number using only the integer portion of the floating point number.

Example 1.5 Assume that you work for the waste water treatment plant. Part of your job dictates that you report the gallons of water treated at the plant. However, your meter reports lbs of water treated. You have been told to to report the amount of treated waste water in gallons and ounces. There are 128 ounces in a gallon and 16 ounces in a pound. Here is a short program that performs the conversion.

```
1  lbs = float(input("Please enter the lbs of water treated: "))
2  ounces = lbs * 16
3  gallons = int(ounces / 128)
4  ounces = ounces - gallons * 128
5  print("That's",gallons,"gallons and", \
6         ounces,"ounces of treated waste water.")
```

In Example 1.5 the lbs were first converted to ounces. Then the whole gallons were computed from the ounces by converting to an integer the result of dividing the ounces float by 128. On line 4 the remaining ounces were computed after taking out the number of ounces contained in the computed gallons.

Several of the operations between ints and floats are given in Fig. 1.18. If you need to round a float to the nearest integer (instead of truncating the fractional portion) you can use the *round* function. Absolute value is taken using *abs*. There are other operations between floats and ints that are not discussed in this chapter. A complete list of all operations supported by integers and floats are given in Appendices and B. If you need to read some documentation about an operator you can use the appendices or you can search for Python documentation on the internet or you can start a Python shell and type *help(float)* or *help(int)*. This help facility is built into the Python programming language. There is extensive documentation for every type within Python. Typing *help(type)* in the Python shell where *type* is any type within Python will provide you with all the operations that are available on that type of value.

Operation	Operator	Comments
Indexing	s[x]	Yields the xth character of the string s. The index is zero based, so s[0] is the first character.
Concatenation	s + t	Yields the juxtaposition of the strings s and t.
Length	len(s)	Yields the number of characters in s.
Ordinal Value	ord(c)	Yields the ordinal value of a character c. The ordinal value is the ASCII code of the character.
Character Value	chr(x)	Yields the character that corresponds to the ASCII value of x.
String Conversion	str(x)	Yields the string representation of the value of x. The value of x may be an int, float, or other type of value.
Integer Conversion	int(s)	Yields the integer value contained in the string s. If s does not contain an integer an error will occur.
Float Conversion	float(s)	Yields the float value contained in the string s. If s does not contain a float an error will occur.

Fig. 1.19 String operations

Practice 1.10 Write a short program that computes the length of the hypotenuse of a right triangle given the two legs as pictured in Fig. 1.23 on page 32. The program should use three variables, *sideA*, *sideB*, and *sideC*. The Pythagorean theorem states that the sum of the squares of the two legs of the triangle equals the square of the hypotenuse. Be sure to assign all three variables their correct values and print the length of *sideC* at the end of the program. HINT: Raising a value to the 1/2 power is the same thing as finding the square root. Try values 6 and 8 for *sideA* and *sideB*.

1.13
Strings

Strings are another type of data in Python. A string is a sequence of characters.

```
name = 'Sophus Lie'
print("A famous Norwegian Mathematician is", name)
```

This is a short program that initializes a variable called *name* to the string 'Sophus Lie'. A string literal is an actual string value written in your program. String literals are *delimited* by either double or single quotes. Delimited means that they start and end with quotes. In the code above the string literal *Sophus Lie* is delimited by single quotes. The string *A famous Norwegian Mathematician is* is delimited by double quotes. If you use a single quote at the beginning of a string literal, you must use a single quote at the end of the string literal. Delimiters must come in matching pairs.

Strings are one type of sequence in Python. There are other kinds of sequences in Python as well, such as lists which we'll look at in a couple of chapters. Python supports operations on sequences. For instance, you can get an individual item from a sequence. Writing,

```
print (name[0])
```

will print the first character of the string that *name* references. The 0 is called an index. Each subsequent character is assigned a subsequent position in the string. Notice the first position in the string is assigned 0 as its index. The second character is assigned index 1, and so on. Strings and their operations are discussed in more detail in Chap. 3.

> **Practice 1.11** Write the three line program given in the two listings on page 24. Then, without writing the string literal "house", modify it to print the string "house" to the screen using string indexing. HINT: You can add strings together to build a new string. So,
>
> ```
> name = "Sophus" + " Lie"
> ```
>
> will result in *name* referring to the string "*Sophus Lie*".

1.14
Integer to String Conversion and Back Again

It is possible in Python to convert an integer to a string. For instance,

```
x = str(83)
print (x[0])
print (x[1])
y = int(x)
print (y)
```

This program converts 83 to '83' and back again. Integers and floats can be converted to a string by using the *str* conversion operator. Likewise, an integer or a float contained in a string can be converted to its numeric equivalent by using the *int* or *float* conversion operator. Conversion between numeric types and string types is frequently used in programs especially when producing output and getting input.

Conversion of numeric values to strings should not be confused with ASCII conversion. Integers may represent ASCII codes for characters. If you want to convert an integer to its

ASCII character equivalent you use the *chr* conversion operator. For instance, *chr*(83) is 'S'. Likewise, if you want to convert a character to its ASCII code equivalent you use the *ord* conversion operator. So *ord*('S') is equal to *83*.

> **Practice 1.12** Change the program above to convert 83 to its ASCII character equivalent. Save the value in a variable and print the following to the screen in the exact format you see here.
>
> ```
> The ASCII character equivalent of 83 is S.
> ```

You might have noticed in Fig. 1.19 there is an operator called *int* and another called *float*. Both of these operators are also numeric operators and appear in Fig. 1.18. This is called an overloaded operator because *int* and *float* are operators that work for both numeric and string operands. Python supports overloaded operators like this. This is a nice feature of the language since both versions of *int* and *float* do similar things.

1.15
Getting Input

To get input from the user you can use the *input* function. When the *input* function is called the program stops running the program, prompts the user to enter something at the keyboard by printing a string called the *prompt* to the screen, and then waits for the user to press the *Enter* key. The user types a string of characters and presses enter. Then the *input* function returns that string and Python continues running the program by executing the next statement after the input statement.

Example 1.6 Consider this short program.

```
name = input("Please enter your name:")
print("The name you entered was", name)
```

The *input* function prints the prompt "Please enter your name:" to the screen and waits for the user to enter input in the Python Shell window. The program does not continue executing until you have provided the input requested. When the user enters some characters and presses enter, Python takes what they typed before pressing enter and stores it in the variable called *name* in this case. The type of value read by Python is always a string. If we want to convert it to an integer or some other type of value, then we need to use a conversion operator. For instance, if we want to get an int from the user, we must use the *int* conversion operator.

> # Python 2 ↝ 3
>
> Python 2 included a way to get input also called *input*. This old version of the *input* function was very confusing to use and was eliminated in Python 3. In Python 2 the equivalent of Python 3's *input* was called *raw_input*. If you are writing a Python 2 program you may replace any call to *input* with a call to *raw_input*. If you are using Python 2, DO NOT use the *input* function. In Python 2 the value that the input function returned partially depended on the variable names in your program! This was a bad idea that led to much confusion in Python programs so almost no one used it and hence it was eliminated in Python 3.[8]

Practice 1.13 Assume that we want to pause our program to display some output and we want to let the user press some key to continue. We want to print "press any key to continue..." to the screen. Can we use the input function to implement this? If so, how would you write the input statement? If not, why can't you use input?

Example 1.7 This code prompts the user to enter their age. The string that was returned by *input* is first converted to an integer and then stored in the variable called *age*. Then the age variable can be added to another integer. It is important to remember that *input* always returns a string. If some other type of data is desired, then the appropriate type conversion must be applied to the string.

```
age = int(input("Please enter your age:"))
olderAge = age + 1
print("Next year you will be", olderAge)
```

1.16
Formatting Output

In this chapter just about every fragment of code prints something. When a value is printed, it appears on the console. The location of the console can vary depending on how you run a program. If a program is run from within the Wing IDE, the console is the *Python Shell* window in the IDE. If the program is debugged from within Wing IDE 101, the output appears in the *Debug I/O* window.

When printing, we may print as many items as we like on one line by separating each item by a comma. Each time a comma appears between items in a print statement, a space appears in the output.

Example 1.8 Here is some code that prints a few values to the screen.

```
name = "Sophus"
print (name,"how are you doing?")
print ("I hope that,", name, "is feeling well today.")
```

The output from this is:

```
Sophus how are your doing?
I hope that Sophus is feeling well today.
```

To print the contents of variables without spaces appearing between the items, the variables must be converted to strings and string concatenation can be used. The + operator adds numbers together, but it also concatenates strings. For the correct + operator to be called, each item must first be converted to a string before concatenation can be performed.

Example 1.9 Assume that we ask the user to enter two floating point numbers, x and y, and we wish to print the result of raising x to the yth power. We would like the output to look like this.

```
Please enter a number: 4.5
Please enter an exponent: 3.2
4.5^3.2 = 123.10623351
```

Here is a program that will produce that output, with no spaces in the exponentiation expression. NOTE: The caret symbol (i.e. ^) is not the Python symbol for exponentiation.

```
1  base = float(input("Please enter a number: "))
2  exp = float(input("Please enter an exponent: "))
3  answer = base ** exp
4  print(str(base) + "^" + str(exp), "=", answer)
```

In Example 1.9, line 4 of the program prints three items to the console. The last two items are the = and the value that the answer variable references. The first item in the print statement is the result of concatenating *str(base)*, the caret, and *str(exp)*. Both *base* and *exp* must be converted to strings first, then string concatenation will be performed by the + operator because the operands on either side of the + are both strings.

Type	Specifier	Comments
int	%wd	Places an integer in a field of width w if specified. %2d would place an integer in a field of width 2. w may be omitted.
int	%wx	Format the integer in hexadecimal. Put it in a field of width w if specified. w may be omitted.
int	%wo	Format the integer in octal. Put it in a field of width w if specified. w may be omitted.
float	%w.df	Format a floating point number with total width w (including the decimal point) and with d digits after the decimal point. Displaying the entire number include the d digits takes precedence over displaying in a field of w characters should w not be big enough. w and d may be omitted.
float	%w.de	Format a floating point number using scientific notation with d digits of precision and w field width. Scientific notation uses an exponent of 10 to move the decimal point so only one digit appears to the left of the decimal point. w and d may be omitted.
str	%ws	Place a string in a field of width w. w may be omitted.
	%%	Include a % sign in the formatted string.

Fig. 1.20 Format specifiers

Practice 1.14 The sum of the first n positive integers can be computed by the formula

$$sum(1..n) = 1 + 2 + 3 + 4 + \cdots + n = n(n+1)/2$$

Write a short Python program that computes the sum of the first 100 positive integers and prints it to the screen in the format shown below. Use variables to represent the 1, the 100, and the result of the computation. Your program must compute the 5050 value. You cannot just print the result to the screen. You must compute it first from the 100.

```
sum(1..100)=5050
```

For advanced control of the format of printing we can use string formatting. String formatting was first used in the C language *printf* function back in the 1970's. It's an idea that has been around a long time, but is still useful. The idea is that we place formatting instructions in a string and then tell Python to replace the formatting instructions with the actual values. This is best described with an example.

Example 1.10 Assume we wish to re-implement the program in Example 1.9. However, in this version of the program, if the user enters more than 2 decimal places for either number we wish to round the numbers to two digits of precision when they are printed to the console. Assume we wish to round the answer to 4 decimal places when displayed. The following code will do this.

```
1  base = float(input("Please enter a number: "))
2  exp = float(input("Please enter an exponent: "))
3  answer = base ** exp
4  print("%1.2f^%1.2f = %1.4f"%(base,exp,answer))
```

Running this program produces the following output.

```
Please enter a number: 4.666666667
Please enter an exponent: 3.3333333333
4.67^3.33 = 169.8332
```

Line 4 in Example 1.10 prints the result of formatting a string. To use Python formatting, a format string must be written first, followed by a percent sign, followed by the replacement values. If there is more than one replacement value, they must be written in parentheses. Each time a % appears inside the format string it is replaced by one of the values that appear after the format string. How a value is formatted when it is placed in the format string is controlled by the format specifier. Figure 1.20 contains some specifiers for common types of data in Python. Every format specifier may include an optional width field. If specified, the width field specifies the actual width of the replaced data. If the width of the data being inserted into the format string exceeds the alloted width, the entire field is included anyway, stretching the width of the formatted string. String formatting can be very useful when generating a printed report of some data.

Practice 1.15 Re-do Practice 1.14 using format specifiers when printing instead of converting each item to a string. The goal is for the output to look exactly the same.

```
sum(1..100)=5050
```

1.17
When Things Go Wrong

As a programmer, you will soon discover that things can go wrong when writing a program. No programmer writes every program correctly the first time. We are all human and make mistakes. What makes a programmer a really good programmer is when they can find their

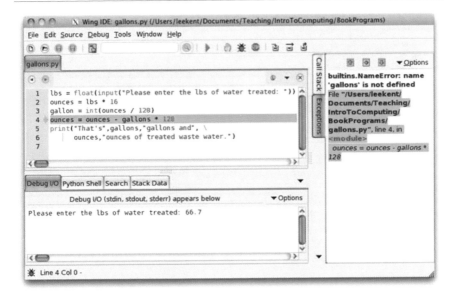

Fig. 1.21   A run-time error

mistakes and correct them. Debugging programs is a skill that can be learned and therefore can be taught as well. But, it takes lots of practice and patience. Fortunately, you will have many chances to practice as you work your way through this book.

Sometimes, especially when you are first learning to debug your programs, it can help to have someone to talk to. Just the act of reading your code to someone else may cause you to find your mistake. Of course, if you are using this text as part of a course you may not want to read your code to another class member as that may violate the guidelines your instructor has set forth. But, nevertheless, you might find that reading your code to someone else may help you discover problems. This is called a code walk-through by programming professionals. It is a common practice and is frequently required when writing commercially available programs.

There is no substitute for thorough testing. You should run your program using varied values for input. Try to think of values that might cause your program to break. For instance, what if 0 is entered for an integer? What if a non-integer value is entered when an integer was required? What happens if the user enters a string of characters when a number was required?

Sometimes the problems in our code are not due to user input. They are just plain old mistakes in programming caused either by temporarily forgetting something, or by our misunderstanding how something works. For instance, in this chapter we learned about assignment statements. You can store a value in the memory of a computer and point a named reference at the value so you can retrieve it later. But, you must assign a name to a value before you can retrieve it. If you don't understand that concept, or if you forgot where you assigned a value a name in your program, you might accidentally write some code that tries to use that value before it is assigned a name. For instance, consider the

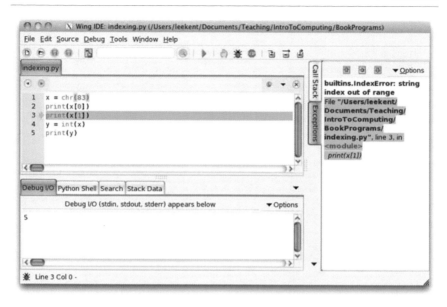

Fig. 1.22 An index out of range error

Fig. 1.23 A right triangle

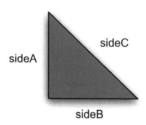

program in Fig. 1.21. The program is trying to use the gallons variable which has not been assigned a value. The error message is on the right side of the window. The line where the error was first detected by Python is highlighted.

In the example in Fig. 1.21 the actual error is not on the line that is highlighted. The highlighted line is the line where Python first *detected* the error. This is a very common occurrence when debugging. Detection of an error frequently occurs after the location of the actual error. To become a good programmer you must learn to look backwards through your code from the point where an error is detected to find the location where it occurred. In this case, the *gallon* variable should have been written as *gallons* on line 3 but was incorrectly typed.

Another common error is the *index out of range* error. This can occur when trying to access a value in a sequence by indexing into the sequence. If the index is for an item that is outside the range of the sequence, an index out of range error will occur. For instance, if you have a string called x that is one character long and you try to access the second element of the string, your program will abort with an index out of range error. Figure 1.22 shows this happening in a snippet of code.

Once again, in the example in Fig. 1.22 the error did not occur on the line that is high-lighted. The error occurred because the programmer meant to take the *str(83)* which would result in "83" as a string instead of the *chr(83)* which results in the string "S". If the string had been "83" then line 3 would have worked and would have printed 3 to the screen.

When an error occurs it is called an uncaught exception. Uncaught exceptions result in the program terminating. They cannot be recovered from. Because uncaught exceptions result in the program terminating it is vital to test your code so that all variations of running the program are tested before the program is released to users. Even so, there are times when a user may encounter an error. Perhaps it has happened to you? In any case, thorough testing is critical to your success as a programmer and learning to debug and test your code is as important as learning to program in the first place. As new topics are introduced in this text, debugging techniques will also be introduced to provide you with the information you need to become a better debugger.

1.18
Review Questions

1. What does the acronym IDE stand for? What does it do?
2. What does the acronym CPU stand for? What does it do?
3. How many bytes are in a GB? What does GB stand for?
4. What is the decimal equivalent of the binary number 01101100?
5. What is the hexadecimal equivalent of the binary number 01101100?
6. What is the binary equivalent of the number -62?
7. What is the ASCII equivalent of the decimal number 62?
8. What is a type in Python? Give an example. Why are there types in Python programs?
9. How can you tell what type of value is stored in 4 contiguous bytes of memory?
10. How can you interactively work with the Python interpreter?
11. What is prototyping as it applies to computer programming?
12. Name two different types of errors that you can get when writing a computer program? What is unique about each type of error?
13. What is a reference in a Python program?
14. Why shouldn't you compare floats for equality?
15. What would you have to write to ask the user to enter an integer and then read it into a variable in your program? Write some sample code to do this.
16. Assume that you have a constant defined for $pi = 3.14159$. You wish to print just 3.14 to the screen using the *pi* variable. How would you print the *pi* variable so it only display 3.14?

1.19
Exercises

1. Write a program that asks the user to enter their name. Then it should print out the ASCII equivalent of each of the first four characters of your name. For instance, here is a sample run of the program below.

```
Please enter your name: Kent
K ASCII value is 75
e ASCII value is 101
n ASCII value is 110
t ASCII value is 116
```

2. Write a program that capitalizes the first four characters of a string by converting the characters to their ASCII equivalent, then adding the necessary amount to capitalize them, and converting the integers back to characters. Print the capitalized string. Here is a sample of running this program.

```
Please enter a four character string: kent
The string capitalized is KENT
```

3. You can keep track of your car's miles per gallon if you keep track of how many miles you drive your car on a tank of gas and you always fill up your tank when getting gas. Write a program that asks the user to enter the number of miles you drove your car and the number of gallons of gas you put in your car and then prints the miles per gallon you got on that tank of gas. Here is a sample run of the program.

```
Please enter the miles you drove: 256
Please enter the gallons of gas you put in the tank: 10.1
You got 25.346534653465348 mpg on that tank of gas.
```

4. Write a program that converts US Dollars to a Foreign Currency. You can do this by finding the exchange rate on the internet and then prompting for the exchange rate in your program. When you run the program it should look exactly like this:

```
What is the amount of US Dollars you wish to convert? 31.67
What is the current exchange rate
(1~US Dollar equals what in the Foreign Currency)? 0.9825
The amount in the Foreign Currency is $31.12
```

5. Write a program that converts centimeters to yards, feet, and inches. There are 2.54 centimeters in an inch. You can solve this problem by doing division, multiplication, addition, and subtraction. Converting a float to an int at the appropriate time will help in solving this problem. When you run the program it should look exactly like this (except possibly for decimal places in the inches):

```
How many centimeters do you want to convert? 127.25
This is 1 yards, 1 feet, 2.098425 inches.
```

6. Write a program that computes the minimum number of bills and coins needed to make change for a person. For instance, if you need to give $34.36 in change you would need one twenty, one ten, four ones, a quarter, a dime, and a penny. You don't have to compute change for bills greater than $20 dollar bills or for fifty cent pieces. You can solve this problem by doing division, multiplication, subtraction, and converting floats to ints when appropriate. So, when you run the program it should look exactly like this:

```
How much did the item cost: 65.64
How much did the person give you: 100.00
The person's change is $34.36
The bills or the change should be:
1 twenties
1 tens
0 fives
4 ones
1 quarters
1 dimes
0 nickels
1 pennies
```

7. Write a program that converts a binary number to its decimal equivalent. The binary number will be entered as a string. Use the powers of 2 to convert each of the digits in the binary number to its appropriate power of 2 and then add up the powers of two to get the decimal equivalent. When the program is run, it should have output identical to this:

```
Please enter an eight digit binary number: 01010011
The decimal equivalent of 01010011 is 83.
```

8. Write a program that converts a decimal number to its binary equivalent. The decimal number should be read from the user and converted to an *int*. Then you should follow the algorithm presented in Example 1.1 to convert the decimal number to its binary equivalent. The binary equivalent must be a string to get the correct output. The output from the program must be identical to this:

```
Please enter a number: 83
The binary equivalent of 83 is 01010011.
```

You may assume that the number that is entered is in the range 0-255. If you want to check your work, you can use the *bin* function. The *bin* function will take a decimal number and return a string representation of that binary number. However, you should not use the *bin* function in your solution.

9. Complete the program started in practice problem 1.10. Write a program that asks the user to enter the two legs of a right triangle. The program should print the length of the hypotenuse. If *sideA* and *sideB* are the lengths of the two legs and *sideC* is the length of the third leg of a right triangle, then the Pythagorean theorem says that $sideA^2 + sideB^2 = sideC^2$. Ask the user to enter *sideA* and *sideB*. Your program should print the value of *sideC*.

```
Please enter the length of the first leg: 3
Please enter the length of the second leg: 4
The length of the hypotenuse is 5.0
```

1.20
Solutions to Practice Problems

These are solutions to the practice problems in this chapter. You should only consult these answers after you have tried each of them for yourself first. Practice problems are meant to help reinforce the material you have just read so make use of them.

Solution to Practice Problem 1.1

The decimal equivalent of the binary number 01010101_2 is 85.

Solution to Practice Problem 1.2

$$58/2 = 29 \quad \textit{remainder } 0$$
$$29/2 = 14 \quad \textit{remainder } 1$$
$$14/2 = 7 \quad \textit{remainder } 0$$
$$7/2 = 3 \quad \textit{remainder } 1$$
$$3/2 = 1 \quad \textit{remainder } 1$$
$$1/2 = 0 \quad \textit{remainder } 1$$

So the answer is 00111010_2.

Solution to Practice Problem 1.3

$$-83_{10} = 10101101_2$$

Solution to Practice Problem 1.4

The ASCII code for space is 32. $32_{10} = 00100000_2$

Solution to Practice Problem 1.5

We, as programmers, determine how bytes in memory are interpreted by the statements that we write. If we want to interpret the bits 01010011 as a character we write 'S' in our program. If we want the same bits to represent an integer, we write 83 in our program.

Solution to Practice Problem 1.6

There is no solution needed for this exercise. Try it out and if you have problems, talk to your instructor or someone who can help to make sure you get this working before proceeding.

Solution to Practice Problem 1.7

1. An assignment statement is written as

```
<variable> = <expression>
```

where a variable is assigned the value of an expression.
2. To retrieve a value from memory we write the name of the variable that refers to that value.
3. If we use a variable before it has been assigned a value Python will complain of a name error, meaning the variable has not been assigned a value yet.

Solution to Practice Problem 1.8

The binary representation of 58 is 00111010. The number is $3A_{16}$ and 72_8. In Python syntax that would be $0x3A$ and $0o72$.

Solution to Practice Problem 1.9

There is no solution needed for this since it is in the text. However, you should make sure you try this so you understand the mechanics of writing a program using the IDE. If you can't get it to work you should ask someone that did get it to work for help or ask your instructor.

Solution to Practice Problem 1.10

```
sideA = 6
sideB = 8
sideC = (sideA*sideA + sideB**2) ** 0.5
print(sideC)
```

Solution to Practice Problem 1.11

Here is one program that you might get as a result.

```
name = 'Sophus Lie'
print("The name is", name)
word = name[3] + name[1] + name[4] + name[5] + name[9]
print(word)
```

Solution to Practice Problem 1.12

Here is one version of the program. Do you understand why + was used at the end of the print statement?

```
x = chr(83)
print("The ASCII character equivalent of",ord(x),"is",x+".")
```

Solution to Practice Problem 1.13

You cannot use input to implement this because the input function waits for the enter key to be pressed, not just any key. You could prompt the user though with "Press Enter to continue...".

Solution to Practice Problem 1.14

Here is a version of the program. It must have variables to 1 and 100 to be correct according to the directions.

```
start = 1
end = 100
sumOfNums = end * (end + 1) // 2
print("sum("+str(start)+".."+str(end)+")="+str(sumOfNums))
```

Solution to Practice Problem 1.15

```
start = 1
end = 100
sumOfNums = end * (end + 1) // 2
print("sum(%d..%d)=%d"%(start,end,sumOfNums))
```

Decision Making

2

In this chapter we explore how to make choices in our programs. Decision making is valuable when something we want to do depends on some user input or some other value that is not known when we write our program. This is quite often the case and Python, along with all interesting programming languages, has the ability to compare values and then take one action or another depending on that outcome.

For instance, you might write a program that reads data from a file and takes one action or another based on the data it read. Or, a program might get some input from a user and then take one of several actions based on that input.

To make a choice in Python you write an *if* statement. An if statement takes one of two forms. It may be just an *if* statement. In this case, if the condition evaluates to true then it will evaluate the *then statements*. If the condition is not true the computer will skip to the statements after the if statement.

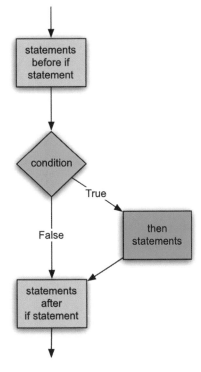

Fig. 2.1 If statement

```
<statements before if statement>
if <condition>:
    <then statements>
<statements after if statement>
```

Figure 2.1 depicts this graphically. An if statement evaluates the conditional expression and then goes to one of two places depending on the outcome. Notice the indentation in the *if* statement above. The indentation indicates the *then statements* are part of the *if* statement. Indentation is very important in Python. Indentation determines the control flow of the program. Figure 2.1 graphically depicts this as well.

K.D. Lee, *Python Programming Fundamentals,* Undergraduate Topics in Computer Science, 41
DOI 10.1007/978-1-84996-537-8_2, © Springer-Verlag London Limited 2011

Fig. 2.2   Relational operators

Operator	Condition
<	Less Than
>	Greater Than
<=	Less Than or Equal to
>=	Greater Than or Equal to
==	Equal to
!=	Not Equal to

Fig. 2.3   Stepping into and over

If the condition evaluates to true, a detour is taken to execute the *then statements* before continuing on after the *if* statement.

Generally, we want to know if some value in our program is equal to, greater, or less than another value. The comparison operators, or relational operators, in Python allow us to compare two values. Any value in your program, usually a variable, can be compared with another value to see how the two values relate to each other.

Figure 2.2 lists the operators you can use to compare two values. Each of these operators is written between the two values or variables you want to compare. They evaluate to either true or false depending on the two values. When the condition evaluates to true, the *then statements* are executed. Otherwise, the *then statements* are skipped.

Example 2.1 An if statement is best described by giving an example. Assume we want to see if a number entered by a user is divisible by 7. We can write the program pictured in Fig. 2.3 to decide this. The program gets some input from the user. Remember that *input* reads a string from the user. The *int* converts the string to an integer. Then, the *num* variable is checked to see if it is divisible by 7. The % is called the modulo or just the mod operator. It gives us the remainder after dividing by the divisor (i.e. 7 in this case). If the remainder after dividing by 7 is 0 then the number entered by the user is divisible by 7.

An important feature of a debugger is the ability to step over our code and watch the computer execute each statement. This is called *stepping over* or *stepping into* our code. Figure 2.3 depicts how this is done. For now stepping into and stepping over code do relatively the same thing. To begin stepping through a program you press the *Step Into* button. Once the program is started, you press the *Step Over* button to avoid jumping to other code that your program might call. Stepping into and over code can be very useful in understanding exactly what your program is doing.

> **Practice 2.1** Write a short program that asks the user to enter the name of a month. If the user enters "December" your program should print "Merry Christmas!". No matter what you enter, your program should print "Have a Happy New Year!" just before the program terminates. Then, use *Step Into* and *Step Over* to execute each statement that you wrote. Run your program at least twice to see how it be-haves when you enter "December" and how it behaves when you enter something else.

Sometimes, you may want your program to do one thing if a condition is true and something else if a condition is false. Notice that the *if* statement does something only when the condition evaluates to true and does not do anything otherwise. If you want one thing to happen when a condition is true and another to happen if the condition is false then you need to use an *if-else* statement. An *if-else* statement adds a keyword of *else* to do something when the condition evaluates to false. An *if-else* statement looks like this.

```
<statements before if statement>
if <condition>:
   <then statements>
else:
   <else statements>
<statements after if statement>
```

If the condition evaluates to true, the *then statements* are executed. Otherwise, the *else statements* are executed. Figure 2.4 depicts this graphically. The control of your program branches to one of two locations, the *then statements* or the *else statements* depending on the outcome of the *condition*.

Fig. 2.4 If-else statement

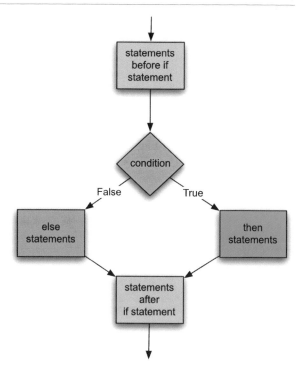

Again, indentation is very important. The *else* keyword must line up with the *if* statement to be properly paired with the *if* statement by Python. If you don't line up the *if* and the *else* in exactly the same columns, Python will not know that the *if* and the *else* go together. In addition, the *else* is only paired with the closest *if* that is in the same column. Both the *then statements* and the *else statements* must be indented and must be indented the same amount. Python is very picky about indentation because indentation in Python determines the flow of control in the program.

In the case of the *if-else* statement, either the *then statements* or the *else statements* will be executed. This is in contrast to the *if* statement that is described in Fig. 2.1. When learning about *if* statements this seems to be where some folks get stuck. The statements that are conditionally executed are those statements that are indented under the *if* or the *else*.

In either case, after executing the *if* or the *if-else* statement control proceeds to the next statement after the *if* or *if-else*. The statement after the *if-else* statement is the next line of the program that is indented the same amount as the *if* and the *else*.

Example 2.2 Consider a program that finds the maximum of two integers. The last line before the *if-else* statement is the *y =* assignment statement. The first line after the *if-else* statement is the *print*("*Done.*") statement.

```
x = int(input("Please enter an integer: "))
y = int(input("Please enter another integer: "))
if x > y:
    print(x,"is greater than",y)
else:
    print(y,"is greater than or equal to",x)
print("Done.")
```

> **Practice 2.2** Modify the program from practice problem 2.1 to print "Merry Christmas!" if the month is December and "You'll have to wait" otherwise. It should still print "Have a Happy New Year!" in either case as the last line of output. Then run the program at least twice using step into and over to see how it behaves when "December" is entered and how the program behaves when anything else is entered.

2.1
Finding the Max of Three Integers

Any statement may be placed within an *if* statement, including other *if* statements. When you want to check multiple conditions there may be a need to put one *if* statement inside another. It can happen, but not very often. For instance, you may need to know if a value entered by a user is between two numbers. This could be written using two if statements, the outer *if* statement checking to see if the value entered is greater than some minimum, and the inner *if* statement checking to see of the value entered is less than some maximum. There are other ways to check to see if a value is between a maximum and minimum, but nested *if* statements can be used in this kind of circumstance.

Let's consider another possibility. Suppose you are asked to write a program that finds the maximum of three integers. This can be accomplished by writing nested *if* statements. Figure 2.5 depicts the flow of control for such a program.

We could determine which of the three integers, x, y and z, was the greatest by first comparing two of them, say x and y. Then, depending on the outcome of that condition, we would compare two more integers. By nesting if statements we can arrive at a decision about which is greatest. This code gets a bit complicated because we have three *if* statements to deal with, two of which are nested inside the third statement.

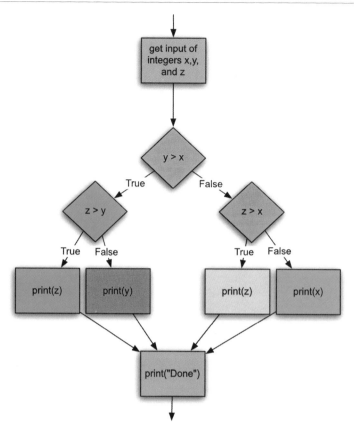

Fig. 2.5 Max of three integers

Example 2.3 While you wouldn't normally write code like this, it is provided here to show how *if* statements may be nested. The code prints the maximum of three integers entered by the user.

```python
x = int(input("Please enter an integer: "))
y = int(input("Please enter another integer: "))
z = int(input("Please enter a third integer: "))
if y > x:
    if z > y:
        print(z, "is greatest.")
    else:
        print(y, "is greatest.")
else:
    if z > x:
        print(z, "is greatest.")
    else:
        print(x, "is greatest.")
print("Done.")
```

2.2
The Guess and Check Pattern

There is no way a good programmer would write a program that included the code that appeared in Example 2.3. It is too complicated. Instead, it would be much better to use a pattern or idiom called *Guess and Check*. Using this pattern involves first making a guess as to a correct solution and storing that guess in a variable. Then, you use one or more *if* statements to check that guess to see if it was correct or not. If it was not a correct guess, then the variable can be updated with a new guess. Finally, when the guess has been thoroughly checked, it should equal the value we were looking for.

Example 2.4 Consider the max of three program in Example 2.3. This could be rewritten using the guess and check pattern if we first make a guess as to the maximum value and then fix it if needed.

```
x = int(input("Please enter an integer:"))
y = int(input("Please enter another integer:"))
z = int(input("Please enter a third integer:"))
# Here is our initial guess
maxNum = x
if y > maxNum: # Fix our guess if needed
    maxNum = y
if z > maxNum: # Fix our guess again if needed
    maxNum = z
print(maxNum, "is greatest.")
print("Done.")
```

The code in Example 2.3 and Example 2.4 get the same input and print exactly the same thing. However, the code in Example 2.4 is much easier to understand, mainly because the control flow is simplified by not having nested *if* statements. Notice that no *else* clauses were needed in Example 2.4. So, the code is simplified by having two *if* statements instead of three. It is simplified by having no nested *if* statements. Finally it is simplified because there are no use of *else* clauses in either of the *if* statements.

> **Practice 2.3** Use the guess and check pattern to determine if a triangle is a perfect triangle. A perfect triangle has side lengths that are multiples of 3, 4, and 5. Ask the user to enter the shortest, middle, and longest sides of a triangle and then print "It is a perfect triangle" if it is and "It is not a perfect triangle" if it isn't. You may assume that the side lengths are integers. Let your guess be that the message you will print is "It is a perfect triangle".

2.3
Choosing from a List of Alternatives

Sometimes you may write some code where you need to choose from a list of alternatives. For instance, consider a menu driven program. You may want to print a list of choices and have a user pick from that list. In such a situation you may want to use an *if* statement and then nest an if statement inside of the *else* clause. An example will help clarify the situation.

Example 2.5 Consider writing a program where we want the user to enter two floats and then choose one of several options.

```
x = float(input("Please enter a number:"))
y = float(input("Please enter a second number:"))

print("1) Add the two numbers")
print("2) Subtract the two numbers")
print("3) Multiply the two numbers")
print("4) Divide the two numbers")

choice = int(input("Please enter your choice: "))

print("The answer is: ",end="")

if choice == 1:
   print(x + y)
else:
   if choice == 2:
      print(x - y)
   else:
      if choice == 3:
         print(x * y)
      else:
         if choice == 4:
            print(x / y)
         else:
            print("You did not enter a valid choice.")
```

Do you notice the stair step pattern that appears in the code in Example 2.5? This stair stepping is generally considered ugly and a nuisance by programmers. Depending on how much you indent each line, the code can quickly go off the right side of the screen or page. The need to select between several choices presents itself often enough that Python has a special form of the *if* statement to handle this. It is the *if-elif* statement. In this statement, one, and only one, alternative is chosen. The first alternative whose condition evaluates to *True* is the code that will be executed. All other alternatives are ignored. The general form of the *if-elif* statement is given on the next page.

```
<statements before if statement>
if <first condition>:
   <first alternative>
elif <second condition>:
   <second alternative>
elif <third condition>:
   <third alternative>
else:
   <catch-all alternative>
<statements after the if statement>
```

There can be as many alternatives as are needed. In addition, the *else* clause is optional so may or may not appear in the statement. If we revise our example using this form of the *if* statement it looks a lot better. Not only does it look better, it is easier to read and it is still clear which choices are being considered. In either case, if the conditions are not mutually exclusive then priority is given to the first condition that evaluates to true. This means that while a condition may be true, its statements may not be executed if it is not the first true condition in the if statement.

Example 2.6 Here is a revision of Example 2.5 that looks a lot nicer.

```
x = float(input("Please enter a number:"))
y = float(input("Please enter a second number:"))

print("1) Add the two numbers")
print("2) Subtract the two numbers")
print("3) Multiply the two numbers")
print("4) Divide the two numbers")

choice = int(input("Please enter your choice:"))

print("The answer is: ",end="")

if choice == 1:
   print(x + y)
elif choice == 2:
   print(x - y)
elif choice == 3:
   print(x * y)
elif choice == 4:
   print(x / y)
else:
   print("You did not enter a valid choice.")
```

Fig. 2.6 Messages

Month	Message
January	Hello Snow!
February	More Snow!
March	No More Snow!
April	Almost Golf Time
May	Time to Golf
June	School's Out
July	Happy Fourth
August	Still Golfing
September	Welcome Back!
October	Fall Colors
November	Turkey Day
December	Merry Christmas!

Practice 2.4 Write a short program that asks the user to enter a month and prints a message depending on the month entered according to the messages in Fig. 2.6. Then use the *step into and over* ability of the debugger to examine the code to see what happens.

2.4
The Boolean Type

Conditions in *if* statements evaluate to *True* or *False*. One of the types of values in Python is called *bool* which is short for Boolean. George Boole was an English Mathematician who lived during the 1800's. He invented the Boolean Algebra and it is in honor of him that *true* and *false* are called Boolean values today [13].

In an *if* statement the condition evaluates to true or false. The Boolean value of the condition decides which branch is to be executed. The only requirement for a condition in an *if* statement is that it evaluates to true or false. So writing *if True ...* would mean that the *then statements* would always be executed. Writing such an *if* statement doesn't really make sense, but using Boolean values in *if* statements sometimes does.

Example 2.7 Consider a program that must decide if a value is between 0 and 1. The program below uses a Boolean expression to discover if that is the case or not.

```
x = int(input("Please enter a number:"))
if x >= 0 and x <= 1:
    print(x, "is between 0 and 1")
```

Fig. 2.7 The and operator

A	B	A and B
False	False	False
False	True	False
True	False	False
True	True	True

Fig. 2.8 The or operator

A	B	A or B
False	False	False
False	True	True
True	False	True
True	True	True

Fig. 2.9 The not operator

A	not A
False	True
True	False

Because an *if* statement only requires that the condition evaluates to true or false, any expression may be used as long as the result of evaluating it is true or false. Compound Boolean expressions can be built from simple expressions by using the logical operators *and*, *or*, and *not*. The *and* of two Boolean values is true when both Boolean values are true as shown in Fig. 2.7. The *or* of two Boolean values is true when one or the other is true, or when both are true as depicted in Fig. 2.8. The *not* of a Boolean value is true when the original value was false. This is shown in Fig. 2.9.

The three figures describe the *truth-tables* for each of the Boolean operators. A truth-table can be constructed for any compound Boolean expression. In each of the truth tables, A and B represent any Boolean expression. The tables show what the Boolean value of the expression *A and B*, *A or B*, and *not A* would be, given the values of A and B in the table. The *and*, *or*, and *not* logical operators can be strung together in all sorts of ways to produce complex Boolean expressions, but writing a program with complex Boolean expressions is generally a bad idea since it is difficult to understand the logic of complex expressions. Keeping track of whether to use *and* or *or* when *not* is involved in the expression is difficult and should be avoided if possible.

There are at least a couple of ways that negation (i.e. the use of the *not* operator) can be avoided in *if* statements. The statement can be rewritten to test the opposite of what you first considered. Another technique is to use the guess and check pattern. The following two examples illustrate how this can be done.

Example 2.8 Consider a club where you must be under 18 and over 15 to join. Here is a first try at a program that tells you whether you can join or not.

```
age = int(input("Please enter your age:"))
if (not age > 15) and (not age < 18):
    print("You can't join")
else:
    print("You can join")
```

Does this program do the job? In fact, as it is written here everyone can join the club. The problem is with the choice of *and* in the Boolean expression. It should have been *or*. The correct program would be written as follows.

```
age = int(input("Please enter your age: "))
if (not age > 15) or (not age < 18):
    print("You can't join")
else:
    print("You can join")
```

While the program above is correct, it is still difficult to understand why it is correct. The problem is the use of negation with the *or* operator. A much better way to write it would be to remove the negation in the expression.

```
age = int(input("Please enter your age:"))
if age > 15 and age < 18:
    print("You can join")
else:
    print("You can't join")
```

Example 2.9 The guess and check pattern can be applied to Boolean values as well. If you need to decide a *yes* or *no* question, you can make a guess and then fix it if needed.

```
age = int(input("Please enter your age:"))
member = True
if age <= 15:
    member = False
if age >= 18:
    member = False
if member:
    print("You can join")
else:
    print("You can't join")
```

The technique used in Example 2.9 is especially useful when there are a number of conditions that must be checked to make sure that the *yes* or *no* answer is correct. In fact, when the exact number of conditions is unknown, this technique may be necessary. How the exact number of conditions to check can be unknown will become clearer in the next chapter.

Practice 2.5 Write a program that determines whether you can run for president. To run for president the constitution states: *No Person except a natural born Citizen, or a Citizen of the United States, at the time of the Adoption of this Constitution, shall be eligible to the Office of President; neither shall any Person be eligible to that Office who shall not have attained to the Age of thirty five Years, and been fourteen Years a Resident within the United States* [7]. Ask three questions of the user and use the guess and check pattern to determine if they are eligible to run for President.

2.5
Short Circuit Logic

Once in a while using the guess and check pattern may not produce the desired results. There are situations where you may want to evaluate one condition only if another condition is true or false. An example should make this clear.

Example 2.10 Consider a program that checks to see if one integer evenly divides another.

```
top = int(input("Please enter the numerator:"))
bottom = int(input("Please enter the denominator:"))

if bottom != 0 and top % bottom == 0:
    print("The numerator is evenly divided by the denominator.")
else:
    print("The fraction is not a whole number.")
```

Dividing *top* by *bottom* would result in a run-time error if *bottom* were 0. However, division by 0 will never happen in this code because Python, and most programming languages, uses short-circuit logic. This means that since both *A* and *B* must be true in the expression *A and B* for the expression to evaluate to *true*, if it turns out that *A* evaluates to *false* then there is no point in evaluating *B* and therefore it is skipped. In other words, Boolean expressions are evaluated from left to right until the truth or falsity of the expression can be determined and the condition evaluation terminates. This is exactly what we want in the code in Example 2.10.

Practice 2.6 In Minnesota you can fish if you are 15 years old or less and your parent has a license. If you are 16 years old or more you need to have your own license. Write a program that uses short circuit logic to tell someone if they are legal to fish in Minnesota. First ask them how old they are, whether they have a license or not, and whether their parent has a license or not.

2.6
Comparing Floats for Equality

In Python, real numbers or *floats* are represented using eight bytes. That means that 2^{64} different real numbers can be represented. This is a lot of real numbers, but not enough. Since there are infinitely many real numbers between any two real numbers, computers will never be able to represent all of them.

Because *floats* are only approximations of real numbers, there is some round-off error expected when dealing with real numbers in a program. Generally this round-off error is small and is not much of a problem unless you are comparing two real numbers for equality. If you need to do this then you need to subtract the two numbers and see if the difference is insignificant since the two numbers may be slightly different.

So, to compare two *floats* for equality you can subtract the two and see if the difference is small relative to the two numbers.

Example 2.11 This program compares a guess with the result of dividing two *floats* and tells you if you are correct or not.

```
top = float(input("Please enter the numerator:"))
bottom = float(input("Please enter the denominator:"))

guess = float(input("Please enter your guess:"))

result = top/bottom
biggest = abs(result)

if abs(guess) > biggest:
    biggest = abs(guess)

# require the answer is within 1/10th Percent
# of the correct value.
if abs((guess-result)/biggest) < .001:
    print("You guessed right!")
else:
    print("Sorry, that's wrong. The correct value was",result)
```

Notice in the program in Example 2.11 that the *abs* function returns the absolute value of the *float* given to it so it doesn't matter if the numbers you are comparing are positive or negative. The code will work either way. In this example, .001 or 1/10th of 1% difference was deemed close enough. Depending on your application, that value may be different.

> **Practice 2.7** Use the guess and check pattern to determine if a triangle is a perfect triangle. You must allow the user to enter any side length for the three sides of the triangle, not just integers. A perfect triangle has side lengths that are multiples of 3, 4, and 5. Ask the user to enter the three side lengths and then print "It is a perfect triangle" if it is and "It is not a perfect triangle" if it isn't.

2.7
Exception Handling

Sometimes things go wrong in a program and it is out of your control. For instance, if the user does not enter the proper input an error may occur in your program. Python includes exception handling so programmers can handle errors like this. Generally, if there is a possibility something could go wrong you should probably use some exception handling. To use exception handling you write a *try-except* statement. The flow of control in a try-except statement is shown in Fig. 2.10. When writing it in your program it looks like this:

```
<statements before try-except>
try:
   <try-block statements>
except [Exception]:
   <except-block statements>
<statements after the try-except code>
```

A try-except block may monitor for any exception or just a certain exception. There are many possible exceptions that might be caught. For instance, a *ValueError* exception occurs when you try to convert an invalid value to an integer. A *ZeroDivisionError* exception occurs when you try to divide by zero. In the general form shown above, the *Exception* is optional. That's what the square brackets (i.e. [ ]) mean. You don't actually write the square brackets. They mean the exception is optional in this case. If the exception is omitted then any exception is caught.

Exception handling can be used to check user input for validity. It can also be used internally in the program to catch calculations that might result in an error depending on the values involved in the calculation. When a *try* block is executed if a run-time error occurs that the try-except block is monitoring then program control immediately skips to the beginning of the except block. If no error occurs while executing the *try* block then

Fig. 2.10 Try-except
statement

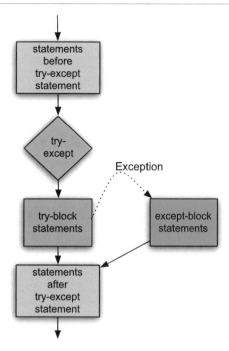

control skips the *except* block and continues with the statement following the *try-except* statement. If an error occurs and the *except* block is executed, then when the except block finishes executing control goes to the next statement after the *try-except* statement.

Example 2.12 Here is a bulletproof version of the program first presented in Example 2.10. This example does not use short-circuit logic. It uses exception handling instead. Notice the use of *exit*(0) below. This is a Python function that exits the program immediately, skipping anything that comes after it.

```
try:
    top = int(input("Please enter the numerator:"))
except ValueError: # This try-except catches only ValueErrors
    print("You didn't enter an integer.")
    exit(0)

try:
    bottom = int(input("Please enter the denominator:"))
except: # This try-except catches any exception
    print("You didn't enter an integer.")
    exit(0)

try:
    if top % bottom == 0:
        print("The numerator is evenly divided by the " + \
            "denominator.")
```

```
else:
    print("The fraction is not a whole number.")
except ZeroDivisionError:
    print("The denominator cannot be 0.")
```

Try-except statements are useful when either reading input from the user or when using data that was read earlier in the program. Example 2.12 uses three *try-except* statements. The first two catch any non-integer input that might be provided. The last catches a division by zero error.

Practice 2.8 Add exception handling to the program in practice problem 2.6 so that if the user answers something other than their age that the program prints "You did not enter your age correctly".

2.8
Review Questions

1. What is the difference between an *if* statement and an *if-else* statement? Be sure to state what the difference in meaning is between the two, not just the addition of the *else* keyword.
2. What type of value is returned by the relational operators?
3. What does it mean to *Step Over* code? What is that referring to?
4. What is a *nested if* statement?
5. How can *nested if* statements be avoided?
6. What is the general pattern for *Guess and Check*?
7. What is the Mathematician George Boole famous for?
8. When is it difficult to determine whether *and* or *or* should be used in an *if* statement?
9. What is short circuit logic? When does it apply? Give an example of when it would apply. Do not use the example in the book.
10. What is the problem with comparing floats for equality?
11. If an exception occurs on line 2 of while executing this code give the line numbers of this program in the order that they are executed. What is the output from the program?

```
try:
    x = int(input("Please enter an integer:"))
    y = int(input("Please enter another integer:"))
except:
    print("You entered an invalid integer.")
print("The product of the two integers is",x*y)
```

Fig. 2.11 Grading scale

Grade	If Greater Than Or Equal To
A	93.33
A-	90
B+	86.67
B	83.33
B-	80
C+	76.67
C	73.33
C-	70
D+	66.67
D	63.33
D-	60
F	0

2.9
Exercises

1. Type in the code of Example 2.6. Execute the code using a debugger like the one included with the Wing IDE 101. Step into and over the code using the debugger. Enter a menu choice of 1. Using the line numbers in Example 2.6, which lines of the program are executed when you enter a 1 for the menu choice. List these lines. Do the same for each of the other menu choice values. If you run the program and enter a menu choice of 5, which lines of the program are executed. If you use the debugger to answer this question you will be guaranteed to get it right and you'll learn a little about using a debugger.

2. Write a program that prints a user's grade given a percent of points achieved in the class. The program should prompt the user to enter his/her percent of points. It should then print a letter grade A, A-, B+, B, B-, C+, C, C-, D+, D, D-, F. The grading scale is given in Fig. 2.11. Use exception handling to check the input from the user to be sure it is valid. Running the program should look like this:

```
Please enter your percentage achieved in the class: 92.32
You earned an A- in the class.
```

3. Write a program that converts centimeters to yards, feet, and inches. There are 2.54 centimeters in an inch. You can solve this problem by doing division, multiplication, addition, and subtraction. Converting a float to an int at the appropriate time will help in solving this problem. When you run the program it should look exactly like this (except possibly for decimal places in the inches):

```
How many centimeters do you want to convert? 127.25
This is 1 yard, 1~foot, 2.098425 inches.
```

This is a modification of the program in exercise 5 of Chap. 1. In this version of it you should print "yard" when there is one yard, and "yards" when there is more than one yard. If there are zero yards then it should not print "yard" or "yards". The same thing applies to "feet". Use an *if* statement to determine the label to print and if the label should be printed at all.

4. Write a program that computes the minimum number of bills and coins needed to make change for a person. For instance, if you need to give $34.36 in change you would need one twenty, one ten, four ones, a quarter, a dime, and a penny. You don't have to compute change for bills greater than $20 dollar bills or for fifty cent pieces. You can solve this problem by doing division, multiplication, subtraction, and converting floats to ints when appropriate. So, when you run the program it should look exactly like this:

```
How much did the item cost: 65.64
How much did the person give you: 100.00
The person's change is \$34.36
The bills or the change should be:
1 twenty
1 ten
4 ones
1 quarter
1 dime
1 penny
```

This is a modification of the program in exercise 6 of Chap. 1. In this version, only non-zero amounts of bills and change should be printed. In addition, when only one bill or coin is needed for a particular denomination, you should use the singular version of the word. When more than one bill or coin for a denomination is needed, the plural of the label should be used.

5. Write a program that asks the user to enter an integer less than 50 and then prints whether or not that integer is prime. To determine if a number less than 50 is prime you only need to divide by all prime numbers that are less than or equal to the square root of 50. If any of them evenly divide the number then it is not prime. Use the guess and check pattern to solve this problem. Use exception handling to check the input from the user to be sure it is valid. A run of the program should look like this:

```
Please enter an integer less than 50: 47
47 is prime.
```

6. Write a program that converts a decimal number to its binary equivalent. The decimal number should be read from the user and converted to an *int*. Then you should follow the algorithm presented in Example 1.1 to convert the decimal number to its binary equivalent. The binary equivalent must be a string to get the correct output. In this version of the program you must handle all 16-bit signed integers. That means that you must handle numbers from -32768 to 32767. In this version of the program you should not print any leading 0's. Leading 0's should be omitted from the output.

If you want to check your work, you can use the *bin* function. The *bin* function will take a decimal number and return a string representation of that binary number. However, you should not use the *bin* function in your solution.

The output from the program must be identical to this:

```
Please enter a number: 83
The binary equivalent of 83 is 1010011.
```

7. Write a program that prompts the user to enter a 16-bit binary number (a string of 1's and 0's). Then, the program should print the decimal equivalent. Be sure to handle both negative and positive binary numbers correctly. If the user enters less than 16 digits you should assume that the digits to the left of the last digit are zeroes. When run the output should look like this:

```
Please enter a 16-bit binary number: 1010011
The binary equivalent of 1010011 is 83.
```

To handle negative numbers correctly you first need to detect if it is a negative number. A 16-digit binary number is negative if it is 16 digits long and the left-most digit is a 1. To convert a negative number to its integer equivalent, first take the 1's complement of the number. Then convert the 1's complement to an integer, then add 1 to the integer and negate the result to get the 2's complement.

The conversion from bits to an integer can be carried out by multiplying each bit by the power of 2 that it represents as described in Sect. 1.5 of Chap. 1.

8. Converting numbers to any base can be accomplished using the algorithm from Example 1.1. For instance, an integer can be converted to hexadecimal using this algorithm. Hexadecimal numbers are base 16. That means there are 16 possible values for one digit. Counting in hexadecimal starts 0, 1, 2, 3, 4, 5, 6, 7, 8, 9, a, b, c, d, e, f, 10, 11, 12, and so on. The algorithm changes so that instead of dividing by 2 you divide by 16. The one gotcha is that if the remainder after dividing is greater or equal to 10 (base 10) then you should not append the base 10 value to the string. Instead you should append a, b, c, d, e, or f. You can use if statements to determine the correct value to append. Write a program that prompts the user to enter an integer and then prints its hexadecimal equivalent. Traditionally, hexadecimal numbers start with a "0x" to identify them as hex, so your output should look like this:

```
Please enter an integer: 255
The hexadecimal equivalent is 0x00ff
```

Your program should handle any base 10 integer from 0 to 65535. There is a function called *hex* in Python that converts integers to their hexadecimal representation. You may not use this in implementing this program, but you may use it to see if your program is producing the correct output. For instance, calling *hex(255)* will return the string 0xff.

You should check the input that the user enters to make sure that it is in the valid range accepted by your program.

2.10
Solutions to Practice Problems

These are solutions to the practice problem s in this chapter. You should only consult these answers after you have tried each of them for yourself first. Practice problems are meant to help reinforce the material you have just read so make use of them.

Solution to Practice Problem 2.1

```
month = input("Please enter a month:")
if month == "December":
    print("Merry Christmas!")
print("Have a Happy New Year!")
```

Solution to Practice Problem 2.2

```
month = input("Please enter a month:")
if month == "December":
    print("Merry Christmas!")
else:
    print("You'll have to wait")
print("Have a Happy New Year!")
```

Solution to Practice Problem 2.3

```
sideone = int(input( \
   "Please enter length of shortest side of triangle:"))
sidetwo = int(input( \
   "Please enter length of middle side of triangle:"))
sidethree = int(input( \
   "Please enter length of longest side of triangle:"))

ratio = sideone // 3

msg = "It is a perfect triangle."

if sidetwo // 4 != ratio:
    msg = "It is not a perfect triangle."

if sidethree // 5 != ratio:
    msg = "It is not a perfect triangle."

print(msg)
```

Solution to Practice Problem 2.4

```
month = input("Please enter a month:")
if month == "January":
    msg = "Hello Snow!"
elif month == "February":
    msg = "More Snow!"
elif month == "March":
    msg = "No More Snow!"
elif month == "April":
    msg = "Almost Golf Time"
elif month == "May":
    msg = "Time to Golf"
elif month == "June":
    msg = "School's Out"
elif month == "July":
    msg = "Happy Fourth"
elif month == "August":
    msg = "Still Golfing"
elif month == "September":
    msg = "Welcome Back!"
elif month == "October":
    msg = "Fall Colors"
elif month == "November":
    msg = "Turkey Day"
elif month == "December":
    msg = "Merry Christmas!"
else:
    msg = "You entered an incorrect month."

print(msg)
```

Solution to Practice Problem 2.5

```
age = int(input("Please enter your age:"))
resident = input( \
  "Are you a natural born citizen of the U.S. (yes/no)?")
years = int(input( \
  "How many years have you resided in the U.S.?"))

eligible = True
if age < 35:
    eligible = False

if resident != "yes":
    eligible = False

if years < 14:
    eligible = False
```

```
if eligible:
    print("You can run for president!")
else:
    print("You are not eligible to run for president!")
```

Solution to Practice Problem 2.6

```
age = int(input("What is your age?"))
license = input( \
   "Do you have a fishing license in MN (yes/no)?")
parentlic = input( \
   "Does your parent have a fishing license (yes/no)?")

if (age < 16 and parentlic == "yes") or license == "yes":
    print("You are legal to fish in MN.")
else:
    print("You are not legal to fish in MN.")
```

Solution to Practice Problem 2.7

```
sideone = float(input( \
  "Please enter length of shortest side of triangle:"))
sidetwo = float(input( \
  "Please enter length of middle side of triangle:"))
sidethree = float(input( \
  "Please enter length of longest side of triangle:"))

ratio = sideone / 3

msg = "It is a perfect triangle."

if abs((ratio - sidetwo / 4) / sidetwo) > 0.001:
    msg = "It is not a perfect triangle."

if abs((ratio - sidethree / 5) / sidethree) > 0.001:
    msg = "It is not a perfect triangle."

print(msg)
```

Solution to Practice Problem 2.8

```
try:
    age = int(input("What is your age?"))
except:
    print("You did not enter your age correctly.")
    exit(0)

license = input( \
  "Do you have a fishing license in MN (yes/no)?")
parentlic = input( \
  "Does your parent have a fishing license (yes/no)?")

if (age < 16 and parentlic == "yes") or license == "yes":
    print("You are legal to fish in MN.")
else:
    print("You are not legal to fish in MN.")
```

Repetitive Tasks
3

When my children were very little I played with them and read books to them. If they were particularly entertained I would get the, "Do it again!", command from them. And, of course, I did it or read it again. Who can say no to a three year-old when they are being so cute. They never seemed to grow tired of repetition when they found something entertaining. Eventually, I grew tired of it myself and would give them the, "One more time...", warning.

Computers are very good at doing repetitive tasks, often called iteration in Computer Science lingo. Computers don't get tired and they don't get bored. Usually, when a task is repeated, it is repeated for the same type of data over and over again. For instance, sending out paychecks is a repetitive job since each employee's deductions must be computed and then a paycheck must be printed or electronically deposited. For large companies, this job would require many people since each person would only be able to compute the withholdings for a relatively small number of people. In fact, before the advent of electronic computers, the word *Computer* referred to people whose job it was to carry out these kinds of calculations. That certainly must have been a mundane and repetitive job. Electronic computers on the other hand don't get tired, can work around the clock, and can work at lightning speed. Repeating a task in a programming language is often called iteration or a loop. In this chapter you learn about loops in Python. You learn how to write various kinds of loops and more importantly, you learn *when* to write various kinds of loops.

When doing a task over and over again it is probably the case that the data that the computer needs to do its job is located in some sort of list or sequence. Python has built-in support for lists. In addition, Python also supports strings, which are sequences of characters. Since so much of what computers do are repetitive tasks, it is important to know how to repeat code and how to manipulate strings and lists. This chapter explores the use of strings and lists. You learn that strings and lists are types of objects and discover what you can do with these objects. In Computer Science sequences and iteration go hand in hand.

So, what is a string? In the first chapter a *string literal* was defined as any sequence of characters surrounded by either single or double quotes. A string literal is used to represent a specific *string object* in Python. So a string literal is written in a Python program when you have a specific string object that you want to use in your program.

K.D. Lee, *Python Programming Fundamentals,* Undergraduate Topics in Computer Science,   **65**
DOI 10.1007/978-1-84996-537-8_3, © Springer-Verlag London Limited 2011

So what is an object? Every value in Python is an object. Types of objects include integers, floats, and strings. An object is a value along with methods that can either change the value of the object or give us more information about its value.

Example 3.1 Consider the string literal "How are you?". The letters in quotes are written to construct a string object. The string object has both a value, the string itself, and methods that may operate on that value. If we write the code below we get the reference called *s* pointing to the string object containing "How are you?" as shown in Fig. 3.1.

```
s = "How are you?"
```

We can interact with an object by sending messages to the object. We send a message by writing the object reference or variable name, followed by a dot (i.e. a period), followed by the method we want to call on the object. In parentheses we may pass some information to the method. The additional information are called arguments. So, calling a *method* on an *object* that is pointed to by a *reference* with zero or more *arguments* looks like this:

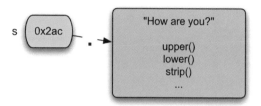

Fig. 3.1 A string object

reference.method(arguments)

Sometimes it helps us to think about this interaction as sending messages to the object and getting the object to respond to these messages. So sending a message to an object or calling a method on the object are the same thing. Whatever we decide to call it, the result is the same. The object's method does something for us.

Methods can either retrieve some information about an object or they can alter the object in some way. The *lower* and *upper* methods of the string class return a new copy of the string with the characters converted to lower or upper case. The *strip* method returns a copy of a string with leading and trailing blanks removed. All the methods on strings are provided in Appendix C.

Example 3.2 When the following code is executed, *t* refers to a new string "how are you?". Notice the first letter of the string that *t* refers to is now lower case. To call the method called *lower()* on *s* you write *s.lower()*.

```
s = "How are you?"
t = s.lower()
print(t)
```

Practice 3.1 Write a short program that asks the user to enter a sentence. Then print the sentence back to the screen with all lower case letters capitalized and all upper case letters in lower case.

Types in Python are sometimes called *classes*. The term *class* is just another name for *type* in Object-Oriented Programming languages. In Object-Oriented Programming (i.e. OOP) terminology a *type* is a *class* and a *value* is an *object*. These are just different names for the same thing in Python because every type is also a class and every value is an object.

Strings have many methods that can be called on them. To find out what methods you can call on a string you can use the internet and search for *python string class* or you can go to the Python Shell Window in the Wing IDE or some other IDE and type *help(str)*. Remember that *str* is the name of the string class in Python. Appendix C contains a table of most of the available string operators and methods as well.

Practice 3.2 Use Appendix C to help you write a program that asks the user to enter "yes" or "no". If they enter a string with any capital letters the program should print a message that says, "Next time please use all lower case letters."

3.1
Operators

If you take a look at Appendix C to peruse the string methods you will notice there are two kinds of methods described there. At the beginning of the appendix there are operators like <=. These operators are just special methods in Python. They describe methods that are not written using the *reference.method(arguments)* format. Instead, the <= method describes an infix operation that can be performed between two string objects to see if one string is less than or equal to another string object.

Example 3.3 Consider the following code.

```
s = input("Please enter a your name:")
t = input("Please enter your mom's name:")
if s <= t:
    print("Your name comes before your mom's name.")
else:
    print("Your mom's name comes before your name.")
```

Operator	Returns	Result	Comments
str(90)	str	"90"	for most argument types
chr(90)	str	"Z"	ASCII character equivalent of int
ord("Z")	int	90	ASCII int equivalent of character
s+t "how"+"are"+"you"	str	"hithere" "howareyou"	same as s.__add__(t)
s in t 'he' in "there"	bool	False True	same as s.__in__(t)
s==t s=='hi'	bool	False True	same as s.__eq__(t)
s>=t	bool	False	same as s.__ge__(t)
s<=t	bool	True	same as s.__le__(t)
s>t	bool	False	same as s.__gt__(t)
s<t	bool	True	same as s.__lt__(t)
len(s)	int	2	same as s.__len__()
t[1:4] t[:3] t[1:]	str	"her" "the" "here"	same as t.__getslice__(1,4) same as t.__getslice__(0,3) same as t.__getslice__(1,len(t))
s.upper()	str	"HI"	does not change s
s.strip()	str	"hi"	removes surrounding whitespace
u.split()	list	["how","are","you"]	splits on whitespace
All examples assume s = "hi", t = "there", and u = " how are you "			

Fig. 3.2 String operators and common methods

The code in Example 3.3 asks the user to enter two strings and compares the two strings. If your name would appear first alphabetically it prints the first message, otherwise it prints the second message. The comparison of $s <= t$ on the third line of code is possible because of the existence of the __le__ method for strings. This is a special method that you will see if you type *help(str)*.

When reading Appendix C most of the operators are really methods that aren't called in the usual way. These methods are sometimes called *hooks*, *syntactic sugar*, or just *operators*. A hook in Python is just a special way of calling a method. Most methods are called in the usual way by writing *reference.method(arguments)*. In fact, even the special hook methods can be called in the usual way. So, comparing two strings, *s* and *t*, to see if one is less than or equal to the other could be written s.__le__(t). Of course, it is more convenient and descriptive to use the operator format and write $s <= t$ when comparing two strings. This is why it is called *syntactic sugar*. It is much nicer to write the comparison operator $s <= t$ than to write s.__le__(t). Syntactic sugar refers to the ability to write a part of a program in a pleasing way as opposed to having to always stick to writing code using the same rules.

Operators are methods that are not called using the *reference.method*(*arguments*) format. Figure 3.2 has examples of calling several of the string operators and some of the string methods. All the string methods can be found in Appendix C. Appendices and B describe operators on integers and floats that are similar to the string operators and are called in a similar fashion.

Practice 3.3 Use Fig. 3.2 and Appendix C to help you write a program that asks the user to enter "yes" or "no". If they enter "yes" then you should print "You entered yes." and likewise if they enter "no". However, make sure you accept "Yes", "yEs", or any other combination of upper and lower case letters for "yes" and for "no". Identify the syntacticly sugared methods that you are calling on the string class in your answer.

3.2
Iterating Over a Sequence

In Python, a string is sometimes thought of as a sequence of characters. Sequences have special status in Python. You can iterate over sequences. *Iteration* refers to repeating the same thing over and over again. In the case of string sequences, you can write code that will be executed for each character in the string. The same code is executed for each character in a string. However, the result of executing the code might depend on the current character in the string. To iterate over each element of a sequence you may write a *for* loop. A *for* loop looks like this:

```
<statements before for loop>

for <variable> in <sequence>:
    <body of for loop>

<statements after for loop>
```

In this code the <variable> is any variable name you choose. The variable will be assigned to the first element of the sequence and then the statements in the body of the for loop will be executed. Then, the variable is assigned to the second element of the sequence and the body of the for loop is repeated. This continues until no elements are left in the sequence.

If you write a for loop and try to execute it on an empty sequence, the body of the for loop is not executed even once. The for loop means just what is says: for each element of a sequence. If the sequence is zero in length then it won't execute the body at all. If there is one element in the sequence, then the body is executed once, and so on.

For loops are useful when you need to do something for every element of a sequence. Since computers are useful when dealing with large amounts of similar data, for loops are often at the center of the programs we write.

Example 3.4 Consider the following program.

```
s = input("Please type some characters and press enter:")
for c in s:
    print(c)
print("Done")
```

If the user enters *how are you?* the output is:

```
h
o
w

a
r
e

y
o
u
?
Done
```

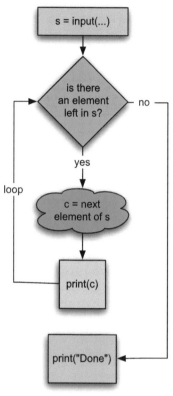

Figure 3.3 depicts what happens when executing the code of Example 3.4. Each character of the sequence is printed on a separate line. Notice that there are blank lines, or what appear to be blank lines, between the words. This is because there are space characters between each of the words in the original string and the for loop is executed once for every character of the string including the space characters. Each of these blank lines really contains one space character.

Fig. 3.3 A for loop

Practice 3.4 Type in the code in Example 3.4. Set a break point on the *print(c)* line. Run it with the debugger and watch it as it runs. Then answer these questions:

1. Does the string *s* change as the code is executed?
2. What happens if the user just presses enter when prompted instead of typing any characters?

Practice 3.5 Modify the code in Example 3.4 to print the characters to the screen as capital letters whether the user enters capital letters or not. For instance, it would print "HOW ARE YOU?" to the screen, with one letter on each line if "how are you?" were entered at the keyboard.

3.3
Lists

A list in Python is any sequence of values surrounded by square brackets (i.e. [ ]). So for instance [0, 1, 2, 3] is a list. So is ['a', 1, 'b', 4.2]. Lists are any sequence of values inside square brackets. The items of the list can be of different types, although it is quite common for all values in a list to be of the same type. The list type is called *list* in Python as you might expect.

A list is a sequence too. A list can be iterated over using a for loop just like a string. Each element of the list is used to execute the body of the for loop once. Appendix D contains a table that outlines the methods and operators that apply to lists. There are several operations on sequences that are useful. For instance, *len(s)* returns the length of a sequence (the number of elements in the sequence). We can concatenate two sequences using +. So writing $s + t$ returns a new string which is the juxtaposition of the strings referenced by s and t. We can get part of a sequence by slicing it. A slice is one or more contiguous elements of a sequence. It is created by using brackets and a colon. For instance, if s refers to the string "how are you?", then $s[0{:}3]$ is the string "how" and $s[4{:}7]$ is the string "are". You can even get a slice starting at the end of a sequence. So, $s[-4{:}]$ gives you the last four items of a sequence, the string "you?" in this case. You can learn more about slicing in Appendices C or D. The length function, concatenation operator, and slicing apply to either strings or lists since they apply to all types of sequences in Python.

Practice 3.6 Write a for loop that prints the following output.

```
0
1
2
3
4
```

The list of integers starting from 0 and going to $n - 1$ is so useful there is a function in Python that we can use to generate such a list. It is called *range*. The range function can be called on an integer, n, and it will generate a list of integers from 0 to $n - 1$. For instance, *range(5)* generates the list $[0, 1, 2, 3, 4]$.

The range function can be used to generate other ranges of integers, too. In general the range function is called by writing *range([start,]stop[,increment])*. For example, *range(10, 110, 10)* generates the list $[10, 20, 30, 40, 50, 60, 70, 80, 90, 100]$ and *range(10, 0, −1)* generates the list $[10, 9, 8, 7, 6, 5, 4, 3,$

Python 2 ⤳ 3
In Python 2 the range function returned a list of integers. Because this was deemed inefficient for large lists of integers, Python 3's range function returns a generator which generates the list of integers as needed. This is called lazy evaluation and is more efficient since each new value is generated only when it is needed. To see the list that range(n) generates in Python 3 you can write list(range(n)) which will convert the generator to a list that you can inspect.

$2, 1]$. In Sect. 1.13 we learned that writing $s[0]$ referred to the first character in the string s. $s[1]$ refers to the second character. Writing $s[−1]$ returns the last element of s. The indexing operations apply to all sequences, not just strings. Using indexing and a for loop together we can write some interesting code.

Example 3.5 This example uses indexing to print each of the characters in a string on separate lines. The output from this program is exactly the same as the output from Example 3.4. Contrast this code to the code that appeared in Example 3.4.

```
s = input("Please type some characters and press enter:")
for i in range(len(s)):
    print(s[i])
print("Done")
```

Notice the use of the *len* function inside the call to the *range* function. When we wish to go through all the elements of a list and we need an index into that list, the *len* function can be used along with *range* to generate the proper list of integers for the indices of the list.

Practice 3.7 Write a program that prints out the characters of a string in reverse order. So, if "hello" is entered, the program prints:

```
o
l
l
e
h
```

To accomplish this, you must use a for loop over the indices of the list since you cannot directly go backwards through a sequence with a for loop. However, you can generate a list with the indices going from the last to first index.

Python includes a few methods that make it much easier to process strings in your programs. One of these methods is called *split*. The split method splits a string into words. Each word is defined as a sequence of characters separated by whitespace in your string. Whitespace are blanks, tabs, and newline characters in your strings. The split method splits a string into a list of strings.

Example 3.6 Contrast the code found here with the code in Example 3.4. Notice that the for loop contains *s.split()* instead of just *s*.

```
s = input("Please type some characters and press enter:")
for word in s.split():
    print(word)
print("Done")
```

If the user enters "how are you?" the output is:

```
how
are
you?
Done
```

Practice 3.8 You can see what the split method does by setting some variable to the result of *s.split()*. For instance, the second line could be:

```
splitWords = s.split()
```

Modify the code to add this line and use *splitWords* in the *for loop*. Run the code in Example 3.6 using the debugger. Step into and over the code and watch the *word* and *splitWords* variables. Run the program several times with different input and make note of what splitWords ends up containing.
What is the type of the value that *s.split()* returns? What does the for loop iterate over?

Another useful operator on sequences is the *in* operator. This operator makes it possible to check to see if an item is in a sequence. For a string, this means you can ask, "Is a character in this string?". For a list it means you can ask if an item is in a list.

Example 3.7 Consider this code that determines if you like something similar to Sophus Lie. The *in* operator let's you find an item in a list and returns True if it does and False otherwise.

```
activity = input("What do you like to do? ")
liesActivities = ["math", "hike", "walk", "gymnastics"]
if activity in liesActivities:
    print("Sopus Lie like to do that, too!")
else:
    print("Good for you!")
```

3.4
The Guess and Check Pattern for Lists

While the *in* operator works well to test for membership in a sequence, it won't work in all situations. Sometimes we need to know if a value with some property other than equality is in a sequence. In these circumstances, the guess and check pattern may be appropriate. The guess and check pattern that we learned about in the last chapter can be applied to sequences, too. You still make a guess at the beginning of the pattern, but then you fix your guess while executing a loop over each element in the sequence you are working with. An example will make things clear.

Example 3.8 Assume we want to know if the user enters an even number in a list of numbers. Here is some code that will decide if one of those numbers is even.

```
s = input("Please enter a list of integers:")
lst = s.split() # Now lst is a list of strings.

# make a guess first
containsEven = False

# the iterate over the list
for element in lst:
    x = int(element)
    # check your guess in the loop
    # and fix it if needed
    if x % 2 == 0:
        containsEven = True

# after the loop you know whether
# your guess was correct or not.
if containsEven:
    print("The list contained an even number")
else:
    print("The list did not contain an even number")
```

The code shown in Example 3.8 works by making a guess and then running through the list of possible counter-examples to fix the guess if needed. Notice the *if containsEven* appears after the *for* loop. It is not indented under the *for* loop. This is very important because other wise you would be checking if the property held for the entire list before you have even looked at the entire list.

Practice 3.9 Type this code and run it using step into and over. Make sure you get the expected output. What would happen in Example 3.8 if the *if containsEven* statement were indented under the for loop?

Practice 3.10 Imagine you work at a rehabilitation center for those that suffer from obsessive-compulsive disorders. You have to write a program that monitors your patients by looking for key words in their daily blogs that they are required to keep. The words are *orderly*, *shopping*, *repeat*, *again*, *gamble*, and *bid*. If any of these words appear in their blog entry then you should print "You really need to talk to someone about this". Otherwise you can print, "Thanks for updating your blog." Here is one possible interaction with this program.

```
Please make your blog entry for today: I am going to eat
    breakfast, then I'll make a bid on some items that I'm
    shopping for.
You really need to talk to someone about this.
```

Write this program using the guess and check pattern to see if any of the sensored words appear in their blog entry. Your blog entry will appear on the first line only. It was wrapped around to fit on the page here.

3.5
Mutability of Lists

Section 1.11 on page 20 introduced you to variables as references to objects. The mental picture of variables pointing at objects was not really all that important at the time. Now, it becomes more crucial that you have this mental picture formed in your mind. Up until this moment, the objects we've looked at were immutable. This means that once an object was created, it could not be modified. For instance, if $x = 6$ is written in a Python program, you

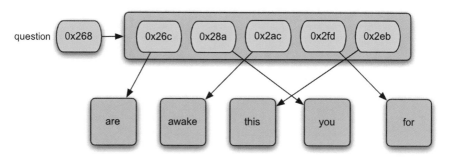

Fig. 3.4 A list object

cannot modify the 6 later on. You *can* modify the reference *x* to point to a new integer, but the 6 itself cannot be modified. Integers are immutable in Python. So are float, bool, and string objects. They are all immutable. Lists, however, are not immutable. A list object can be changed. This is because of the way list objects are constructed.

Example 3.9 Consider the code given here. The code builds a list called *question*. The question object is pictured in Fig. 3.4.

```
question = ['are','you','awake','for','this']
```

What we learned on page 20 says that *question* is a reference to an object. However, all the elements of the list are also objects. The way a list is formed, the elements of a list are actually references that point to the individual items of the list. A list is really a list of references. Unlike strings, individual references within a list can be made to point to new objects using indexed assignment.

It is valid to write:

```
<list reference>[<index>] = <value>
```

Writing this changes a reference within the list object to point to a new object. This mutates the list object. A list object is mutable because of indexed assignment. It should be noted that indexed assignment is not valid on strings. Strings in Python are immutable and therefore attempting to use indexed assignment on a string will result in an error.

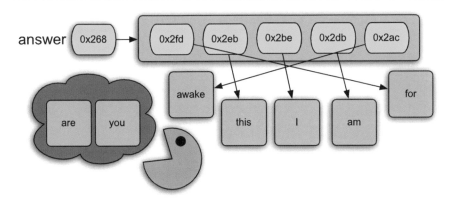

Fig. 3.5 A mutated list object

Example 3.10 Assume we want to change the sentence contained in the list from "are you awake for this" to "for this I am awake". But, we want to avoid creating any more string objects than necessary. The code below does this and prints ['*for*', '*this*', '*I*', '*am*', '*awake*'] since *answer* is a list. Figure 3.5 depicts what *answer* looks like in memory after the code below has been executed.

```
answer = question
answer[0] = answer[3]
answer[1] = answer[4]
answer[4] = answer[2]
answer[2] = 'I'
answer[3] = 'am'
print(answer)
```

> **Practice 3.11** Given what you now know about references, what would print if the *question* variable were printed after executing the code in Example 3.10? Run this code with the debugger.

In Example 3.10 the *answer* list started out with ['*are*', '*you*', '*awake*', '*for*', '*this*'] and ended up containing ['*for*', '*this*', '*I*', '*am*', '*awake*']. It's not a new list. The existing list was updated. In addition, as you just discovered, the variable *question* was also mutated because both *question* and *answer* refer to the same list. This can be seen in Fig. 3.6, which shows the code in Example 3.10 while it is being executed and just before *answer[4]* is assigned its new value. In Wing, and in many IDEs, it looks as if there are two separate lists, the *answer* and the *question* lists. However, if you look carefully, both lists have the same reference. They are both located at 0x644bc0. If you were to type in this code and

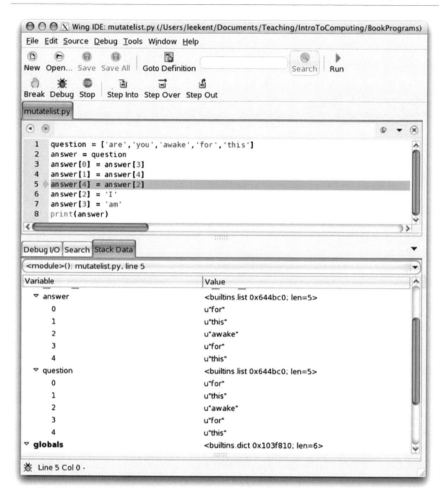

Fig. 3.6   Using Wing to inspect a list

execute it you would see that the two lists truly update in synchronization with each other. When one is updated, the other simultaneously updates.

Also worth noting is that sometimes you can see the reference value when using a debugger and other times you may not. For instance, in Fig. 3.6 you can see the two references to the *question* and *answer* list. However, you cannot see the references to any of the strings contained in the list. The creators of the Wing IDE chose not to show references for strings for two reasons: Including all the references would clutter up the debugger and make it harder to use and in the case of strings, references are not really necessary since strings are immutable. Nevertheless, it does not mean that the list does not contain references to the individual items. It does; the Wing designers have just chosen not to show them in this case.

The idea that variables are really references to objects is important when objects are mutable, like lists. Understanding how the code works depends on you having the correct mental picture. Lists are the only objects we've seen so far that are mutable. Objects of type integer, floats, booleans, and strings are not mutable. There are other types of objects that are mutable in Python including dictionaries.

3.6
The Accumulator Pattern

Iterating over sequences can be useful when we want to count something. Counting is a common occurrence in computer programs. We may want to count the number of people who are taking an Introduction to Computer Science, we may want to add up the amount of money made from ticket sales to a concert. The applications of counting could go on and on. To count we can use what is called the *Accumulator Pattern*. This pattern works by initializing a variable that keeps track of how much we have counted so far. Then we can write a for loop to go through a list of elements in a sequence and add each element's value to the accumulator. The pattern looks like this:

```
<accumulator> = <identity>
for <element> in <sequence>:
    <accumulator> = <accumulator> <operator> <element>
```

This pattern is pretty abstract. With an example it should make some more sense.

Example 3.11 Here is a program that counts the number of elements in a list. Of course, we could use the *len(lst)* function to give us the number of elements in the list, but this illustrates the accumulator pattern for us. This code counts the number of integers in a list. Actually, it counts the number of whitespace separated strings in the list since the code never converts the strings to integers.

```
s = input("Please enter a list of integers:")
lst = s.split() # Now lst is a list of strings.
count = 0 # Here is the beginning of the accumulator pattern
for e in lst:
    count = count + 1

print("There were", count, "integers in the list.")
```

The Accumulator pattern can be used in a multitude of ways. It can be used to count by adding one each time through the loop, it can be used to count the number of items that satisfy some constraint. It can be used to add some number of items in the list together. It can be used to compute a product if needed.

Practice 3.12 Modify the code in Example 3.11 to count the number of even integers entered by the user.

Practice 3.13 Write a program that asks the user to enter an integer and computes the factorial of that integer, usually written $n!$ in mathematics. The definition of factorial says that $0! = 1$ and for $n > 0$, $n! = 1 * 2 * 3 \ldots * n$. You can write this program by using the range function and the accumulator pattern to multiply all the numbers from 1 to n together. If you need to review how to use the range function you can refer to page 72.

In the previous exercise it is worth mentioning that if written correctly not only will it compute $n!$ when $n > 0$, but it will also compute $0!$ correctly. When $0!$ is computed, the body of the for loop is not executed at all. Take a look at your code or at the solution to the practice exercise to confirm this. This sometimes happens when writing code and is called a *boundary condition*. A boundary condition happens when there is a special case that causes the program control to take a slightly different path. In this case, computing $0!$ is a boundary condition and the body of the for loop is not executed. When testing code you have written it is important that you consider your boundary conditions and that you test them to be sure that your program handles them correctly.

3.7
Reading from and Writing to a File

A file is a grouping of related data that can be read by a computer program. Files may be stored in many different places including the hard drive, a thumb drive, on a CD, at a network location, really any place where a program could have access to it. While files occur in many forms and sizes, a *text file* is a bunch of text written using an editor and usually stored on a hard drive. Files can be read and written from Python programs. Files are another type of sequence as far as Python programs are concerned and we can iterate over them just as we would any sequence. Files are sequences of strings, one string for each line of the file. To read from a file we open it and then iterate over the lines of the file.

Example 3.12 A commonly used command in the Linux operating system is called *cat* which stands for catalog but actually prints the contents of a file to the screen. We can write a similar program in Python. Here is the code. For this to work, you must enter the name of a file in the same directory or folder as the program that you are running.

```
filename = input("Please enter the name of a file: ")
catfile = open(filename,"r")
for line in catfile:
    print(line)
catfile.close()
```

Practice 3.14 If you run the program in Example 3.12 you will notice an extra blank line between the lines of the file. This is because there is a '*n*' newline character at the end of each line read from the file. You can't see the newline character, but it is there. The *print* statement prints another newline at the end of each line. Modify the code in Example 3.12 to eliminate the extra line. Look at Appendix C for a method that will help you eliminate the extra newline character at the end of each line.

The program in Example 3.12 reads one line at a time from the file. The second line of the example opens the file for *reading*. To write a file it may be opened for *writing* by using a "w" instead of a "r". You can also open a file with "a" for append to add to the end of an existing file.

Example 3.13 The program below writes to a file named by the user. The file is opened and it is closed. Closing is important when writing a file so you know when the file as been completely written. Otherwise, in some situations, the data may still be in memory and waiting to be written out. Closing the output file insures that the data has actually made it to the file.

```
filename = input("Please enter the name of a file: ")
yourName = input("What is your name? ")
age = int(input("How old are you? "))
outfile = open(filename,"w")
outfile.write("Hello " + yourName + ". How are you?\n")
outfile.write("Next year you will be "+str(age+1) \
        +" years old\n")
outfile.close()
```

When writing to a file you use the *file.write* method. Unlike the *print* function, you cannot write multiple items by separating them with commas. The write method takes only one argument, the string to write. To write multiple items to a line of a file, you must use string concatenation (i.e. the + operator) to concatenate the items together as was done in Example 3.13. When comma separated items in a print statement are printed, a space character is automatically added between comma separated items. This is not true of string concatenation. If you want a space in the concatenated strings, you must add it yourself.

If you have non-string items to write to a file, they must be converted to strings using the *str* function. Otherwise, you'll get a run-time error when Python tries to concatenate a string to a non-string item. In Example 3.13 the *age* variable is an integer because of the *int* conversion on the third line. In the sixth line, one is added to the age and then the sum *age* + 1 is converted to a string so it can be concatenated to the string literals and then written to the file.

3.8
Reading Records from a File

It is frequently the case that a file contains more than one line that relate to each other in some way. For example, consider an address book program. Each entry in your address book may contain last name, first name, street, city, zip code, home phone number, and mobile number. Typically, each of these pieces of information would be stored on a separate line in a file. A program that reads such a file would need to read all these lines together and a *for loop* will not suffice. In this case it can be done if we use a *while loop*. A *while loop* looks like this:

```
<statements before while loop>
while <condition>:
    <body of while loop>
<statements after the while loop>
```

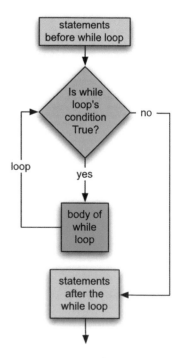

The condition of the while loop is evaluated first. If the condition evaluates to true, then the body of the while loop is executed. The condition is evaluated again and if the condition evaluates to true, the body of the while loop is performed again. The body of the while loop is repeated until the condition evaluates to false. It is possible the body of the while loop will never be executed if the condition evaluates to false the first time as graphically depicted in Fig. 3.7.

A *while loop is* used to read records from a file that are composed of multiple lines. A *for loop* will not suffice because a *for loop* only reads one line per iteration. Since multiple lines must be read, a *while loop* gives you the extra control you need. To read a multi-line record from a file we can use the pattern shown on the next page.

Fig. 3.7 A while loop

```
<read first line from first record>
while <line> != "":
   <read the rest of the record>
   <process the record>
   <read the first line of the next record>
<close the file>
```

This pattern can be illustrated by looking at part of an address book application where each address book record resides on 6 lines of a file.

Example 3.14 Here is a program that counts the number of entries in your phonebook. This assumes that the file looks something like the following:

```
Lie
Sophus
2234 Valdres Rd
Decorah, IA 52101
777-555-1234
777-554-4765
Lee
Kent D.
700 College Drive
Decorah, IA 52101
777-555-1212
777-554-0789
...
```

To read this file and count the entries the code would look like this:

```
1  phonebook = open("addressbook.txt","r")
2  numEntries = 0
3  # reads the first line of the first record
4  lastName = phonebook.readline().rstrip()
5  while lastName != "":
6     # when the file is completely read the lastName string
7     # will be empty. Since the lastName wasn't an empty
8     # string, read the rest of the record.
9     firstName = phonebook.readline().rstrip()
10    street = phonebook.readline().rstrip()
11    citystatezip = phonebook.readline().rstrip()
12    homephone = phonebook.readline().rstrip()
13    mobilephone = phonebook.readline().rstrip()
14
15    # Process the record by adding to the accumulator
16    numEntries = numEntries + 1
17
18    # Read the first line of the next record
19    lastName = phonebook.readline().rstrip()
20
21  print("You have", numEntries, "entries in your address book.")
```

The code in Example 3.14 reads the first line of a record, or at least it tries to. Every opened file has a current position that is set to the beginning of the file when the file is opened. As lines are read from the file, the current position advances through the file. When the current position is at the end of the file, the program in Example 3.14 will attempt to read one more line on either line 4 or line 19, depending on whether the file is empty or not. When the current position is at the end and it attempts to read a line, the *lastName* variable will be a reference to an empty string. This is the indication in Python that the current position is at the *end of file* sometimes abbreviated *EOF*. When this happens the code exits the while loop and prints the output on line 21. If the *lastName* variable is not empty, then the code assumes that because one line was present, all six lines will be present in the file. The code depends on each record being a six line record in the input file called *addressbook.txt*.

When you read a line from a file using the *readline* method you not only get the data on that line, but you also get the newline character at the end of the line in the file. The use of the *rstrip* method on the string read by *readline* strips away any white space from the right end of the string. If you need to look at the data at all you probably don't want the newline character on the end of each line of the record.

Whether you are writing code in Python or some other language, this *Reading Records From a File* pattern comes up over and over again. It is sometimes called the loop and a half problem. The idea is that you must attempt to read a line from the file before you know whether you are at the end of file or not. This can also be done if a boolean variable is introduced to help with the while loop. This boolean variable is the condition that gets you out of the while loop and the first time through it must be set to get your code to execute the while loop at least one.

Example 3.15 As with nearly every program, there is more than one way to do the same thing. The loop and a half code can be written differently as well. Here is another variation that while slightly different, accomplishes the same thing as Exampe 3.14.

```
 1  phonebook = open("addressbook.txt","r")
 2  numEntries = 0
 3  eof = False
 4  while not eof:
 5      # when the file is completely read the lastName string
 6      # will be empty. So will the other lines, but if the
 7      # lastName is empty then we know not to process the record.
 8      lastName = phonebook.readline().rstrip()
 9      firstName = phonebook.readline().rstrip()
10      street = phonebook.readline().rstrip()
11      citystatezip = phonebook.readline().rstrip()
12      homephone = phonebook.readline().rstrip()
13      mobilephone = phonebook.readline().rstrip()
14
15      # if lastName is empty then we didn't really read a record.
16      if lastName != "":
17          # Process the record by adding to the accumulator
18          numEntries = numEntries + 1
19      else:
20          eof = True
21  print("You have", numEntries, "entries in your address book.")
```

Example 3.14 and Example 3.15 do exactly the same thing. They each perform a loop and a half. The half part is one half of the body of the loop. In Example 3.14 this was reading the *lastName* variable before the loop started. In Example 3.15 this was the first half of the body of the while loop. Some may feel one is easier to memorize than the other. Some experienced programmers may even prefer another way of writing the loop and a half. The important thing is that one of these patterns should be memorized. You can use it any time you need to read multi-line records from a file.

William Edward Deming was a mathematician and consultant who is widely recognized as an important contributor to the rebuilding of Japan after the second world war [15]. One of his principles emphasized that you should not repeat the same process in more than one location. In Computer Science this translates to "You should avoid writing the same code in more than one location in your program". If you write code more than once and have to make a change later, you have to remember to change it in every location. If you've only written the code once, you only have to remember to change it in that one location. Copying code within your program increases the risk of there being a bug introduced by changing only some of the locations and not all of them when new function is being added or when a bug is being fixed. This guiding principle should be followed whenever possible. Example 3.14 appears to violate this principle with one line of repeated code. That's the tradeoff for not having to include an extra *if* statement in the body of the while loop as was done in Example 3.15.

3.9
Review Questions

1. Where did the term *computer* originate?
2. What is a sequence in Python? Give an example.
3. How do you call a method on an object? What is the general form? Give an example that's not in the book.
4. What is a *class* in Python?
5. What is a *type* in Python?
6. *Definite iteration* is when the number of iterations is known before the loop starts. What construct in Python is used for definite iteration?
7. *Indefinite iteration* is what happens when the exact number of iterations is not known before the loop begins (but still may be calculable if you know the input). What construct in Python is used for indefinite iteration?
8. How can you get at the last element of a list? Give two examples of expressions that return the last element of a list.
9. If you wanted to print all the items of a list in reverse order using a while loop, how would you do it? Write some example code that demonstrates how this might be accomplished. Remember, you must use a while loop in your answer.
10. How would you use the *Guess and Check* pattern to find a name in a phonebook? Write some code that searches a list of names for someone's name. Is there a more efficient way of finding a name in a phonebook?

11. Lists and strings are similar in many ways. One major difference is that lists are mutable and strings are not. What does that mean? Give an example of an operation that lists support but strings do not.

12. Why does mutable data sometimes lead to confusion when programming?

13. What is the *accumulator pattern*? Give an example of how it might be used.

14. There are two ways to read from a file that are presented in the text. Describe both of them. When is one more appropriate than the other?

3.10
Exercises

1. Write a program that prints all the prime numbers less than 1000. You can write this program by creating a list of prime numbers. To begin, the list is empty. Then you write two nested for loops. The outer for loop runs through all the numbers from 2 to 999. The inner for loop runs through the list of prime numbers. If the next number in the outer for loop is not divisible by any of the prime numbers, then it is prime and can be printed as a prime and added to the list of primes. To add an *element*, e, to a *list*, lst, you can write *lst.append(e)*. This program uses both the guess and check pattern and the accumulator pattern to build the list of prime numbers.

2. Write a menu driven program that works with an address book file as described in Example 3.14. You may want to consult Example 2.6 to see how to print a menu to the user and get input from them. Your program should have three menu items, look up a name, add a contact, and quit. Interacting with your program should look something like this:

```
1) Look up a person by last name
2) Add a person to the address book.
3) Quit

Enter your choice: 1
Please enter the last name to look up: Lie

Sophus Lie
2234 Valdres Rd
Decorah, IA 52101
home: 777-555-1234
mobile: 777-554-4765

1) Look up a person by last name
2) Add a person to the address book.
3) Quit

Enter your choice: 3
Done
```

You will want to create your own address book file for this problem. Call the file "addressbook.txt". You can create it by selecting *New* in your IDE and then saving it in the same directory as your program. You should call the file "addressbook.txt". Don't add a ".py" to the end of this text file. Be sure when you write to the file that you put a newline character at the end of each line. If you create your own file there should be a newline character at the end of each line. If you don't do this then when you try to write another record to the file it may not end up formatted correctly. You can always open the text file with Wing to take a look at it and see if it looks like the format presented in Example 3.14.

3. Write a program that asks the user to enter a list of numbers and then prints the count of the numbers in the list and the average of the numbers in the list. Do not use the *len* function to find the length of the list. Use the accumulator pattern instead. The program would print this when run.

```
Please enter a list of numbers: 1.0 10 3.5 4.2 10.6
There were 5 numbers in the list.
The average of the numbers was 5.86
```

4. Write a program that asks the user to enter a list of numbers. The program should take the list of numbers and add only those numbers between 0 and 100 to a new list. It should then print the contents of the new list. Running the program should look something like this:

```
Please enter a list of numbers: 10.5 -8 105 76 83.2 206
The numbers between 0 and 100 are: 10.5 76.0 83.2
```

5. Write a program that asks the user to enter a list and then builds a new list which is the reverse of the original list.

6. Draw a picture of the variable references and values that result from running the code in exercise 5.

7. Write a program that asks the user to enter a list and then reverses the list in place so that after reversing, the original list has been reversed instead of creating a new list.

8. Draw a picture of the variable references and values that result from running the code in exercise 7.

9. Write a program that asks the user to enter a list of integers one at a time. It should allow the user to terminate the list by entering a −1. Running the program would look something like this.

```
Enter a list of integers terminated by a -1.
Please enter the first integer and press enter: 5
Please enter another integer: 4
Please enter another integer: 3
Please enter another integer: 8
Please enter another integer: -1
The list of integers is 5 4 3 8
```

10. Write a program that computes a user's GPA on a 4 point scale. Each grade on a 4 point scale is multiplied by the number of credits for that class. The sum of all the credit, grade products is divided by the total number of credits earned. Assume the 4 point scale assigns values of 4.0 for an A, 3.7 for an A-, 3.3 for a B+, 3.0 for a B, 2.7 for a B-, 2.3 for a C+, 2.0 for a C, 1.7 for a C-, 1.3 for a D+, 1.0 for a D, 0.7 for a D-, and 0 for an F. Ask the user to enter their credit grade pairs using the following format until the enter 0 for the number of credits.

```
This program computes your GPA.
Please enter your completed courses.
Terminate your entry by entering 0 credits.
Credits? 4
Grade? A
Credits? 3
Grade? B+
Credits? 4
Grade? B-
Credits? 2
Grade? C
Credits? 0
Your GPA is 3.13
```

11. Example 1.1 on page 11 presented a nice algorithm for converting a base 10 integer to binary. It turns out that this algorithm works for both positive and negative integers. Write this algorithm one more time. This time, use a loop to avoid duplicating any code. Write the algorithm so it will convert any 32-bit signed integer to its binary equivalent. Thirty-two bit signed integers are integers in the range of -2^{31} to $2^{31} - 1$. That would be integers in the range $-2,147,483,648$ to $2,147,483,647$. Be sure to eliminate any leading 0's from the result before it is printed. Your loop should terminate when the number you are converting has reached zero (according to the algorithm) or when you've reached the requisite 32 bits for your number.

3.11
Solutions to Practice Problems

These are solutions to the practice problems in this chapter. You should only consult these answers after you have tried each of them for yourself first. Practice problems are meant to help reinforce the material you have just read so make use of them.

Solution to Practice Problem 3.1

```
sentence = input("Please enter a sentence: ")
print("Here is the sentence with the case swapped.")
print(sentence.swapcase())
```

Solution to Practice Problem 3.2

```
answer = input("Please answer yes or no: ")
if not answer.islower():
  print("Next time please user all lower case letters.")
```

Solution to Practice Problem 3.3

The else would be optional for this exercise.

```
answer = input("Please answer yes or no: ")
if answer.lower()=="yes":
  print("You entered yes.")
elif answer.lower()=="no":
  print("You answered no.")
else:
  print("You answered neither yes or no.")
```

Solution to Practice Problem 3.4

1. Does the string *s* change as the code is executed?
     No it does not.
2. What happens if the user just presses enter when prompted instead of typing any characters?
     The body of the for loop is not executed at all.

Solution to Practice Problem 3.5

```
s = input("Please type some characters and press enter:")
for c in s:
    print(c.upper())
```

Solution to Practice Problem 3.6

```
for i in range(5):
    print(i)
```

Solution to Practice Problem 3.7

```
s = input("Please type some characters and press enter:")
for i in range(len(s)-1,-1,-1):
    print(s[i])
```

Solution to Practice Problem 3.8

The split method returns a list of strings. The for loop iterates over the list. Each time through the loop the word variable is referencing the next string in the list.

Solution to Practice Problem 3.9

If the containsEven *if* statement were indented, then the for loop would check to see if *containsEven* were true or false each time through the loop. The program would print that the list did not contain an even number (even though it might) over and over again until an even number was found. Then it would print it did contain an even number over and over again. It would print one line for each element of the list.

Solution to Practice Problem 3.10

```
entry = input("Please make your blog entry for today: ")
found = False
for word in entry.split():
    if word in ['orderly', 'shopping', 'repeat', 'again', \
                'gamble', 'bid']:
        found = True

if found:
    print("You really need to talk to somone about this.")
else:
    print("Thanks for you entry.")
```

Solution to Practice Problem 3.11

If the *question* variable were printed it would be the same as if the *answer* variable were printed. Both *question* and *answer* refer to the same list.

Solution to Practice Problem 3.12

```
s = input("Please enter a list of integers:")

lst = s.split() # Now lst is a list of strings.

count = 0 # Here is the beginning of the accumulator pattern

for e in lst:
    if int(e) % 2 == 0:
        count = count + 1

print("There were", count, "even integers in the list.")
```

Solution to Practice Problem 3.13

```
n = int(input("Please enter a non-negative integer: "))

factorial = 1
for i in range(1,n+1):
  factorial = factorial * i

print(str(n)+"! =",factorial)
```

Solution to Practice Problem 3.14

```
filename = input("Please enter the name of a file:")
catfile = open(filename,"r")
for line in catfile:
    print(line.rstrip())
catfile.close()
```

Using Objects

4

In this chapter we explore objects and code re-use. Python is an object-oriented language and learning to use objects can make programming fun and productive. In this chapter we'll explore object-oriented programming by using the turtle module.

If we had to write every program from scratch, we wouldn't be able to get very much done. Part of the fun of programming is using something someone else has written to solve a problem quickly. Another fun aspect of programming is writing code that others may want to use in their programs. In fact, programmers sometimes become famous among their peers by writing code that turns out to be very valuable: people like Yukihiro Matsumoto [2], who created the Ruby programming language, or Robin Milner [6] who described the type inference system used by Standard ML, or Guido van Rossum the creator of the Python Programming Language [10]. There are many, many computer scientists that could be named here.

Python makes it easy for programmers who want to share code with others to do just that. A *module* is a file containing Python code. When a programmer needs to use code another programmer wrote, he or she can import the module containing the code they want to use into their program. Modules can be imported into other modules so one programmer can easily use code that another programmer wrote. One such module is called *turtle*. The *turtle* module includes code that helps us draw figures in the sand. A turtle can walk around a beach dragging his or her tail in the sand or raising that tail. When the tail is down, the turtle leaves a track. When the tail is up the turtle leaves no trail. With this simple analogy we can draw some pretty interesting pictures. The idea has been around since at least the late 1960's when Seymour Papert added turtle graphics to the Logo programming language [14]. Gregor Lingl, an Austrian high school teacher, has implemented a version of turtle graphics for Python that now is part of the Python programming environment.

To use a module it needs to be imported into your program. There are two ways to import a module. The decision of which to use is partly based on convenience and partly based on safety of your program. The safe way to import a module is to write `import module` where *module.py* is the name of a module. The module must be in the current directory or in one of the directories where your installation of Python knows to look. When importing a module in this way you must prefix any use of code within the module with the module name. If you want to call a function or use a type, t, that is defined in

K.D. Lee, *Python Programming Fundamentals,* Undergraduate Topics in Computer Science,   93
DOI 10.1007/978-1-84996-537-8_4, © Springer-Verlag London Limited 2011

the imported module, you must write *module.t*. This is safe because there will never be the possibility of using the same name within two different modules since all names must be *qualified* with the module name. Using *qualified* names makes importing safe, but is not the most convenient when writing code.

Example 4.1 Here is a program that imports the turtle code and uses it to draw a square.

```
import turtle

t = turtle.Turtle()
screen = t.getscreen()
t.forward(25)
t.left(90)
t.forward(25)
t.left(90)
t.forward(25)
t.left(90)
t.forward(25)
screen.exitonclick()
```

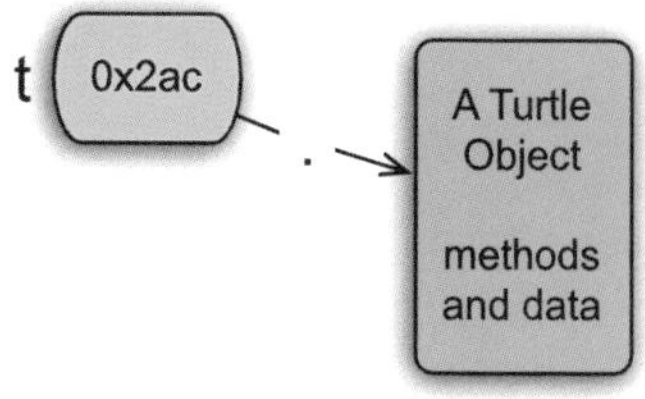

Fig. 4.1 A turtle object

If you are going to try this code, DO NOT call it turtle.py. If you name your own program the same as a module name, then Python will no longer import the correct module. If you already did this you must delete the turtle.pyc file in your folder and rename your module to something other than turtle.py.

Example 4.1 imports the turtle module using *import turtle*. Once the module is imported, a Turtle object can be created. In this case, the programmer must write *turtle.Turtle()* to create an object of type *Turtle*. Because the Turtle type or *class* resides in the turtle module the fully qualified name of *turtle.Turtle()* must be written to create a Turtle object. Figure 4.1 shows the *turtle* reference pointing to a *Turtle* object just like integer variables are references that point to *int* objects and string variables are references that point to *str* objects. Initializing a Turtle object and making a reference point to it is just like creating any other object in Python.

Practice 4.1 Write some code that uses a for loop to draw a square using the turtle module.

A more convenient way to import a module is to write *from module import **. In this case we could import the turtle module by writing *from turtle import **. This imports the turtle module as before but merges all the names of functions, types, and classes in the turtle module with the names of functions, variables, and types in your program.

Example 4.2 Here is a program that draws a pentagon using the other form of import.

```
from turtle import *

t = Turtle()
screen = t.getscreen()
t.forward(25)
t.left(72.5)
t.forward(25)
t.left(72.5)
t.forward(25)
t.left(72.5)
t.forward(25)
t.left(72.5)
t.forward(25)
screen.exitonclick()
```

Example 4.2 imports by merging the namespace of the turtle module and the program in the example. Both Example 4.1 and 4.2 demonstrate how to call a *method* on an *object*. This means that any variables defined in the turtle module will be overridden if they are also defined in the code in Example 4.2. For example, we would want to be careful and not name something *Turtle* in our code since that would mean that we would no longer be able to create a Turtle object in our program. Redefining a name like this is not permanent though. The problem only exists within the program. Once the program terminates, the next time we import the turtle module, the Turtle class would be available again.

Not every class must be imported from a module. Python already makes the *int*, *float*, *bool*, and *str* classes available without importing anything. These classes are called *built-in* classes in Python. But, the *Turtle* class is not built-in. It must be imported from the *turtle* module.

In both examples the variable *t* is a reference that points to a *Turtle* object. The turtle object can be told to do things. Turtles understand certain messages or methods. We've already learned how to call methods on objects in Chap. 3. For instance, we've called the *split* method on a *string* object. Sending a message to a Turtle object is no different. For instance in Example 4.2 we sent the *forward* message to the turtle *t* passing 25 as the number of steps to move forward. The *forward* method, and other methods that turtles understand, are described in Appendix F. Methods for the *TurtleScreen* class are described in Appendix G.

Practice 4.2 Write a short program that prompts the user to enter the number of sides of a regular polygon. Then draw a regular polygon with that many sides. You can use the *textinput* method described in Appendix G to get the input or you can just use *input* to get the input from the Debug I/O tab of Wing IDE 101.

While actual turtles are slow and perhaps not very interesting, turtle objects can be fun. A turtle object can be used in a lot of different ways. It can change color and width. It can be used to draw filled in shapes. It can draw circles and even display messages on the screen. Turtle graphics is a great way to become familiar with object-oriented programming. The best way to learn about object-oriented programming is just to have fun with it. Refer to Appendix F and use it to write some programs that draw some interesting pictures with color, interesting shapes, filled in polygons, etc.

Fig. 4.2 A 4WD truck

Practice 4.3 Use the turtle module to write a program that draws a 4WD truck like that pictured in Fig. 4.2. A truck consists of two tires and a top of some sort. You should use some color. You may use *penup* and *pendown* while drawing. However, don't use *goto* once you have started drawing. The reason for this will become evident in the exercises at the end of the chapter.

You may want to change color, fill in shapes, etc. Be creative and try things out. Just be sure the last line of your program is *screen.exitonclick()*. Without the call to *screen.exitonclick()* the turtle graphics window may appear to freeze up.

4.1
Constructors

To create an object of a certain type or *class* we must write

```
<objectref> = <Class>(<args>)
```

This creates an object of type *Class* and then points the *objectref* variable at the object that was just created. Figure 4.1 shows what happens in memory as a result of executing the *t = Turtle()* line of code in Examples 4.1 and 4.2. Several things happen when we create an object. Python first reserves enough space in memory to hold the object's data. Then, the object is initialized with the data that must be stored in it. All objects have some data associated with them. For instance, a Turtle object knows its current location on the screen, its direction, and its color, among other things. When a Turtle object is created, all the information is stored in the object. This is called *constructing an object* and it happens when we call the constructor. So, when we write the following line of code or similar lines of code for other types of objects:

```
t = Turtle()
```

we are instructing Python to create a Turtle object using the constructor and we make the variable *t* point to the turtle object that was just created. There are lots of constructors that are available to us for creating different types of objects in Python.

Example 4.3 Here are some examples of objects being created using constructors. The types (i.e. classes) *str, int, float, Turtle,* and *list* each have their own constructors. In fact, sometimes a class has more than one constructor. Look at the float examples below. There are at least two ways to create a float object. You can either pass the constructor a string and it will convert the float in the string to a float object, or you can pass an integer to the float constructor.

```
s = str(6)
x = int("6")
y = float("6.5")
z = float(6)
t = Turtle()
lst = list("a b c")
u = 6
r = "hi there"
```

Except in a few special circumstances, a constructor is always called by writing the name of the class then a left paren, then any arguments to pass to the constructor, followed by a right paren. Calling a *constructor* returns an instance of the *class*, called an *object*. For a few of the built-in classes there is some *syntactic sugar* available for creating objects. In Example 4.3, the variables *u* and *r* are initialized to point to an integer object and a string object, respectively. *Syntactic sugar* makes constructing objects for some of the built-in classes more convenient and it is necessary in some cases. Without some *syntactic sugar*, how would you create an object containing the integer 6?

Practice 4.4 Using Wing, or some other IDE, run the code in Example 4.2. Set a breakpoint at the line where *screen* is initialized. Then, look at the *Stack Data* and specifically at the *t* variable. Expand it out so you can see the state of the turtle and specifically the *_position* of the turtle. This is the (*x, y*) location of the turtle on the screen. When the turtle is at the peak of the pentagon from Example 4.2 what is its (*x, y*) location?

4.2
Accessor Methods

When we have an object in our program, we may wish to learn something about the state of that object. To ask for information about an object you must call an *accessor* method. Accessor methods return information about the state of an object.

Example 4.4 To learn the heading of the turtle we might call the *heading* method.

```
import turtle

t = turtle.Turtle()

print(t.heading())
```

Calling the heading method on the turtle means writing *t* followed by a dot (i.e. a period) followed by the name of the method, in this case *heading*. The accessor method, *heading*, returns some information about the object, but does not change the object. Accessor methods do not change the object. They only access the state of the object.

> **Practice 4.5** Is the *forward* method an accessor method? What about the *xcor* method? You might have to consult Appendix F to figure this out.

4.3
Mutator Methods

Mutator methods, as the name suggests, change or mutate the state of the object. Section 3.5 introduced the mutability of lists. Mutator methods are called the same as accessor methods. Where an accessor method usually gives you information back, a mutator method may require you to provide some information to the object.

Example 4.5 Here are some calls to mutator methods.

```
turtle.right(90)
turtle.begin_fill()
turtle.penup()
```

One misconception about object-oriented programming is that assigning one reference to another creates two separate objects. This is not the case as is demonstrated by the

Fig. 4.3 Two references to one object

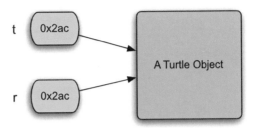

following code. This isn't a problem if the object doesn't change. However, when the object may be mutated it is important to know that the object is changing and this means that it changes for all references that point at the object.

Example 4.6 Here is an example of one turtle with two different references to it. Both *t* and *r* refer the same turtle.

```
t = Turtle()
t.forward(50)

r = t

r.left(90)
r.forward(100)

t.left(90)
t.forward(50)
```

In Example 4.6 more than one reference points to the same Turtle object as depicted in Fig. 4.3. Writing *r* = *t* does not create a second Turtle. It only points both references to the same Turtle object. This is clear from Example 4.6 when one Turtle seems to pick up where the other left off. In fact, they are the same turtle.

Practice 4.6 How would you create a second Turtle object for *r* if that's really what you wanted?

4.4
Immutable Classes

Section 3.5 first defined immutable classes. An immutable class is a type with no mutator methods. If an object has no mutator methods then it is impossible to tell if two references point to the same object or if they point to different objects. In fact it doesn't really matter since neither reference can be used to change the object. This may happen frequently in Python for objects of type *int, float, string*, and *bool*. All these classes are immutable. These classes of objects can never be changed once they are created since they have no mutator methods!

Practice 4.7 If strings cannot be changed, what happens in the following code? Draw a picture to show what happens in the following code.

```
x = "hello"
x = x + " world"
print(x)
```

While string objects can't be changed, references can be. That's what happens in the exercise above. *str* objects never change once they are created. Immutable classes are nice to work with because we can forget about their being objects and references and just concentrate on using them without fear of changing the object accidentally.

4.5
Object-Oriented Programming

Turtles are fun to program because they make drawing easy by remembering many of the details of generating computer graphics for us. That's really the motivation behind object-oriented programming and using objects. What we've seen in this short chapter are all the mechanics for creating and using objects. Objects make our lives as programmers simpler. Every object maintains some state information, its data, and every object lets us either access that data through an accessor function or it allows its data to be changed by calling mutator methods. Many objects have both accessor and mutator methods.

The power of object-oriented programming is in the ability to organize the data in our programs into logical entities that somehow make sense. A turtle is a great way to embody many of the elements of graphics programming while giving us a way of visualizing how the turtle works by thinking about how a real turtle might leave marks in the sand.

4.6
Working with XML Files

Now that you know how to use objects and in particular how to use turtle graphics you can put it to use. There are many applications for Turtle graphics. It can be used to draw pictures as we've seen. Turtle graphics can also be used to visualize data. In the next few sections you'll learn how to visualize workout data retrieved from an exercise computer. Workout data like heart rate in beats per minute, distance, and cadence is available from many workout devices. The particular device used in examples in this text was a Garmin Forerunner 305. The Garmin Training Center program comes with the exercise computer and it can be used to capture the data from the computer. Garmin Training Center will display a graphical representation of the workout data similar to that shown in Fig. 4.4. Our goal is to gather information on a workout and plot it using turtle graphics.

Once data has been captured from the Garmin 305, the data can be exported to an XML file. XML files have a fairly straight-forward structure but also may contain a lot of formatting information that is not really part of the data. It would be painful to have to write code that reads an XML file and extracts just the information you need. Fortunately, it is because XML files contain this extra formatting information that it is possible for someone else to write code that we can use to read an XML file. That code is called an XML parser. Parsing refers to reading data and selecting out the individual components or elements of that data.

To parse an XML file you must import an XML parser. We'll use the minidom XML parser in this text. The import statement looks like this:

```
from xml.dom import minidom
```

Once you have imported the XML parser you create a parser object by telling the minidom to parse the XML file.

```
xmldoc = minidom.parse("trainingdata.xml")
```

That's all there is to parsing an XML file. The call to the parse function above may take some time to execute depending on the size of your XML file. That's because the entire file is being parsed and depending on how many exercise sessions are in your database, that file can be quite large. Once it is parsed we want to go through the parsed XML file and extract the information we want from the file.

Looking at Fig. 4.4 we can determine that we need several pieces of information. This graph is of a biking exercise session. It includes heart rate, cadence, and distance. Cadence is a measure of the revolutions of the pedals on a bike per minute. Other information may be available, too, but this introduction to data visualization will concentrate on just these three measures. Not as obvious, but just as important, time is also being measured in the workout.

A tag in an XML file is a string of characters that appears within angle brackets (i.e. a less than/greater than sign pair). There are *start-tags* and *end-tags* within XML files. For instance, `<Activities>` is a start-tag. Each start-tag has a matching end-tag that ends one *element* of an XML file. For instance, the Activities element of an XML file would start with `<Activities>` and end with `</Activities>`. The matching end-tag always has the same name as the start-tag. A start-tag may have certain attributes that are a part of the tag. For instance, the `<Activity Sport="Other">` tag has a *Sport* attribute.

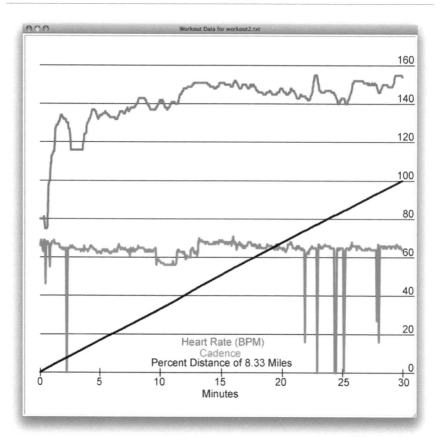

Fig. 4.4 Workout data visualization

Start-tags and end-tags always occur in matching pairs. In between the tags there may be other start-tag/end-tag pairs. There may also be plain text between a start-tag and matching end-tag. This plain text is called *data*.

Example 4.7 The Training Center database file has a fairly complex structure, but can be read easily enough using an XML parser. Here is an example of the Training Center database XML file. The file largely consists of a series of *Activity* elements. Within each activity are a series of Laps. Within each lap is some summary information and a series of Trackpoints. Each trackpoint reflects the information collected from the sensors at some moment in time during a workout.

This is only a small sample of part of a Training Center database XML file. The actual files can get very large depending on the number of workouts recorded and the duration of each workout.

```xml
<?xml version="1.0" encoding="UTF-8" standalone="no" ?>
<TrainingCenterDatabase xmlns="http://www.garmin.com...">

  <Folders/>

  <Activities>
    <Activity Sport="Running">
      <Id>2008-10-28T20:00:37Z</Id>
      <Lap StartTime="2008-10-28T20:00:37Z">
        <TotalTimeSeconds>2244.6000000</TotalTimeSeconds>
        <DistanceMeters>4828.8569336</DistanceMeters>
        <MaximumSpeed>3.2622104</MaximumSpeed>
        <Calories>486</Calories>
        <AverageHeartRateBpm xsi:type="HeartRateInBeats...">
          <Value>142</Value>
        </AverageHeartRateBpm>
        <MaximumHeartRateBpm xsi:type="HeartRateInBeats...">
          <Value>166</Value>
        </MaximumHeartRateBpm>
        <Intensity>Active</Intensity>
        <TriggerMethod>Manual</TriggerMethod>
        <Track>
          <Trackpoint>
            <Time>2008-10-28T20:00:37Z</Time>
          </Trackpoint>
          <Trackpoint>
            <Time>2008-10-28T20:00:38Z</Time>
            <Position>
              <LatitudeDegrees>43.2554457</LatitudeDegrees>
              <LongitudeDegrees>-91.7153302</LongitudeDegrees>
            </Position>
            <AltitudeMeters>348.6152344</AltitudeMeters>
            <DistanceMeters>0.0000000</DistanceMeters>
            <HeartRateBpm xsi:type="HeartRateInBeats...">
              <Value>93</Value>
            </HeartRateBpm>
            <SensorState>Absent</SensorState>
          </Trackpoint>
```

4.7
Extracting Elements from an XML File

XML is a very common file format. Many applications use XML to store their data. Some that you might be familiar with include the Apple iTunes application or the registry in Microsoft Windows. Mac OS X uses it as well in its application structure. XML is popular because the definition of XML makes it possible to add additional elements to an XML file later without affecting code that was written before the new fields were added. This ability to add to an XML file without breaking existing code means there is a huge advantage to using XML as the format for data in practically any application.

So, learning to extract elements from an XML file is a very practical skill to learn. Since an XML file is a collection of start-tag/end-tag pairs, to extract elements from an XML file you begin by asking for a list of all elements that match a given tag-name. In Example 4.7 the main element was named with the *TrainingCenterDatabase* tag. To ask for the list of all elements that match the TrainingCenterDatabase tag we can write:

```
elements = xmldoc.getElementsByTagName("TrainingCenterDatabase")
```

This returns a list of all tags that match the tag name *TrainingCenterDatabase*. We know there is only one of these tags in the file, so we can get just the first one by using index 0 into the list.

```
root = xmldoc.getElementsByTagName("TrainingCenterDatabase")[0]
```

The root variable is the first of the DOM elements returned by the minidom parser. DOM stands for Document Object Model. Now that we have the root element we can get sub-elements from the root. The sub-elements of the root are the list of *Activities* elements.

```
activitiesList = root.getElementsByTagName("Activities")
```

Again, there is only one *Activities* tag within a database so using index 0 gives us the first *Activities* element. To get the *Activity* tags from the single Activities tag we can write the following:

```
activities = activitiesList[0].getElementsByTagName("Activity")
```

Finally, to collect the list of different activities we can traverse the list of activities and add the sport name to a list of exercise activities if it has not already been added.

```
exerciseActivities = []

for activity in activities:
  sport = activity.attributes["Sport"]
  sportName = sport.value

  if not sportName in exerciseActivities:
    exerciseActivities.append(sportName)
```

4.8
Dictionaries

In the code presented in Sect. 4.7 you can see how the value of the *Sport* attribute is retrieved from an element. If the element's tag contains an attribute or attributes, you can use the name of the attribute to retrieve its value. The attribute and value pairs of a tag make up a dictionary.

A dictionary is a little like a list. You can use indexing to look up values within the dictionary just like you use indexing to look up values within a list. The difference is that instead of using only integers as the index values, you can use any value you like.

Example 4.8 A list and a dictionary have similarities. Both data types hold a collection of values. The difference between a list and a dictionary are in the values used to index into them. In a list, the index values must be non-negative integers and the locations within the list are numbered sequentially starting at 0.

Within a dictionary there is no ordering of the index values. An index value, called a *key* when working with dictionaries, can be nearly any value. A dictionary is a list of *key*, *value* pairs. Each key is mapped to a value. Keys must be unique, values do not have to be unique in the dictionary.

Here is some code that creates both a list and a dictionary and demonstrates similar operations on the two datatypes.

```
lst = [] # an empty list
dct = {} # an empty dictionary

# The append method adds items to a list.
lst.append("Biking")
lst.append("Running")
lst.append("Other")

# The next line adds Sport/Running as a key/value pair
dct["Sport"] = "Running"
dct["Day"] = "June 18, 2010"
dct["Time"] = "1850PM CDT"

# We can iterate over a list by using a for loop.
for i in range(len(lst)):
    print(i, lst[i])

# We can iterate over a dictionary using a for loop
# to go through the list of keys to the dictionary.
for key in dct.keys():
    print(key, dct[key])
```

Appendix E contains a complete listing of dictionary operators and methods.

4.9
Getting at the Data in an XML File

The purpose of at least some of the start/end-tag pairs in an XML file is to delineate data within the file. For instance, within each Activity element is one Id element. This Id element contains the date and time when the activity was performed. In Example 4.7 the

Running activity shown there was performed at about 8 pm Zulu time on October 28th, 2008. Zulu is just another name for GMT (Greenwich Mean Time).

To display workout data we must let the user pick a workout based on the date and time it was performed so we must read the date and time from the Id tag. To do this, we get the *Id* element much like we have extracted other elements. Then we ask for the Id element's data.

Example 4.9 Here is code that will get the date and time of a workout.

```
dVal = activity.getElementsByTagName("Id")[0].firstChild.data
year = int(dVal[0:4])
month = int(dVal[5:7])
day = int(dVal[8:10])
hour = int(dVal[11:13])
minutes = int(dVal[14:16])
seconds = int(dVal[17:19])
dateOfWorkout = datetime(year,month,day,hour,minutes,seconds)
```

The *getElementsByTagName* method returns a list of all elements containing the *Id* tag (there is only one in an activity). The index 0 gives us the only Id element in the list. The *firstChild* field returns just the data between the start and end *Id* tag. Finally, the *data* field gives us the data of the Id tag. Anytime you need the plain text data contained in an element, you can use *firstChild.data* to retrieve it.

In Example 4.9 the datetime class is defined in the *datetime* module. To use the datetime class the module must be imported at the top of the program file. A datetime object constructed as is done in Example 4.9 can be useful, especially when computing the difference between to timestamps. Slicing is used to extract the year, month, day, hour, minutes, and seconds of the workout date. Then a datetime object is constructed from those parts.

Practice 4.8 Write some code that finds all the times that "Biking" was the workout type. You should write your code so it prints a menu of the times to the screen like this:

```
1) 2010-01-26 23:02:14
2) 2010-01-28 19:58:33
Please enter your choice (1-2) :
```

4.10
Working with Time

To graph a workout from data presented in Example 4.7 a workout must be selected and matched by searching through the XML file. You can search through the elements looking for the workout that matches the date a user of the program selected (see the previous practice exercise). Once the workout has been found, then you have to go to the *Lap* element. In the *Lap* element you can get the *Track* element. From the *Track* you get read the *Trackpoint* elements.

Each Trackpoint element is recorded at a particular date and time. You can construct a datetime object for the trackpoint using the same technique used to construct a datetime object above. It would make sense to build a list of all the datetime objects for the trackpoints in a workout. Then, you can compute the total time of the workout by subtracting the last datetime object from the first.

Example 4.10 Here is some code that will compute the total time of a workout assuming that you have built a list of all the datetimes of a workout.

```
duration = timeList[-1] - timeList[0]
totalWorkoutTime = duration.seconds
```

Example 4.10 provides the code necessary for computing the total time of a workout assuming that *timeList* is a list of datetime objects for each *Trackpoint* element of a workout. Subtracting two *datetime* objects yields a *timedelta* object. A *timedelta* object has a seconds field that contains the actual seconds separating the two datetimes.

4.11
Parallel Lists

To graph the data from a workout you first have to collect the required information. To plot data as shown in Fig. 4.4, the list of trackpoint times, heart rate measurements, and distances must be recorded. Cadence can also be recorded in a list if it exists in the trackpoint information. A separate list can be built for each type of information. One list for time, one list for heart rate measurements, one list for cadence, and one for distance. Each index within the separate lists contains data of one trackpoint. For instance, the first entry in each list (i.e. index 0) contains the time, distance, cadence, and heart rate of the first trackpoint in the workout.

This technique of using multiple lists to hold data that are related to each other is called *parallel lists*. The lists are in a sense parallel to each other because each list contains information that is related to the others at the same index value within the list. Each index location within the four lists contains the four elements of one trackpoint. Since we will need to go through the data more than once, it makes sense to store this information in parallel lists so we can go through it as often as we need.

4.12
Visualizing a Workout

To create the graph of a workout a Turtle is created as seen earlier in this chapter. It is necessary to set the world coordinates of the screen to match the data that has just been read. To set the world coordinates we need a maximum in the *x* direction (i.e. horizontal) and the *y* direction (i.e. vertical). The horizontal direction was chosen to be time. The vertical direction needs to be set to the maximum of the numbers we wish to graph. Maximum heart rate will always be greater than cadence and greater than 100 (for the percent of distance). So, we need two numbers: the duration of the workout and the maximum heart rate.

> **Practice 4.9** How can you find the maximum heart rate for the workout? How would you write that code? Try to use as few loops as possible while still getting the information you need.

If *duration* is the result of subtracting the first datetime object from the last datetime object in the list of trackpoint times, then *duration.seconds* is the number of seconds in the workout. The horizontal maximum can be set to *duration.seconds*+60 to add a little space to the right edge of the window. The vertical maximum can be set to *maxHeartRate*+20 to add a little space to the top edge of the window. To add a little space at the left and bottom edge the window coordinates can be set to start at $(-60, -20)$. The call to set the world coordinates ends up looking like:

```
xMax = duration.seconds+60
yMax = maxHeartRate+20
screen.setworldcoordinates(-60, -20, xMax, yMax)
```

Draw the Axes

Both the *x* and *y* axes need to be drawn on the graph. The vertical *y* axis is drawn as a series of lines in Fig. 4.4. To do this draw lines from 0 to xMax. This needs to be repeated every 20 units in the vertical direction. It can be done with a for loop and the *range* function. Writing the 20, 40, 60, 80, ... text along the right-hand side of the window means positioning the turtle and using "right" alignment when writing the text.

To draw the ticky marks along the bottom another for loop can be used. Since the horizontal dimension is in seconds, every 300 seconds would be 5 minutes which is a reasonable label for a workout. To write the minute labels specify "center" alignment.

Plotting the Data

To plot the data the turtle must be positioned to the first point of the data with the pen up. The color can be set by calling the *color* method. Then the pen should be put down and plotting can commence by going to the next data point with the *goto* method. Each data point is an (x, y) pair. The x coordinate is the time since the beginning of the workout. This can be computed by subtracting the current time from the beginning of the workout. The current time was stored in the time list. The y coordinate is the particular data point being plotted. For instance, heart rate is stored in the heart rate list.

At this point, if you are writing this code, you may think of writing something like this:

```
for timeStamp in timeList:
    time = timeStamp - timeList[0]
    ...
```

The problem with this code is that we are working with parallel lists. Parallel lists mean that corresponding locations in the lists are related. For example, index 0 in each list is one trackpoint. This means that if we need the corresponding data from more than one list, the code above will not do what we want. Instead, we need to index into the list. By doing this, we can use the same index to get the corresponding data from more than one list. When working with parallel lists it is necessary to write:

```
for i in range(len(timeList)):
    timeStamp = timeList[i]
    hr = heartRate[i]
    ...
```

By writing the *for loop* this way, the index i can be used to retrieve the corresponding information from more than one list. In this case, the ith element of both the time list and the heart rate list is the (x, y) pair that should be plotted. Graphing cadence can be done the same way.

Graphing distance is a bit more challenging, but not too much. Distance in the data is given in meters travelled from the beginning of the workout. If meters were plotted, it would go way off the top of the chart. If meters were converted to miles it would be way at the bottom of the chart. Instead, a percent of distance completed so far provides a good visualization of the workout distance. To compute a percent of distance, the total distance is needed which would be in the last element of the distance list. So, the y coordinate of the distance plot, is the percentage of distance covered so far in the workout.

Any good graph should contain a legend for the information being visualized. This information can be provided in a variety of ways. While color may not be visible in the text, using a different color for each plot and for the legend makes sense visually. Each label matches the color of its plotted data.

Finally, if you write this program, you will probably get impatient with the turtle and how slow it plots the data. Once you've seen that the turtle is doing what you want, you can speed up the program by using the tracer function on the screen. Writing *screen.tracer(100)* causes the program to run significantly faster.

4.13
Review Questions

1. What are the two ways to import a module? How do they differ? What are the advantages of each method of importing?
2. How do you construct an object? In general, what do you have to write to call a constructor?
3. What happens when you construct an object?
4. What is the purpose of an accessor method?
5. What is the purpose of a mutator method?
6. Does every class contain both mutator and accessor methods? If so, why? If not, give an example when this is not true.
7. What does an XML file contain?
8. How do you read an XML file in a program?
9. What is an attribute in an XML file? Give an example.
10. What type of value does the method *getElementsByTagName* return when it is called?
11. What is a dictionary?
12. What is a timedelta object and how do you create one in your program?
13. What are parallel lists? Why are they necessary?
14. How are parallel lists used in the program that visualizes workout data?

4.14
Exercises

1. Write the program described starting in Sect. 4.6 on page 100. The program should plot data like it appears in Fig. 4.4. Sample XML Training Center Database files can be found on the text's web site. Be sure to read from Sect. 4.6 to the end of the chapter for hints on how to write this code.
2. Write a program that plots the function

$$g(x) = x^4/4 - x^3/3 - 3x^2$$

You can use the setworldcoordinates method to plot the function on the screen from -20 to 20 on the x-axis and -20 to 20 on the y-axis. When you are done, if you did it right, you should have a screen that looks like Fig. 4.5. To plot the function the x values can go from -20 to 20. The y values can be found by using the definition of the function g. Be sure to include the dots for the units on the graph.
3. Write a program that uses the workout data to compare percent of maximum speed to cadence. Speed can be computed by determining the distance travelled in a trackpoint and dividing it by the time it took to reach that trackpoint from the previous one. Percent of maximum speed can be found by first finding the maximum speed. For each speed found, percent of maximum speed is $(speed/maxSpeed) * 100$. Plot the percent

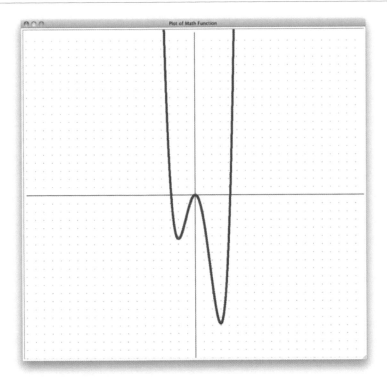

Fig. 4.5 The plot of $g(x) = x^4/4 - x^3/3 - 3x^2$

of maximum speed and then overlay it with cadence. From this visualization of the data you can see where a higher gear was used. Anytime cadence drops or stays about the same but percent of maximum speed seems to increase, a higher gear was used.

4. Write a program that uses the workout data to graph the average speed up to a particular time, t, as a percentage of the total average speed for the workout. You can compute the overall average speed by taking the total distance travelled in the workout divided by the total time of the workout. The average speed at any point in time during a workout is computed by taking the distance travelled to the trackpoint divided by the time to that trackpoint. The graph of this will likely fluctuate wildly at first, but will settle down and should show the general effort being expended at various periods within the workout assuming all other factors remain constant. A good, nearly straight line would indicate a constant effort during the workout.

5. On the website for the text there are three files, *Toyota4Runner.csv*, *NissanVersa.csv*, and *SuzukiS40.csv* that all contain gas mileage information for their corresponding vehicles. Write a program that reads this data and plots average miles per gallon in one dimension and time in the other dimension. Since the first line of each file is not a record, but a description of the columns, you might want to use a *while loop* to read the data so you can throw away the first line before starting the while loop.

HINT: Since each field of the records is in double quotes you can read the line from the file and put square brackets around it as follows.

```
x = "[" + '"Gas","0.0","2010-01-19","10:38 PM", ...' + "]"
y = eval(x)
```

The call to the *eval* function will force the evaluation of the string. Calling *eval* like this returns a list of the elements; in this case a list of strings as the fields of the record. Using this technique will make parsing the input extremely easy. You can get the number of days from two datetime objects by subtracting them and then using the difference as follows:

```
timeDelta = firstDay - lastDay
days = timeDelta.days
```

It might first appear that the difference should be computed as *lastDay–firstDay*. However, this yields a negative number of days so the example in the listing above is correct when computing days.

6. When looking at average EPA MPG for gas powered vehicles there is always a city MPG and a highway MPG, with highway MPG being greater. Since filling the car multiple times within a short amount of time would seem to indicate that a person is taking a trip, there should be a correlation between filling up over short amounts of time (i.e. highway miles) and the observed MPG. Use the *Toyota4Runner.cvs* or the *NissanVersa.cvs* files to plot days since last fill up and observed MPG. You will want to do this as a scatter plot. A scatter plot is simply a dot for each data point. A dot can be made using the *dot* method of the Turtle class. Observe the data that you find there and draw a regression line through that data. A regression line is a best fit line. It minimizes the total distance of points to the line.

To draw a regression line you need to keep track of a few things.

- The sum of all the *x* values
- The sum of all the *y* values
- The sum of all the x^2 values
- The sum of all the $x \times y$ values

Decide what your *x* and *y* axis represent. Compute the values given above. When you have gathered these values you need to use the values in the formula below.

$$y = \bar{y} + m(x - \bar{x})$$

where

$$m = \frac{\sum_{i=1}^{n} x_i y_i - n\bar{x}\,\bar{y}}{\sum_{i=1}^{n} x_i^2 - n\bar{x}^2}$$

All the values you need in the formulas are available in the values you kept track of above. *n* is the number of data points. $\bar{x}$ is the average of the *x* values and likewise for $\bar{y}$. The sum of all the x^2 values is the sum of the squares, NOT the square of the sum.

   To plot the regression line you can choose two x values and then compute their corresponding y values given the formula $y = \overline{y} + m(x - \overline{x})$. This will give you the two end points of the regression line. Once you have the two end points of the line, use the turtle to draw the line between them. Plot this regression line to see the correlation between highway miles and MPG. While this program will compute a linear regression line, it should be noted that the correlation between number of highway miles and MPG is definitely NOT a linear function so observed results should be understood in that context.

7. In practice problem 4.3 you drew a truck using a turtle. You should not have used any *goto* method calls in that practice problem. In this exercise you are to draw trucks of random size at random places on the screen. To generate random numbers in a program you need to import the *random* module. You create a random number generator as follows:

```
from random import *

rand = Random()
```

Their are three methods that Random objects support that you may want to use:

- **rand.randrange(start, stop, step)**—*start* default is 0, *step* default is 1. It returns a random integer in the range [start, stop) that is on one of the *steps*.
- **rand.randint(start, stop)**—*start* default is 0. It returns a random integer in the range [start, stop).
- **rand.random()**—Returns a random floating point number in the range [0,1).

For this exercise you should repeatedly draw trucks at different locations on the screen. You can use the *goto* method to move to a randomly selected location on the screen. By default the screen goes from -500 to 500 in both directions so generating a screen location in the range -400 to 400 in both directions will work well.

   Once you have moved to a random location on the screen, draw the truck as you did in practice problem 4.3. However, to make the trucks different sizes, randomly generate a floating point number between 0 and 1 using the *random* method. This random number is a scale for your truck. Multiply each forward or circle argument by the scale when drawing the truck. By multiplying the forward and circle arguments by a number between 0 and 1 you are creating scaled versions of your truck from 0 (no truck at all) to 1 (a full-size truck).

   Note Do not multiply turns times the scale. All angles are the same in any scaled version of the truck.

4.15
Solutions to Practice Problems

These are solutions to the practice problem s in this chapter. You should only consult these answers after you have tried each of them for yourself first. Practice problems are meant to help reinforce the material you have just read so make use of them.

Solution to Practice Problem 4.1

```
import turtle

t = turtle.Turtle()
screen = t.getscreen()
for k in range(4):
    t.forward(25)
    t.left(90)

screen.exitonclick()
```

Solution to Practice Problem 4.2

```
from turtle import *

t = Turtle()
screen = t.getscreen()
sides = int(screen.textinput("Polygon", \
            "Please Enter the Number of Sides:"))
for k in range(sides):
    t.forward(200//sides)
    t.left(360/sides)

screen.exitonclick()
```

Solution to Practice Problem 4.3

```
from turtle import *

t = Turtle()
screen = t.getscreen()

t.fillcolor("black")
t.begin_fill()
t.circle(20)
t.end_fill()
t.penup()
t.forward(120)
t.pendown()
t.begin_fill()
t.circle(20)
t.end_fill()
t.penup()
t.left(90)
```

```
t.forward(40)
t.right(90)
t.forward(30)
t.right(180)
t.pendown()
t.fillcolor("yellow")
t.begin_fill()
t.forward(180)
t.right(90)
t.forward(30)
t.right(90)
t.forward(90)
t.left(90)
t.forward(30)
t.right(90)
t.forward(30)
t.right(45)
t.forward(43)
t.left(45)
t.forward(30)
t.right(90)
t.forward(30)
t.end_fill()
t.ht()

screen.exitonclick()
```

Solution to Practice Problem 4.4

The turtle's location is (12.0388, 38.18233) at the peak of the pentagon.

Solution to Practice Problem 4.5

The *forward* method is not an accessor method. The *xcor* method is an accessor method. It accesses the *x* coordinate of the turtle.

Fig. 4.6 Concatenation of two
strings

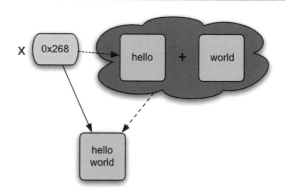

Solution to Practice Problem 4.6

You create a second turtle the same way you created the first.

```
from turtle import *

t = Turtle()
screen = t.getscreen()
t.forward(100)
secondTurtle = Turtle()
secondTurtle.left(90)
secondTurtle.forward(100)
screen.exitonclick()
```

Solution to Practice Problem 4.7

Figure 4.6 depicts what happens when the following code is executed. This is pretty much
identical to what happens with the integers on page 21 in Chap. 1.

```
x = "hello"
x = x + " world"
print(x)
```

Solution to Practice Problem 4.8

This requires you to parse the XML file and extract the data.

```
dates = []
for activity in activities:
```

```
  sport = activity.attributes["Sport"]
  sportName = sport.value
  dateValue = \
      activity.getElementsByTagName("Id")[0].firstChild.data
  year = int(dateValue[0:4])
  month = int(dateValue[5:7])
  day = int(dateValue[8:10])
  hour = int(dateValue[11:13])
  minutes = int(dateValue[14:16])
  seconds = int(dateValue[17:19])
  dateOfWorkout = \
      datetime(year,month,day,hour,minutes,seconds)
  if sportName == sportChoice:
    dates.append(dateOfWorkout)

print("Please pick a date to plot.")

for i in range(len(dates)):
  print(str(i+1)+")", dates[i])

exChoice = int(input( \
    "Please enter your choice (1-"+str(len(dates))+") : "))
dateChoice = dates[exChoice-1]
```

Solution to Practice Problem 4.9

To find the maximum heart rate you can use the guess and check pattern or just the max function. If you have a list of heart rate values called hrList, then *max(hrList)* will give you the maximum heart rate.

Defining Functions

Functions are something most of us are familiar with from Mathematics. A function g might be defined as

$$g(x) = x^4/4 - x^3/3 - 3x^2$$

When a function is defined this way we can then call the function g with the value 6—usually written $g(6)$—to discover that the value returned by the function would be 144. Of course, we aren't only limited to passing 6 to g. We could pass 0 to g and $g(0)$ would return 0. We could pass any of number into g and compute its result.

The identifier g represents the *definition* of a function and calling a function by writing $g(6)$ is called *function application* or a *function call*. These two concepts are part of most programming languages including Python. In Python, functions can be both *defined* and *called*.

Example 5.1 The function $g(x) = x^4/4 - x^3/3 - 3x^2$ can be defined in Python as shown below. It can also be called as shown here. This program calls g and prints 144.0 to the screen.

```
def g(x):
    return x**4/4.0 - x**3/3.0 - 3 * x * x

print(g(6))
```

To call a function in Python we write $g(6)$ for instance, just they way we do in Mathematics. It means the same thing, too. Executing $g(6)$ means calling the function g with the value 6 to compute the value of the function call. A function in Python can do more than a function in Mathematics. Functions can execute statements as well as return a value. In Mathematics a value is computed and returned. There are no side-effects of calling the function. In Python (and in just about any programming language), there can be side-effects. A function can contain more than one statement just like our programs contain statements.

K.D. Lee, *Python Programming Fundamentals,* Undergraduate Topics in Computer Science, **119**
DOI 10.1007/978-1-84996-537-8_5, © Springer-Verlag London Limited 2011

Example 5.2 Here is a function that computes and prints a value along with some code that calls the function. Running this program prints "You called computeAndPrint(6,5)" followed by the value 149.0 to the screen. This function is passed two arguments instead of just one.

```
def computeAndPrint(x, y):
    val = x**4/4.0 - x**3/3.0 - 3 * x * x + y
    print("You called computeAndPrint("+str(x)+","+str(y)+")")

    return val

print(computeAndPrint(6,5))
```

5.1
Why Write Functions?

The ability to define our own functions helps programmers in two ways. When you are writing a program if you find yourself writing the same code more than once, it is probably best to define a function with the repeated code in it. Then you can call the function as many times as needed instead of rewriting the code again and again.

It is important that we avoid writing the same code more than once in our programs. Writing code is error-prone. Programmers often make mistakes. If we write the same code more than once and make a mistake in it, we must fix that mistake every place we copied the code. When writing code that will be used commercially, mistakes might not be found until years later. When fixing code that hasn't been looked at for a while it is extremely easy to fix the code in one place and to forget to fix it everywhere.

If we make a mistake in coding a *function*, and then fix the code in the function, we have automatically fixed the code in every spot that uses the function. This principle of modular programming is a very important concept that has been around since the early days of computer programming. Writing code once leads to well-tested functions that work as expected. When we use a well-tested function we can be fairly confident it will work the first time. It also leads to smaller code size, although that is not as much of an issue these days.

Writing functions also helps make our code easier to read. When we use good names for variables and functions in our programs we can read the code and understand what we have written not only as we write it, but years later when we need to look at the code we wrote again. Typically programmers work with a group of three to eight other people. It is important for others in the group to be able to read and understand the code we have written. Writing functions can lead to nice modularized code that is much easier to maintain by you and by others in a group.

5.2
Passing Arguments and Returning a Value

When we write a function we must decide four things:

1. What should our function be called? We should give it a name that makes sense and describes what the function does. Since a function does something, the name of a function is usually a verb or some description of what the function returns. It might be one word or several words long.
2. What should we give to our function? In other words, what arguments will we pass to the function? When thinking about arguments to pass to a function we should think about how the function will be used and what arguments would make it the most useful.
3. What should the function do? What is its purpose? The function needs to have a clearly defined purpose. Either it should return a value or it should have some well-defined side-effect.
4. Finally, what should our function return? The type and the value to be returned should be considered. If the function is going to return a value, we should decide what type of value it should return.

By considering these questions and answering them, we can make sure that our functions make sense before writing them. It does us no good to define functions that don't have a well-defined purpose in our program.

Example 5.3 Consider a program where we are asked to reverse a string. What should the function be called? Probably *reverse*. What should we give to the function? A *string* would make sense. What does *reverse* compute? The reverse of the given string. What should it return? The reversed string. Now we are ready to write the function.

```
def reverse(s):

    # Use the Accumulator Pattern
    result = ""
    for c in s:
        result = c + result

    return result

t = input("Please enter a string: ")
print("The reverse of", t, "is", reverse(t))
```

It is important to decide the type of value *returned* from a function and the types of the arguments *given* to a function. The words *returned* and *given* are words that give us a clue about what the function should look like and what it might do. When presented with a specification for a function look for these words to help you identify what you need to write.

The word *parameter* refers to the identifier used to represent the value that is passed as an *argument* to the function. Sometimes the parameter is called a formal parameter. When a function is called, it is passed an argument as in $g(6)$ where 6 is the argument. When the function is applied the parameter called x takes on the value of 6. If it is called as $g(5)$ then the parameter x takes on the value 5. In this way we can write the function once and it will work for any argument passed to the function. In Example 5.3 the argument is the value that t refers to, the value entered by the user when the program is run. The parameter, s, takes on the value that t refers to when the function is called in the print statement. The parameter passing mechanism makes it possible for us to write a function once and use it in many different places in our program with many different values passed in.

Practice 5.1 Write a function called explode that given a string returns a list of the characters of the string.

Practice 5.2 Write a function called implode that given a list of characters, or strings, returns a string which is the concatenation of those characters, or strings.

5.3
Scope of Variables

When writing functions it is important to understand scope. Scope refers to the area in a program where a variable is defined. Normally, a variable is defined after it has been assigned a value. You cannot reference a variable until it has been assigned a value.

Practice 5.3 The following program has an run-time error in it. Where does the error occur? Be very specific.

```
x = x + 1
x = 6
print(x)
```

When we define functions there are several identifiers we write. First, the name of the function is written. Like variables, a function identifier can be used after it is defined. In

Example 5.3 you will notice that the function is defined at the top of the program and the function is called on the last line of the program. A function must be defined before it is used.

However, the variables *s*, *c*, and *result* are not available where *reverse(t)* is called. This is what we want to happen and is due to something called *scope*. The *scope* of a variable refers to the area in a program where it is defined. There are several scopes available in a Python program. Mark Lutz describes the rules of scope in Python with what he calls the *LEGB* rule [3]. Memorizing the acronym *LEGB* will help you memorize the scope rules of Python.

The *LEGB* rule refers to *Local Scope, Enclosing Scope, Global Scope,* and *Built-in Scope*. Local scope extends for the body of a function and refers to anything indented in the function definition. Variables, including the parameter, that are defined in the body of a function are local to that function and cannot be accessed outside the function. They are *local variables*.

The *enclosing scope* refers to variables that are defined outside a function definition. If a function is defined within the scope of other variables, then those variables are available inside the function definition. The variables in the enclosing scope are available to statements within a function.

Example 5.4 While this is not good coding practice, the following code illustrates the enclosing scope. The *values* variable keeps track of all the arguments passed to the reverse function.

```python
def reverse(s):

    values.append(s)

    # Use the Accumulator Pattern
    result = ""
    for c in s:
        result = c + result

    return result

# The values variable is defined in the enclosing scope of
# the reverse function.
values = []

t = input("Please enter a string: ")
while t.strip() != "":
    print("The reverse of", t, "is", reverse(t))
    t = input("Enter another string or press enter to quit: ")

print("You reversed these strings:")
for val in values:
    print(val)
```

Accessing a variable in the enclosing scope can be useful in some circumstances, but is not usually done unless the variable is a constant that does not change in a program. In the program above the *values* variable is accessed by the reverse function on the first line of its body. This is an example of using *enclosing* scope. However, the next example, while it does almost the same thing, has a problem.

Example 5.5 Here is an example of almost the same program. Instead of using the mutator method *append* the list concatenation (i.e. the +) operator is used to append the value *s* to the list of values.

```
def reverse(s):

    # The following line of code will not work.
    values = values + [s]

    # Use the Accumulator Pattern
    result = ""
    for c in s:
       result = c + result

    return result

# The values variable is defined in the enclosing scope of
# the reverse function.
values = []

t = input("Please enter a string: ")
while t.strip() != "":
    print("The reverse of", t, "is", reverse(t))
    t = input("Enter another string or press enter to quit: ")

print("You reversed these strings:")
for val in values:
    print(val)
```

The code in Example 5.5 does not work because of a subtle issue in Python. A new variable, say *v*, is defined in Python anytime $v = \cdots$ is written. In Example 5.5 the first line of the reverse function is *values* = *values* + [*s*]. As soon as *values* = $\cdots$ is written, there is a new local variable called *values* that is defined in the scope of the *reverse* function. That means there are two variables called *values*: one defined in reverse and one defined outside of reverse. The problem occurs when the right-hand side of *values* = *values* + [*s*] is evaluated. Which *values* is being concatenated to [*s*]. Is it the local or the enclosing *values*. Clearly, we would like it to be the enclosing *values* variable. But, it is not. Local scope overrides enclosing scope and the program in Example 5.5 will complain that *values* does not yet have a value on the first line of the reverse function's body.

The problem with Example 5.5 can be fixed by declaring the *values* variable to be *global*. When applied to a variable, global scope means that there should not be a local copy of a variable made, even when it appears on the left hand side of an assignment statement.

Example 5.6 The string concatenation operator can still be used if the *values* variable is declared to be global in the *reverse* function.

```
def reverse(s):
    global values

    #values.append(s)
    values = values + [s]

    # Use the Accumulator Pattern
    result = ""
    for c in s:
        result = c + result

    return result

# The values variable is defined in the enclosing scope of
# the reverse function.
values = []

t = input("Please enter a string: ")
while t.strip() != "":
    print("The reverse of", t, "is", reverse(t))
    t = input("Enter another string or press enter to quit: ")

print("You reversed these strings:")
for val in values:
    print(val)
```

Example 5.6 demonstrates the use of the global scope. The use of the *global* keyword forces Python to use the variable in the enclosing scope even when it appears on the left hand side of an assignment statement.

The final scope rule is the built-in scope. The built-in scope refers to those identifiers that are built-in to Python. For instance, the *len* function can be used anywhere in a program to find the length of a sequence.

The one gotcha with scope is that local scope trumps the enclosing scope, which trumps the global scope, which trumps the built-in scope. Hence the LEGB rule. First local scope is scanned for the existence of an identifier. If that identifier is not defined in the local scope, then the enclosing scope is consulted. Again, if the identifier is not found in enclosing scope then the global scope is consulted and finally the built-in scope. This does have some implications in our programs.

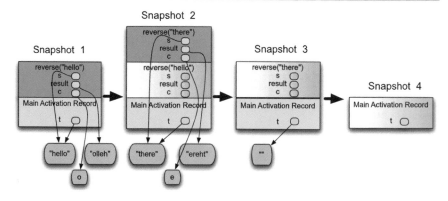

Fig. 5.1 The run-time stack

Practice 5.4 The following code does not work. What is the error message? Do you see why? Can you suggest a way to fix it?

```
def length(L):
    len = 1
    for i in range(len(L)):
        len = len + 1

    return len

print(length([1,2,3]))
```

5.4
The Run-time Stack

The run-time stack is a data structure that is used by Python to execute programs. Python needs this run-time stack to maintain information about the state of your program as it executes. A *stack* is a data structure that lets you push and pop elements. You push elements onto the top of the stack and you pop elements from the top of the stack. Think of a stack of trays. You take trays off the top of the stack in a cafeteria. You put clean trays back on the top of the stack. A stack is a *first in/first out* data structure. Stacks can be created to hold a variety of different types of elements. The *run-time stack* is a stack of *activation records*.

An activation record is an area of memory that holds a copy of each variable that is defined in the local scope of a function while it is executing. As we learned in Example 5.5, a variable is defined when it appears on the left-hand side of an equals sign. Formal parameters of a function are also in the local scope of the function.

Example 5.7 In this example code the reverse function is called repeatedly until the user enters an empty string (just presses enter) to end the program. Each call to reverse pushes an activation record on the stack.

```python
def reverse(s):

    # Use the Accumulator Pattern
    result = ""
    for c in s:
        result = c + result

    return result

t = input("Please enter a string: ")
while t.strip() != "":
    print("The reverse of", t, "is", reverse(t))
    t = input("Enter another string or press enter to quit: ")
```

In Example 5.7, each time the reverse function returns to the main code the activation record is popped. Assuming the user enters the string "hello", snapshot 1 of Fig. 5.1 shows what the run-time stack would look like right before the result is returned from the function call.

In snapshot 2, the activation record for reverse ("hello") had been popped from the stack but is shown grayed out in snapshot 2 to make it clear that the top activation record is a *new* activation record. Snapshot 2 was taken right before the *return result* statement was executed for the second call to reverse.

Snapshot 3 shows what the run-time stack looks like after returning from the second call to reverse. Again, the grayed out activation record is not there, but is shown to emphasize that it is popped when the function returns. Finally, snapshot 4 shows what happens when the main code exits, causing the last activation record to be popped.

Each activation record holds a copy of the local variables and parameters that were passed to the function. Local variables are those variables that appear on the left-hand side of an equals sign in the body of the function or appear as parameters to the function. Recall that variables are actually references in Python, so the references or variables point to the actual values which are not stored in the activation records.

The run-time stack is absolutely critical to the implementation of modern programming languages. Its existence makes it possible for a function to execute and return independently of where it is called. This independence between functions and the code that calls them is crucial to making functions useful in our programs.

```
          8  |        result = c + result
          9
         10 ●     return result
         11
         12  # The values variable is defined in the enclosing scope of
         13  # the reverse function.
         14  values = []
         15
         16  t = input("Please enter a string: ")
         17  while t.strip() != "":
         18 ▶    print("The reverse of", t, "is", reverse(t))
         19       t = input("Enter another string or press enter to quit: ")
         20
         21  print("You reversed these strings:")
         22  for val in values:
         23       print(val)
```

Fig. 5.2   The run-time stack in the Wing IDE

Practice 5.5   Trace the execution of the code in Example 5.2 on paper showing the contents of the run-time stack just before the function call returns.

The run-time stack is visible in most debuggers including the Wing IDE. To view the activation records on the run-time stack you have to debug your program and set a breakpoint during its execution. Figure 5.2 shows the Wing IDE running the program from Example 5.4. A breakpoint was set just before the reverse function returns: the same point at snapshot one in Fig. 5.1. In Wing you can click on the *Stack Data* tab to view the run-time stack. The drop-down combobox directly below the *Stack Data* tab contains one entry for each activation record currently on the run-time stack. In Fig. 5.2 the *<module>* activation record is selected which is Wing's name for the *Main* activation record. When an activation record is selected in the *Stack Data* tab, its local variables are displayed below. In Fig. 5.2 the *t* and *values* variables are displayed from the *Main* activation record. The program is currently stopped at line 10 but the *reverse* function was called from line 18 so that line is highlighted since we are displaying the activation record corresponding to the code *reverse* was called from.

Practice 5.6 Trace the execution of the code in Example 5.2 using the Wing IDE to verify the contents of the run-time stack just before the function call returns match your answer in practice problem 5.5.

5.5
Mutable Data and Functions

If you consider Fig. 5.1, it should help in understanding that a function that mutates a value passed to it will cause the code that called it to see that mutated data. The program presented in Example 5.7 does not mutate any of the data passed to the reverse function. In fact, since strings are immutable, it would be impossible for reverse to mutate the parameter passed to it. However, Example 5.4 mutates the *values* list. The result of appending to the list is seen in the code that called it. Lists are not immutable. They can be changed in place. In Example 5.4 the reference to the *values* list is not changed. The *contents* of the values list is changed. The changed contents are seen by the main code after the function returns.

As another example, consider a reverse function that doesn't return a value. What if it just changed the list that was given to it. If the parameter to the list function was called *lst*, then writing *lst*[0] = "*h*" will change the first element of the list *lst* to the string *h*. That's what is meant by mutating a data. A new list is not created in this case. The existing list is modified. If a list is passed to a function and the function mutates the list, the caller of the function will see the reversed list. That's what the *append* method does. It mutates the existing list as well.

When a function is called that mutates one or more of its parameters, the calling code will see that the data has been mutated. The mutation is not somehow *undone* when the function returns. Since strings, ints, floats, and bools are all immutable, this never comes up when passing arguments of these types. But, again, lists are mutable, and a function may mutate a list as seen in the next example.

Example 5.8 Consider the following code that reverses a list in place. It does not build a new list. It reverses the existing list.

```
def reverseInPlace(lst):
    for i in range(len(lst)//2):
        tmp = lst[i]
        lst[i] = lst[len(lst)-1-i]
        lst[len(lst)-1-i]=tmp

s = input("Please enter a sentence:")
lst = s.split()
reverseInPlace(lst)
print("The sentence backwards is:",end="")
for word in lst:
    print(word,end=" ")
print()
```

Notice that the *reverseInPlace* function in Example 5.8 does not return anything. In addition, when *reverseInPlace* is called it is not set to some variable, nor is the return value printed. It is just called on a line by itself. That's because it modifies the list passed to it as an argument.

Practice 5.7 Why would it be very uninteresting to call *reverseInPlace* like this? What would the next line of code be?

```
print(reverseInPlace([1,2,3,4,5]))
```

In practice problem 5.7 the value printed to the screen is *None*. None is a special value in Python. It is returned by any function that does not *explicitly* return a value. All functions return a value in Python. Those that don't have a *return* statement in them to explicitly return a value, return *None* by default. Obviously, printing *None* wouldn't tell us much about the reverse of [*1, 2, 3, 4, 5*].

Practice 5.8 What would happen if you tried to use reverseInPlace to reverse a string?

5.6
Predicate Functions

A predicate is an answer to a question with respect to one or more objects. For instance, we can ask, *Is x even?*. If the value that *x* refers to is even, the answer would be *Yes* or *True*. If *x* refers to something that is not even then the answer would be *False*. In Python, if we write a function that returns `True` or `False` depending on its parameters, that function is called a *Predicate* function. Predicate functions are usually implemented using the *Guess and Check* pattern. However, applying this pattern to a function can look a little different than the pattern we learned about in Chap. 2.

Example 5.9 Assume we want to write a predicate function that returns True if one number evenly divides another and false otherwise. Here is one version of the code that looks like the old *Guess and Check* pattern.

```
def evenlyDivides(x,y):
    # returns true if x evenly divides y

    dividesIt = False

    if y % x == 0:
        dividesIt = True

    return dividesIt

x = int(input("Please enter an integer:"))
y = int(input("Please enter another integer:"))

if evenlyDivides(x,y):
    print(x,"evenly divides",y)
else:
    print(x,"does not evenly divide",y)
```

In Example 5.9 the guess and check pattern is applied to the function *evenlyDivides*. Observing that the function returns *True* or *False* it could be rewritten to just return that value instead of using a variable at all as in Example 5.10 below.

Example 5.10 In this example the value is just returned instead of storing it in a variable and returning at the bottom. This is equivalent to the code in Example 5.9 because it returns *True* and *False* in exactly the same instances as the other version of the function. NOTE: If *y* % *x* == *0* then the *return True* is executed. This terminates the function immediately and it never gets to the statement *return False* in that case. If *y* % *x* == *0* is false, then the code skips the *then* part of the *if* statement and executes the *return False*.

```
def evenlyDivides(x,y):
    # returns true if x evenly divides y
    if y % x == 0:
        return True

    return False

x = int(input("Please enter an integer:"))
y = int(input("Please enter another integer:"))

if evenlyDivides(x,y):
    print(x,"evenly divides",y)
else:
    print(x,"does not evenly divide",y)
```

Since the function in Examples 5.9 and 5.10 returns *True* when *y % x == 0* and *False* when it does not, there is one more version of this function that is even more concise in its definition. Any time you have an if statement where you see *if c is true then return true else return false* it can be replaced by *return c*. You don't need an if statement if all you want to do is return true or false based on one condition.

Example 5.11 Here is the same program one more time. This is the elegant version.

```
def evenlyDivides(x,y):
    return y % x == 0

x = int(input("Please enter an integer:"))
y = int(input("Please enter another integer:"))

if evenlyDivides(x,y):
    print(x,"evenly divides",y)
else:
    print(x,"does not evenly divide",y)
```

While the third version of the *evenlyDivides* function is the most elegant, this pattern may only be applied to predicate functions where only one condition needs to be checked. If we were trying to return write a predicate function that needed to check multiple conditions, then the second or first form of *evenlyDivides* would be required.

Practice 5.9 Write a function called *evenlyDividesList* that returns true if every element of a list given to the function is evenly divided by an integer given to the function.

5.7
Top-Down Design

Functions may be called from either the main code of a program or from other functions. A function call is allowed any place an expression may be written in Python. One technique for dealing with the complexity of writing a complex program is called *Top-Down Design*. In top-down design the programmer decides what major actions the program must take and then rather than worry about the details of how it is done, the programmer just defines a function that will handle that later.

Example 5.12 Assume we want to implement a program that will ask the users to enter a list of integers and then will answer which pairs of integers are evenly divisible. For instance, assume that the list of integers 1, 2, 3, 4, 5, 6, 8, and 12 were entered. The program should respond:

```
1 is evenly divisible by 1
2 is evenly divisible by 1 2
3 is evenly divisible by 1 3
4 is evenly divisible by 1 2 4
5 is evenly divisible by 1 5
6 is evenly divisible by 1 2 3 6
8 is evenly divisible by 1 2 4 8
12 is evenly divisible by 1 2 3 4 6 12
```

To accomplish this, a top down approach would start with getting the input from the user.

```
s = input("Please enter a list of ints separated by spaces:")
lst = []
for x in s.split():
    lst.append(int(x))

evenlyDivisible(lst)
```

Without worrying further about how *evenlyDivisible* works we can just assume that it will work once we get around to defining it. Of course, the program won't run until we define *evenlyDivisible*. But we *can* decide that *evenlyDivisible* must print a report to the screen the way the output is specified in Example 5.12. Later we can write the *evenlyDivisible* function. In a top-down design, when we write the *evenlyDivisible* function we would look to see if we could somehow make the job simpler by calling another function to help with the implementation. The *evenlyDivides* function could then be defined. In this way the main code calls a function to help with its implementation. Likewise, the *evenlyDivisible* function calls a function to aid in its implementation. This top-down approach continues until simple functions with straightforward implementations are all that is left.

5.8
Bottom-Up Design

In a *Bottom-Up Design* we would start by defining a simple function that might be useful in solving a more complex problem. For instance, the *evenlyDivides* function that checks to see if one value evenly divides another, could be useful in solving the problem presented in Example 5.12. Using a bottom-up approach a programmer would then see that *evenlyDivides* solves a slightly simpler problem and would look for a way to apply the *evenlyDivides* function to the problem we are solving.

> **Practice 5.10** Using the last version of the *evenlyDivides* function, write a function called *evenlyDivisibleElements* that given an integer, *x*, and a list of integers, returns the list of integers from the given list that evenly divide *x*. This would be the next step in either the bottom-up design or the top-down design of a solution to the problem in Example 5.12.

> **Practice 5.11** Write the function *evenlyDivisible* from Example 5.12 using the *evenlyDivisibleElements* function to complete the program presented in Example 5.12 and practice problem 5.10.

5.9
Recursive Functions

Sections 5.7 and 5.8 taught us that functions can call other functions and that sometimes this helps make a complex problem more manageable in some way. It turns out that not only can functions call other functions, they can also call themselves. This too can make a problem more manageable. If you've ever seen a proof by induction in Mathematics, recursive functions are somewhat like inductive proofs. In an inductive proof we are given a problem and told we know it is solvable for a smaller sized problem. Induction says that if we can use that smaller solution to arrive at a bigger solution, then we can conclude every instance of that problem has a solution. What makes an inductive proof so powerful is that we don't have to worry about the existence of a solution to the smaller problem. It is guaranteed to exist by the nature of the proof.

Recursion in functions works the same way. We may assume that our function will work if we call our function on a smaller value. Let's consider the computation of factorial from

Mathematics. $0! = 1$ by definition. This is called the base case. $n!$ is defined as $n \times (n-1)!$. This is the recursive part of the definition of factorial.

Example 5.13 Factorial can be written in Python much the same way it is defined in Mathematics. The *if* statement must come first and is the statement of the base case. The recursive case is always written last.

```python
def factorial(n):
    if n == 0:
        return 1

    return n * factorial(n - 1)

print(factorial(5))
```

Practice 5.12 What would happen if the base case and the recursive case were written in the opposite order in Example 5.13? HINT: What happens to the run-time stack when a function is called?

A function is recursive if it calls itself. Recursion works in Python and other languages because of the run-time stack. To fully understand how the factorial function works, you need to examine the run-time stack to see how the program prints 120 to the screen.

Practice 5.13 Recalling that each time a function is called an activation record is pushed on the run-time stack, how many activation records will be pushed on the run-time stack at its deepest point when computing factorial(5)?

Practice 5.14 Run the factorial program on an input of 5 using Wing or your favorite IDE. Set a breakpoint in the factorial function on the two return statements. Watch the run-time stack grow and shrink. What do you notice about the parameter n?

Many problems can be formulated in terms of recursion. For instance, reversing a string can be formulated recursively. To reverse a string we only need to reverse a shorter string, say all but the first letter, and then tack the first letter onto the other end of the reversed string. Here is the beautiful part of recursion. We can assume that reversing a shorter string already works!!!

Example 5.14 Here is a recursive version of a function that reverses a string. Remember, the base case must always come first. The base case usually defines the simplest problem we could come up with. The result of reversing an empty string is pretty easy to find. It is just the empty string.

```python
def reverse(s):
    # Base Case: Always FIRST
    if s == "":
        return ""

    # Recursive Case: We may assume it works for
    # smaller problems. So, it works for the slice starting
    # at index 1 of the string.
    return reverse(s[1:]) + s[0]

print(reverse("hello"))
```

Practice 5.15 Write a recursive function that computes the nth Fibonacci number. The Fibonacci numbers are defined as follows: $\text{Fib}(0) = 1$, $\text{Fib}(1) = 1$, $\text{Fib}(n) = \text{Fib}(n - 1) + \text{Fib}(n - 2)$. Write this as a Python function and then write some code to find the tenth Fibonacci number.

5.10
The Main Function

In most programming languages one special function is identified as the *main* function. The main function is where everything gets started. When a program in Java runs, the main function is executed first and the code in the main function determines what the program does. The same is true in C, C++, Pascal, Fortran, and many other languages. In Python this is not required by the language. However, it is good programming practice to have a main function anyway.

One advantage to defining a main function is when you wish to write a module that others may use. When importing a module a programmer probably does not want the main function in the imported module to run since he or she is undoubtably writing their own main function. The programmer writing the module that is imported may want to write a main function to test the code they are providing in the module. Python has some special handling of imported modules that allow both the provider and the importer of a module to get the behavior they desire.

By writing a main function, all variables defined in the main function are no longer available to the whole program module. An example might help in explaining why this might be important.

Example 5.15 This code works, but it is accessing the variable *l* in the *drawSquare* function from the enclosing scope. It is generally a bad idea to access the enclosing scope of a function except in some specific circumstances. Of course, this was a mistake. It should have been *length* that was used in the *drawSquare* function.

```python
# Imports always go at the top
import turtle

# Function definitions go second
def drawSquare(turtle, length):
    for k in range(4):
        turtle.forward(l)
        turtle.left(90)

# Main code goes at the end
t = turtle.Turtle()
screen = t.getscreen()

l = int(input("Please enter a side length: "))
drawSquare(t,l)

screen.exitonclick()
```

While the code in Example 5.15 works, it is not desirable because if a programmer changes the main code he or she may affect the code in the drawSquare function. For instance, if the programmer renames *l* to *length* at some future time, then the drawSquare function will cease to work. In addition, if drawSquare is moved to another module at some point in the future it will cease to work. A function should be as self-contained as possible to make it independent of where it is defined and where it is used.

The problem in the code above is easy to miss at first. You could easily think the program is fine since it does what it is supposed to do. The problem is due to the fact that up to this point we have not used a main function in our programs. Python programmers sometimes write a main function and sometimes do not. However, it is safer to write a main function and most experienced Python programmers will stick to the convention of writing one.

Example 5.16 Here is the draw square program again, this time with a main function. When the Python interpreter scans this file, two functions are defined, *drawSquare* and *main*. The *if* statement at the end of the program is the first statement to be executed.

```python
# Imports always go at the top
import turtle

# Function definitions go second
def drawSquare(turtle, length):
    for k in range(4):
        turtle.forward(length)
        turtle.left(90)

# main function definition goes second to last.
def main():
    t = turtle.Turtle()
    screen = t.getscreen()
    l = int(input("Please enter a side length: "))
    drawSquare(t,l)
    screen.exitonclick()

# the if statement that calls main goes last.
if __name__ == "__main__":
    main()
```

When a program has a main function in Python, the convention is to write an *if* statement at the end of the program that starts everything executing. There is a special hook in Python that controls how a Python program is started. When a program is imported as a module the special variable called _ _*name*_ _ is set to the name of the module. When a program is NOT imported, but run as the main module of a Python program, the special variable _ _*name*_ _ is set to the value "_ _*main*_ _". When running the code in Example 5.16 the *if* statement's condition is True and therefore *main* is called to get the program started. However, this code implements a useful function, the *drawSquare* function. It might be the case that some programmer would like to use this function in their code. If this code resides a file called *square.py* and a programmer has a copy of this module and writes *import square* in their code, then when this module loads the _ _*name*_ _ variable will be set to the name of the module and not "_ _*main*_ _". If you run this code as a program then the *main* function gets called. If you import this module into some other program, then the *main* function does not get called. When a module is written that is intended to be imported into other code, the main function often contains code to test the functions provided in the module.

In Example 5.16, if the programmer were to mistakenly write *turtle.forward(l)* instead of *turtle.forward(length)*, Python would complain the first time the *drawSquare* function was called. It would say that *l* is undefined. This is much more desirable since we would like to catch errors like that right away as opposed to some later time.

Example 5.17 Here are a few lines from the *turtle.py* module that would be executed when the turtle module is run as a program instead of being imported.

```
if __name__ == "__main__":
    def switchpen():
        if isdown():
            pu()
        else:
            pd()

    def demo1():
        """Demo of old turtle.py - module"""
        reset()
        ...

    def demo2():
        """Demo of some new features."""
        speed(1)
        ...

    demo1()
    demo2()
    exitonclick()
```

5.11
Keyword Arguments

Up to this point we have learned that arguments passed to a function must be in the same order as the formal parameters in the function definition. For instance, in Example 5.16, to call the *drawSquare* function we would write *drawSquare(t,l)* as is done in the *main* function of the example.

It turns out that Python allows programmers to call functions using keyword arguments as well [5]. This is not possible in every language, but this is one of the very powerful features of Python. A formal parameter in the function definition is the name given to a value that will be passed to the function. For instance, in Example 5.16 the formal parameters to drawSquare are *turtle* and *length*. These two names are also keywords that may be used when calling drawSquare. The drawSquare function can be called by writing *drawSquare(length=l,turtle=t)* using the keyword style of parameter passing.

5.12
Default Values

When the keyword style of parameter passing is used, some keyword values may or may not be supplied depending on what the function does. In this case, a function definition can supply a default value for a parameter.

Example 5.18 Here is the *drawSquare* function with a default length value for the side length of the square. This means that the following calls to *drawSquare* would all be valid.

```
def drawSquare(turtle,length=20):
    for k in range(4):
        turtle.forward(length)
        turtle.left(90)

drawSquare(t,40)
drawSquare(t)
drawSquare(length=30,turtle=t)
```

5.13
Functions with Variable Number of Parameters

Python functions may have a variable number of parameters passed to them. To deal with this a special form of parameter is defined in Python by writing an asterisk in front of it. Writing *args* as a formal parameter defines *args* as a list (see [5]). Every argument that is passed starting at *args* position will be passed in a list that *args* will refer to.

Example 5.19 Consider a function called *drawFigure* that draws a figure by making a series of forward and left moves with a turtle. Since there could be a variable number of forward and left turns, they are represented by the formal parameter *args* which is a list of all the arguments after the named *turtle* argument.

```
import turtle

def drawFigure(turtle, *args):
    for i in range(0,len(args),2):
        turtle.forward(args[i])
        turtle.left(args[i+1])

def main():
    t = turtle.Turtle()
    screen = t.getscreen()
    drawFigure(t,50,90,30,90,50,90,30,90)
    screen.exitonclick()

if __name__ == "__main__":
    main()
```

5.14
Dictionary Parameter Passing

Using keyword/value pairs to pass values to functions is much like building a dictionary. A dictionary is a set of keys and associated values. For instance, you can assign width=20 and height=40 in a dictionary. Appendix E describes the operators and methods of dictionaries.

Example 5.20 Here is a dictionary called *dimensions* with keys *width* and *height*.

```
dimensions = {}
dimensions['width'] = 20
dimensions['height'] = 40
```

As an added convenience for programmers, a dictionary of keyword/value pairs may be specified as a parameter to a function [5]. The dictionary is automatically defined as the set of all keyword/value pairs passed to the function. A keyword/value dictionary parameter is defined by writing two asterisks in front of the parameter name.

Example 5.21 Here is a *drawRectangle* function that gets its width and height as keyword/-value arguments. The function definition specifies a *dimensions* keyword/value dictionary argument. The code below shows how it can be used.

```
import turtle

def drawRectangle(turtle, **dimensions):
    width = 10
    height = 10
    if "width" in dimensions:
        width = dimensions["width"]
    if "height" in dimensions:
        height = dimensions["height"]
    drawFigure(turtle,width,90,height,90,width,90,height,90)

def drawFigure(turtle, *args):
    for i in range(0,len(args),2):
        turtle.forward(args[i])
        turtle.left(args[i+1])

def main():
    t = turtle.Turtle()
    screen = t.getscreen()
    drawRectangle(t,width=40,height=20)
    screen.exitonclick()

if __name__ == "__main__":
    main()
```

5.15
Review Questions

1. What is the difference between defining a function and calling a function? Give an example of each and describe what happens when a function is both defined and called.
2. What are two reasons to write functions when possible in your code?
3. What is an argument and what is a formal parameter?
4. What is scope and what is the name of the rule for determining the scope of a variable? Describe what each letter means in the acronym for determining scope.
5. What is an activation record? When is one pushed and when is it popped?
6. How do activation records and scope relate to each other?
7. If a function is called and passed a string it can make all the changes it wants to the string but when the function returns the changes will be lost. This isn't necessarily the case if a function is passed a list. Why?
8. What is a predicate function? What programming pattern is a predicate function likely going to use?
9. What is the difference between top-down and bottom-up design?
10. What is a recursive function? What two things must a recursive function contain?
11. Why is a *main* function beneficial in a program? Give two reasons a main function might help in the implementation of a module.
12. What is a keyword parameter/argument? How does it differ from a regular argument?
13. What is a dictionary? How can a dictionary be used in parameter passing?

5.16
Exercises

1. Write a program that contains a drawTruck function that given an *x*, *y* coordinate on the screen draws a truck using Turtle graphics. You may use the goto method on the first line of the function, but after that use only left, right, forward, and back to draw the truck. You may use color when drawing if you would like to.
2. Modify the program in the previous exercise to add a *scale* parameter to the drawTruck function. You should multiply the scale times each forward or back method call while drawing the truck. Then use the drawTruck function at least three times in a program to draw trucks of different sizes.
3. Write a program that contains a function called drawRegularPolygon where you give it a Turtle, the number of sides of the polygon, and the side length and it draws the polygon for you. NOTE: This function won't return a value since it has a side-effect of drawing the regular polygon. Then write some code that uses this function at least three times to draw polygons of different sizes and shapes.
4. Write a predicate function called isEven that returns True if a number is even and False if it is not. Use the function in a program and test your code on several different values.
5. Write a function called allEvens that given a list of integers, returns a new list containing only the even integers. Use the function in a program and test your code on several different values.

6. Write a function called isPalindrome that returns True if a string given to it is a palindrome. A palindrome is a string that is the same spelled backwards or forwards. For instance, *radar* is a palindrome. Use the function in a program and test your code on several different values.

7. Write a function called isPrime that returns True if an integer given to the function is a prime number. Use the function in a program and test your code on several different values.

8. A tuple is a sequence of comma separated values inside of parens. For instance (5,6) is a two-tuple. Write a function called *zip* that is given two lists of the same length and creates a new list of two-tuples where each two-tuple is the tuple of the corresponding elements from the two lists. For example, zip([1, 2, 3], [4, 5, 6]) would return [(1, 4), (2, 5), (3, 6)]. Use the function in a program and test your code on several different values.

9. Write a function called *unzip* that returns a tuple of two lists that result from unzipping a zipped list (see the previous exercise). So unzip([(1, 4), (2, 5), (3, 6)]) would return ([1, 2, 3], [4, 5, 6]). Use the function in a program and test your code on several different values.

10. Write a function called sumIt which is given a list of numbers and returns the sum of those numbers. Use the function in a program and test your code on several different values.

11. Write a recursive function called recursiveSumIt which given a list of numbers, returns the sum of those numbers. Use the function in a program and test your code on several different values.

12. Use top-down design to write a program with three functions that capitalizes the first letter of each word in a sentence. For instance, if the user enters "hi there how are you" the program should print back to the screen "Hi There How Are You". Don't forget to define at least three functions using top-down design. Write comments to show what function you wrote first, followed by the second function you wrote, followed by the third function you wrote assuming you employed a top-down design.

13. Use bottom-up design to write a program with three functions that capitalizes the first letter of each word in a sentence. For instance, if the user enters "hi there how are you" the program should print back to the screen "Hi There How Are You". Don't forget to define at least three functions using bottom-up design. Write comments to show what function you wrote first, followed by the second function you wrote, followed by the third function you wrote assuming you employed a bottom-up design. HINT: The answer to this problem and exercise 12 should only differ in the order that you wrote the functions. The solutions should otherwise be identical.

14. Write a function called *factors* that given an integer returns the list of the factors of that integer. For instance, *factors*(6) would return [1, 2, 3, 6].

15. Write a function called *sumFactors* that given an integer returns the sum of the factors of that integer. For instance, *sumFactors*(6) would return 12 since $1 + 2 + 3 + 6 = 12$.

16. Write a function called *isPerfect* that given an integer returns True if the number is the sum of its factors (not including itself) and False otherwise. For instance, 6 is a perfect number because its factors, 1, 2, and 3 add up to 6.

17. Write a function called *sumRange* that given two integers returns the sum of all the integers between the two given integers inclusive. For instance, *sumRange*(3, 6) would return 18. Use a second function in the definition of sumRange to show that you can employ some top-down design to decompose this problem into a simpler problem and then use that simpler solution to solve this problem. HINT: Look for a function in these exercises you might use in defining *sumRange*.

18. Write a function called *reverseWords* that given a string representing a sentence, returns the same sentence but with each word reversed. For instance, *reverseWords*("*hi there how are you*") would return "ih ereht woh era uoy". Use another function in the definition of this function to make the task of writing this program simpler.

19. Write a function called *oddCharacters* that given a string, returns a string containing only the odd characters of the given string. The first element of a string (i.e. index 0) is an even element. *oddCharacters*("*hi there*") should be "*itee*".

20. Write a function called *oddElements* that given a list, returns a list containing only the odd elements of the list. The first element of a list (i.e. index 0) is an even element. *oddElements*([1,2,3,4]) should be [2,4]. What do you notice about this and the previous problem?

21. Write a function called *dotProduct* that computes the dot product of two lists of numbers given to the function. Use the *zip* function in your solution.

22. Review exercise 2 from Chap. 3. Use top-down design to write at least two functions that implement an addressbook application as described there. When you write it this time use the technique of parallel lists introduced in Chap. 4. The program should read all the records from the file and place the contents of the fields of each record in parallel lists so the file does not have to be read more than once in the application. But, be sure to write the contents of the parallel lists to the file when the user chooses to quit. Otherwise, you won't be able to add entries to the address book.

23. Write a program that computes a user's GPA on a 4 point scale. Each grade on a 4 point scale is multiplied by the number of credits for that class. The sum of all the credit, grade products is divided by the total number of credits earned. Assume the 4 point scale assigns values of 4.0 for an A, 3.7 for an A-, 3.3 for a B+, 3.0 for a B, 2.7 for a B-, 2.3 for a C+, 2.0 for a C, 1.7 for a C-, 1.3 for a D+, 1.0 for a D, 0.7 for a D-, and 0 for an F. Ask the user to enter their credit grade pairs using the following format until the enter 0 for the number of credits.

   In this version of the program you should read the data from the user and build parallel lists. Then, write a function called computeWeightedAverage that given the two parallel lists computes the average and returns it. Use this function in your program.

```
This program computes your GPA.
Please enter your completed courses.
Terminate your entry by entering 0 credits.
Credits? 4
Grade? A
Credits? 3
Grade? B+
Credits? 4
Grade? B-
```

```
Credits? 2
Grade? C
Credits? 0
Your GPA is 3.13
```

5.17
Solutions to Practice Problems

These are solutions to the practice problems in this chapter. You should only consult these answers after you have tried each of them for yourself first. Practice problems are meant to help reinforce the material you have just read so make use of them.

Solution to Practice Problem 5.1

```python
def explode(s):
  lst = []
  for c in s:
    lst.append(c)

  return lst

print(explode("hello"))
```

Solution to Practice Problem 5.2

```python
def implode(lst):
  s = ""
  for e in lst:
    s = s+e

  return s

print(implode(['h', 'e', 'l', 'l', 'o']))
```

Solution to Practice Problem 5.3

The error is *variable referenced before assignment*. It occurs on the first line, the second occurrence of *x*. At this point *x* has no value.

Fig. 5.3 The run-time stack
for Example 5.2

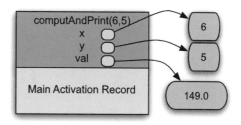

Solution to Practice Problem 5.4

The error message is below. The problem is that the *len* function's name was overridden
in the local scope by the *len* variable. This means that within the local scope of the *length*
function, *len* cannot be called as a function. The error message says that an *int* is not
callable.

```
Traceback (most recent call last):
  File "/Applications/WingIDE.app/...", line 8, in <module>
  File "/Applications/WingIDE.app/...", line 3, in length
    pass
builtins.TypeError: 'int' object is not callable
```

Solution to Practice Problem 5.5

Figure 5.3 show the contents of the run-time stack just before the return from the function.
There are no variables in the main activation record.

Solution to Practice Problem 5.6

Refer to Fig. 5.3 to compare to what you see using your IDE.

Solution to Practice Problem 5.7

None is returned by the function since it does not explicitly return a value. So printing
None is not very interesting, But, more importantly, since the list is reversed in place then
how should the list be accessed? There is no reference stored to the list once the function
returns so the garbage collector comes along and reclaims the space throwing away the
work that was just done. The correct way to call it is shown in Example 5.8.

Solution to Practice Problem 5.8

The *reverseInPlace* function cannot be used to reverse a string since indexed assignment is not possible on strings. In other words, strings are immutable. The line of code $lst[i] = lst[len(lst) - 1 - i]$ is the line of code where the program would terminate abnormally.

Solution to Practice Problem 5.9

```
def evenlyDividesList(x,lst):

   for e in lst:
     if not evenlyDivides(x,e):
       return False

   return True
```

Solution to Practice Problem 5.10

```
def evenlyDivisibleElements(x,lst):
   result = []

   for e in lst:
     if evenlyDivides(e,x):
       result.append(e)

   return result
```

Solution to Practice Problem 5.11

```
def evenlyDivisible(lst):

   for e in lst:
     print(e,'is evenly divisible by ',end="")
     elements = evenlyDivisibleElements(e,lst)
     for f in elements:
       print(f,end=" ")

     print()
```

Solution to Practice Problem 5.12

Each time a function call is made an activation record is pushed on the stack. Each activation record takes some space. Without the base case first, the program would repeatedly call the *factorial* function until the run-time stack overflowed (i.e. ran out of space). This is called *infinite recursion* even though it will not continue indefinitely.

Solution to Practice Problem 5.13

There would be 7 activation records at its deepest point, one for the *main* activation record, and one for each of the arguments recursively passed to *factorial*(5): 5, 4, 3, 2, 1, 0.

Solution to Practice Problem 5.14

When you run the program you should notice that there are 6 different n variables, each with a different value from 5 to 0. This is why it is important to understand the run-time stack and how it works when dealing with recursion. Recursive functions cannot work without the run-time stack.

Solution to Practice Problem 5.15

Here is the solution. However, you would never, ever, write such a program and use it in a commercial setting. It is too slow for anything but small values of n. There are much better solutions to finding fibonacci numbers that are available.

```
def recfib(n):
    if n == 0:
        return 1

    if n == 1:
        return 1

    return fib(n-1) + fib(n-2)
```

Event-Driven Programming

6

When a program runs in Python the Python interpreter scans the program from top to bottom executing the first statement that is not part of a function definition. The program proceeds by executing the next statement and the next. Sequential execution is redirected by iteration (i.e. *for* and *while* loops) and function calls. Nevertheless, the program sequentially executes until Python interprets the last statement at which point the program terminates.

In an event-driven program sequential execution is in response to events happening while the program is executing. Event-driven programs arise in many areas of programming including Operating Systems, Internet Programming, Distributed Computing, and Graphical User Interfaces, often abbreviated GUI programs. An event-driven application begins as a sequential program executing one statement after another until it enters a never-ending loop. This loop, sometimes called the event dispatch loop looks for an incoming event and then dispatches that event to an event handler. Events come in a wide variety of flavors including:

- An interrupt indicating the completion of a disk operation.
- A network packet has become available
- A network connection has become unavailable
- A button was pressed in a GUI application
- A menu item was selected in a GUI application
- An incoming request has been received by a web server.

In an event-driven program, the event dispatch loop looks for events like these. Each event will generally have its own event handler. An event handler is a function that is called to process the event. Each time an event is found, the corresponding event handler is called to process the event. Once the event is processed, the program returns from the event handler to the event dispatch loop to look for the next event. This process repeats forever or until some event is dispatched that causes the program to terminate. For example, if a user chooses to exit a GUI application, the event handler may tell the the event dispatch loop to quit and exit.

K.D. Lee, *Python Programming Fundamentals,* Undergraduate Topics in Computer Science, **149**
DOI 10.1007/978-1-84996-537-8_6, © Springer-Verlag London Limited 2011

Tk is a powerful Application Programming Interface, or API, designed to make GUI programming easy on a variety of operating systems including Mac OS X, Windows, and Linux [11]. An API is a set of classes, or types, and functions that can be useful when implementing a program. In the case of Python, the Tkinter API was designed to allow Python programs to work with the Tk package to implement GUI programs that will run on Windows, Mac OS X, or Linux [5]. The Tkinter API is included in a module called *tkinter*. The module is included with most distributions of Python and may be imported to use in your Python programs.

Fig. 6.1   A Tk root window

Tk programs use widgets to build a GUI application. The term widget has been used at least since the 1980's to refer to any element of a GUI application including windows, buttons, menus, text entry fields, frames, listboxes, etc. There are many different widgets available in tkinter. Typically, any element you can see (and some you can't see, like frames) in a GUI application is a widget. The next sections will introduce several widgets while building a *Reminder!* note application.

6.1
The Root Window

To begin using the Tk API you open a root window. Tk applications can have more than one open window, but the main window is called the root window. It is opened by calling a function called *Tk()*.

Example 6.1   Here is code to open a Tk window.

```python
import sys
import tkinter

def main():
    root = tkinter.Tk()

    root.title("Reminder!")
    root.resizable(width=False,height=False)

    tkinter.mainloop()
if __name__ == "__main__":
    main()
```

The code in Example 6.1 opens a window as pictured in Fig. 6.1. The call to the *title* method sets the title of the window. The call to *resizable* makes the window a non-resizable window. The *Tkinter.mainloop()* calls the Tk event dispatch loop to process events from the windowing application. Even with a simple window like this, the call to mainloop is required because there are events that even a simple window must respond to. For example, when a

---

Python 2 ⤳ 3

In Python 2 the module name for Tkinter was *Tkinter*. In Python 3 the module name become *tkinter*. If you are using Tkinter in Python 2.6 you write:

```
import Tkinter
```

to import the Tkinter module.

---

window is moved on the screen it must respond to its redraw event. Redrawing the window is done automatically by the Tk code once the mainloop function is called.

6.2
Menus

A menu can be added to the application by creating a Menu widget and adding it to the root window. On Windows and Linux the menu will appear right at the top of the window. On a Mac, the menu appears at the top of the screen on the menu bar. This menu contains a *File->Exit* menu item that quits the application when selected.

Example 6.2 Here is the code that, when added right before the call to mainloop, creates a File menu with one menu item to exit.

```
def quit():
    root.destroy()
bar = tkinter.Menu(root)
fileMenu = tkinter.Menu(bar,tearoff=0)
fileMenu.add_command(label="Exit",command=quit)
bar.add_cascade(label="File",menu=fileMenu)
root.config(menu=bar)
```

When adding a menu, you associate a command (i.e. a function) with each menu item added to the menu. The *Exit* menu item is associated with the *quit* function which calls the root's *destroy* method. Notice the *quit* function has no parameters. Most event handlers do not have parameters but do have access to the enclosing scope.

Practice 6.1 Write a Tkinter program that creates a main window with a menu that says *Help*. Within the *Help* menu item should be another menu item that says *About*. When the About menu is selected, your program should print "About was Selected" to the screen.

6.3
Frames

A Frame is an invisible widget that can be used as a container for other widgets. Frames are sometimes useful in laying out a GUI application. Layout refers to getting all the widgets in the right place and making them stay there even when the window is resized. We don't have to worry about resizing the window in the Reminder! application so layout will be a little easier.

In Fig. 6.2 there is a Frame widget. The frame is invisible. The text entry area is inside the frame and so is the *New Reminder!* button. Frames can be useful to group widgets together. They can also have a border around them. The border around this frame is 5 pixels wide. Adding the frame with a border gives a little edge to the window.

Fig. 6.2 The main Reminder! window [9]

Example 6.3 This is the code that creates the frame for the Reminder! application.

```
mainFrame = tkinter.Frame(root,borderwidth=1,padx=5,pady=5)
mainFrame.pack()
```

When the frame is created the first parameter to the Frame constructor is the window that the frame is to be packed into. This is true of every widget. The first parameter to the constructor when creating a widget is the widget it belongs to. In this way, widgets can be nested inside of widgets to form the GUI application. So, the *mainFrame* frame is a part of the *root* window. Recall that in Example 6.1 the variable *root* was set to the root Tk window.

Packing the mainFrame means to add it into the root window and make the contents of the frame visible. While a frame itself is invisible, by packing it the contents of the frame will be visible once the window is drawn. Packing is one method of making a widget visible. Other methods of making widgets visible are discussed in Sect. 6.9.

Practice 6.2 Create a frame and pack it in a root window.

6.4
The Text Widget

The Text widget is a powerful multi-line editing window that can embed graphics and other objects within it. In the Reminder! application it holds the message to be posted. The

Text widget in this application is added to the *mainFrame*. By creating a Text widget and packing it into the main frame the user can enter text into it. The widget handles all the text entry itself without any intervention by the programmer.

Example 6.4 Here is the code to create a Text widget in the Reminder! application.

```
note = tkinter.Text(mainFrame,bg="yellow",width=30,height=15)
note.pack()
```

Practice 6.3 Create a text widget of 3 rows and 20 columns and place it in your practice GUI's frame.

6.5
The Button Widget

The Button widget is used to get button press input from a user. Buttons appear in the native button format of the operating system you are using so they may not look exactly like the button displayed in Fig. 6.2. Since a button must respond to being pressed, when you create a button you specify an event handler to handle the button presses. An event handler is added to the button in the same way a command was added to a menu item in Sect. 6.2.

Example 6.5 Here is the code to create a Button and its associated event handler.

```
def post():
    print("Post")
    addReminder(note.get("1.0",tkinter.END), \
      root.winfo_rootx()+5,root.winfo_rooty()+5, \
      notes,reminders)
    note.delete("1.0",tkinter.END)

tkinter.Button(mainFrame,text="New Reminder!", \
    command=post).pack()
```

Example 6.5 shows a button being created, being added to the main frame, and then being packed within the frame. The keyword argument *text* specifies the text to go on the button. The keyword *command* is used to specify a parameterless function to call when the button is pressed. The function *post* is a parameterless function and is defined in the same scope as the Button. Normally, a function is not defined within the scope of another function. However, in Tk programming it is much more common. Event handlers are almost always nested functions. By nesting the event handler in the main function, it has access to all the variables defined in the main function. In this example the *post* function needs to have access to the *root* variable as well as the *notes* and *reminders* variables. By defining *post* within the same scope as the *root* variable, the *post* function can use these values as needed. Since the function *post* cannot have any parameters as dictated by Tkinter API, the *post* function must access the *root* variable from the enclosing scope. To see the whole program in context refer to Appendix H.

The *post* function gets the contents of the text field, called *note*, by using the *get* method on the note. Calling the *get* method with "1.0" and *tkinter.END* gets the text from beginning to end. The *winfo_rootx()* and *winfo_rooty()* methods get the x and y coordinates for the upper left corner of the root window. The post function then passes that information along with a couple of lists called *notes* and *reminders* to the *addReminder* function. The *addReminder* function adds a new reminder note to the screen as appears in Fig. 6.3.

Fig. 6.3 A Reminder!

Notice that when a command like *post* is provided to a button it is not written *post()*. This is because we are not calling post when the button is created. Instead, we are specifying that when the button is pressed the *post* function should be called. By providing the function name *post* to the button widget it can remember to call that function when it is pressed.

Practice 6.4 Create a button that says "Now!" on it. Connect it to a command that prints "Oh, now you've done it!" to the screen.

6.6
Creating a Reminder!

To create a Reminder! window another top level window is created. To do this, the button calls the *addReminder* function. There are two parts to a reminder, the window itself and the Text widget within the window. A list of reminder windows is maintained in a list called *notes*. A list of the text widgets is maintained in a list called *reminders*. These lists are *parallel* lists. This means that the first entry in both lists corresponds to the first reminder, the second element in both lists is the second reminder and so on. Parallel lists were first introduced in Sect. 4.11 on page 107. Both the window and the Text widget are needed to maintain the information about a *reminder* in the program.

Example 6.6 Here is the code that adds reminders to the screen. The *notes* and *reminders* lists keep track of the windows and Text widgets.

```
def addReminder(text,x,y,notes,reminders):
    notewin = tkinter.Toplevel()
    notewin.resizable(width=False,height=False)
    notewin.geometry("+"+str(x)+"+"+str(y))

    reminder = tkinter.Text(notewin,bg="yellow", \
        width=30,height=15)

    reminder.insert(tkinter.END,text)
    reminder.pack()

    notes.append(notewin)
    reminders.append(reminder)

    def deleteWindowHandler():
        print("Window Deleted")
        notewin.withdraw()
        notes.remove(notewin)
        reminders.remove(reminder)

    notewin.protocol("WM_DELETE_WINDOW", deleteWindowHandler)
```

To add a *reminder* to the screen a toplevel window is created, the new window is not resizable and is positioned over the top of the existing window using the *geometry* method. Calling geometry on a window with a string like "+10+10" positions the window at (10, 10) pixels measured from the upper left corner of the screen. Since the root window's coordinates were passed to the function, the new window is positioned approximately on top of the root window.

The text is copied into the reminder. Then the window and the Text widget are copied into the notes and reminders lists, respectively. The last line of the method adds an event handler for the window deletion event. If the reminder window is closed, the user is getting rid of that reminder. In that case, the reminder window and corresponding Text widget are removed from the notes and reminders lists. The remove method looks for a matching element of the list and removes it. The only matching element of a window or Text entry widget is the original window or widget added to the list.

The *deleteWindowHandler* function is a case where accessing the enclosing scope is exactly what we want. We can't pass parameters to the *deleteWindowHandler* function, but we can access the notes, reminders, reminder, and notewin variables from the enclosing scope to remove the window from the program when it is closed.

6.7
Finishing up the Reminder! Application

There is only a little more code needed to finish the Reminder! application. It is more
interesting if the reminders are saved to a file when the program is closed. Then the reminder windows can be redisplayed when the program is started again. The application
saves the information in a file called *reminders.txt*. The file starts with the *X*, *Y* coordinate of the root window on the screen. Then, each reminder record starts with an *X*,
Y coordinate of the reminder window followed by some text on multiple lines followed
by a line of underscores and periods in a pattern that should never be seen by accident.
The application reads from the file until this special line is found and then makes a reminder out of the text it just read. Then it continues reading the file looking for the next
reminder.

Example 6.7 Here is the code that reads and writes the *reminders.txt* file.

```
try:
    print("reading reminders.txt file")
    file = open("reminders.txt","r")
    x = int(file.readline())
    y = int(file.readline())
    root.geometry("+"+str(x)+"+"+str(y))

    line = file.readline()
    while line.strip() != "":
        x = int(line)
        y = int(file.readline())
        text = ""
        line = file.readline()
        while line.strip() != "____....____._._._":
            text = text + line
            line = file.readline()

        text = text.strip()
        addReminder(text,x,y,notes,reminders)
        line = file.readline()
except:
        print("reminders.txt not found")

def appClosing():
    print("Application Closing")
    file = open("reminders.txt","w")
    file.write(str(root.winfo_x())+"\n")
    file.write(str(root.winfo_y())+"\n")

    for i in range(len(notes)):
        print(notes[i].winfo_rootx())
        print(notes[i].winfo_rooty())
```

```
        print(reminders[i].get("1.0",tkinter.END))
        file.write(str(notes[i].winfo_rootx())+"\n")
        file.write(str(notes[i].winfo_rooty())+"\n")
        file.write(reminders[i].get("1.0",tkinter.END)+"\n")
        file.write("____....____._._._\n")

    file.close()
    root.destroy()
    root.quit() # May or may not be necessary
    sys.exit()

root.protocol("WM_DELETE_WINDOW", appClosing)
```

The code in the *try ... except* block attempts to read the information when the application starts. This code is located in the main function of the application. When the window deletion event occurs for the main window, the appClosing handler is called. The appClosing function writes the file, overwriting any file that was read when the application started. The complete code for the Reminder! application can be found in Appendix H.

6.8
Label and Entry Widgets

Fig. 6.4 A titled Reminder! application

Assume we wish to enhance the Reminder! application by allowing the user to set the title of each reminder. Instead of the reminder note just having *Reminder!* as its title, it could have a user-defined title. So when the *New Reminder!* button was pressed for the application in Fig. 6.4 a new window would appear with "Don't forget trash!" as its title. This can be done by adding a label and an entry widget to the application.

The Label widget is the text "Title:" that appears in the figure. The Entry widget is the one line text field. While a Text widget can handle multiple lines, an Entry widget holds just one line of text.

Example 6.8 Here is the code for the Entry and Text widgets in this application.

```
titleFrame = tkinter.Frame(mainFrame)
titleFrame.pack()

noteTitle = tkinter.StringVar()
titleLabel = tkinter.Label(titleFrame,text="Title:")
titleLabel.grid(row=1,column=1,sticky=tkinter.E)
titleText = tkinter.Entry(titleFrame,textvariable=noteTitle)
titleText.grid(row=1,column=2,columnspan=2, \
    sticky=tkinter.E+tkinter.W)
```

A new frame is created because it will need to contain the two elements on one line in the application. Without a new frame, the "Title:" label would be packed above the Entry widget. Within the *titleFrame* frame, the *titleLabel* and *titleText* widgets are added using the *grid* layout instead of the *pack* layout. In a grid layout you specify which row and column of the grid the widget should be placed in. The *columnspan* argument specifies that the *titleText* widget should span 2 of the three columns of the row.

A *StringVar* is an object with a *get* and a *set* method. The *titleText* Entry widget is created specifying a textvariable called *noteTitle* which is required to be of type *StringVar*. To retrieve the text of the Entry widget we can write *noteTitle.get()* and to set the text of the widget we can write *noteTitle.set("Whatever Text We Want")*. StringVars make it easy to set and retrieve text from an Entry widget.

There is a little more code to write to complete the extension of this application to include the title information in the reminders and in the text file that stores the reminders. This code is left as an exercise.

> **Practice 6.5** Add a label that says "What do you want?" to the practice Tk application from this chapter.

6.9
Layout Management

When widgets are packed or gridded in an application, their appearance within the application is called their layout. Sometimes, when widgets are placed within an application they appear in the right place when the application starts, but if the window is resized, they don't look right. Understanding something about layout management can help you correctly plan your application's layout and avoid these kinds of problems.

Packing widgets places them one above another in what is sometimes called a flow layout. Each widget appears above the next when packed. The Tk packer is responsible for packer layout management. There are some options that can affect how packing is done. Normally the packer places one widget above another in a flow layout. But these options let the programmer have some control about how that flow is managed.

- **fill =** You can specify that if a widget can use the extra space, then it should fill the available space. Valid values for fill are *tkinter.X*, *tkinter.Y*, or *tkinter.BOTH*. X means to fill in the horizontal direction, Y means to fill in the vertical direction, *BOTH* means to fill in both directions. For a label to fill in the horizontal direction you would write:

```
titleLabel = tkinter.Label(titleFrame,text="Title:", \
    bg="green",fg="blue")
titleLabel.pack(fill=tkinter.X)
```

The *bg* and *fg* parameters set the background and foreground color, respectively.

- **side** = This specifies which side to flow from. For example, writing *titleLabel.pack(side=tkinter.LEFT)* will flow from the left rather than the top. Other valid values are *TOP*, *BOTTOM*, or *RIGHT*.

The Tk gridder is responsible for grid layout management. Grid layout allows widgets to be placed in a specific column and/or row of a container widget. As we have seen, it is possible for one widget to span more than one column or row in a grid. The *rowspan* parameter sets the number of rows a widget should span. The *columnspan* option was used in Example 6.8. It is also possible to tell the gridder how it should use the space within a row and column. Normally a widget is centered within the available space, But, if the widget can use it, the gridder can be told to expand the widget to take up the available space. The *sticky* option tells the gridder to stick the widget to one or more sides of the available area. The *tkinter.E* and *tkinter.W* constants stand for east and west. By adding east and west together in Example 6.8 the entry widget will expand to the full width of its allowable size. In that example it has no affect on the layout, since the window cannot be resized anyway, but nonetheless it demonstrates its use.

While packing and gridding are the two most common forms of layout management, there is also a placer. The placer places widgets explicitly within the X,Y plane of the application. The packer, gridder, and placer are the three layout managers for Tkinter. Each of these layout managers have more options available for layout that are not discussed here but can be found by searching for "tkinter layout management" on the internet.

Practice 6.6 Make the entry widget and the button widget in your practice application appear next to each other at the bottom of the window.

6.10
Message Boxes

Sometimes it is necessary to pop up a message box in a GUI application to warn the user of some invalid operation they are trying to perform. Sometimes the application just needs to provide some quick feedback, like "Job Completed" or some other status. Tk provides a few message boxes for these occasions. To use the message boxes you must import *tkinter.messagebox*.

Here are three examples.

- **tkinter.messagebox.showinfo("Invalid Entry","Type a reminder first.")**

    This displays an informational box with an informational icon. You can change the icon displayed in the box by specifying the *icon* = parameter. More information is available online. The dialog box appears on the screen and the application waits for *OK* to be pressed.

- **tkinter.messagebox.showwarning("Invalid Entry","Type a reminder first.")**

  This works the same as the *showinfo* dialog box but displays a warning icon instead of an informational icon.

- **answer = tkinter.messagebox.askyesno("Really?","Are you sure you want to create a blank reminder?")**

  This displays a dialog with *Yes* and *No* buttons. If *Yes* is pressed, the function call returns *True*. If *No* is pressed, the function returns *False*.

Python 2 ↝ 3

In Python 2 the module name for message boxes was *tkMessageBox*. In Python 3 the module name became *tkinter.messagebox*. If you are using Tkinter in Python 2.6 you write:

```
import tkMessageBox
```

to import the Tkinter message box module.

There are other dialogs available including a color chooser and file chooser. There are also several other options that are possible with each of these dialogs. Again, more information can be found online.

> **Practice 6.7** When the button of your practice application is pressed, take the information in the entry widget and display it in a message box of your choice with some appropriate text to go with it.

6.11
Review Questions

1. How are a event-driven program and simple sequential program the same?
2. What distinguishes an event-driven program from a sequential program?
3. What is an API?
4. Name two APIs that are available in Python. What does each API do for you as a programmer?
5. What is a widget?
6. When writing a Tkinter application, what is the purpose of the call to *mainloop*?
7. What is the purpose of a frame in Tkinter?
8. What does the term *layout* refer to in a GUI application? Be complete in your answer.
9. What is the purpose of the StringVar class in Tkinter applications?
10. Why are event handlers generally defined within the scope of the main function?

Fig. 6.5 A titled Reminder!

Fig. 6.6 A GUI for the
AddressBook application

11. What are two methods of arranging widgets in a Tkinter application? Describe the differences between the two methods.

6.12
Exercises

1. Extend the Reminder! application so that each Reminder! is given the title assigned in the main application window. For example, if the *New Reminder!* button is pressed for the application as it appears in Fig. 6.4, the reminder window would appear as shown in Fig. 6.5. Be sure to clear both the text and the title from the root application window after the *New Reminder!* button is pressed.

2. Implement a GUI front-end to the address book application. The GUI should be similar to that presented in Fig. 6.6. Each of the buttons in the application should work as described here.

   a. The add button should add a new entry to the phonebook. This must append an entry to the phonebook. The event handler for this function should look something like this (depending on how you write the rest of your program).

```
def addAddress():
    print "Add"

    if lname.get().strip() == "":
        tkMessageBox.showwarning("Missing Last Name", \
            "You must enter a non-empty last name.")
        return

    if fname.get().strip() == "":
        tkMessageBox.showwarning("Missing First Name", \
            "You must enter a non-empty first name.")
        return

    file = open("addressbook.txt","a")

    file.write(lname.get().strip()+"\n")
    file.write(fname.get().strip()+"\n")
    file.write(street.get().strip()+"\n")
    file.write(city.get().strip()+", "+state.get().strip()+ \
        " "+zip.get().strip()+"\n")
    file.write(phone.get().strip()+"\n")
    file.write(mobile.get().strip()+"\n")

    file.close()

    tkMessageBox.showinfo("Entry Added", \
        "The entry was successfully added.")
```

b. The update button should update an existing entry or display a message saying the entry was not found. Update must find an entry that matches the first and last name displayed in the GUI. If found, the entry in the file is updated to reflect the new information found in the GUI. You find an entry by matching the first and last name in the address book so updating the name will not work. In that case a new entry needs to be added and the old one deleted. If the entry is not found a warning message should be displayed.

Since entries cannot be deleted from files, to update an entry you must open a new file for writing. Then you copy all the entries to the new file that don't match the entry to be updated. Once you find the entry to be updated you write the GUI information to the new file. Finally, you must write the rest of the non-matching entries to the new file. After you are done, you can remove the old file and rename the new file to the *addressbook.txt* file name. The following lines of code will delete the addressbook.txt file and rename a file called __newbook.txt to *addressbook.txt*.

```
os.remove("addressbook.txt")
os.rename(".__newbook.txt","addressbook.txt")
```

c. The delete button deletes an existing entry. To delete an existing entry the last and first name should match the entry being deleted. Since you cannot delete a record from a file, you must create a new file, writing all records to the new file except for the one to be deleted. Then remove the old file and rename the new file to *addressbook.txt*. See the description of the *update* button implementation to see how to delete and rename the files.

d. The find button finds the entry with the same first and last name as typed. It should at least work when both last and first name are supplied by the user. However, you can extend this by making it work if the last name is empty. Then it should match only on first name. Likewise, if the first name is empty then it should only match on last name. In either case it should display the first matching entry in the address book.

e. The next button displays the next address after the current entry and wraps around to the beginning when the last entry was displayed.

3. Implement a GUI front-end for the addressbook application as described in exercise 2, but use parallel lists to hold the fields of each record instead of reading from and writing to the file immediately. You should write code to read the entire file when the application starts and it should be written again when the application closes.

   Each of the buttons should be implemented but instead of reading or writing to the file, the buttons should use the parallel lists as the source of the addressbook entries.

4. Using the Reminder! application code from Appendix H as a reference, rewrite the code so that the reminders are read from an XML file when the application starts and are written to an XML file when the application terminates. To write an XML file you open a text file for writing and you write the data and the XML tags for each XML element.

5. Implement a GUI front-end for the addressbook application but in this version of the application define an XML file format to hold the data. Then, write the program to read the XML file when the application starts and write the XML file when the application terminates. Use parallel lists to hold the fields of each record while the application is running. To write an XML file you open a text file for writing and you write the data and the XML tags for each XML element.

6.13
Solutions to Practice Problems

These are solutions to the practice problems in this chapter. You should only consult these answers after you have tried each of them for yourself first. Practice problems are meant to help reinforce the material you have just read so make use of them.

Solution to Practice Problem 6.1

```python
import tkinter

def main():
    def about():
        print("About was Selected")

    root = tkinter.Tk()

    root.title("Silly Program")

    bar = tkinter.Menu(root)

    fileMenu = tkinter.Menu(bar,tearoff=0)
    fileMenu.add_command(label="About",command=about)
    bar.add_cascade(label="Help",menu=fileMenu)
    root.config(menu=bar)

if __name__ == "__main__":
    main()
    tkinter.mainloop()
```

Solution to Practice Problem 6.2

The window will probably resize to a very tiny window when run because there isn't anything in the frame yet.

```python
mainFrame = tkinter.Frame(root,borderwidth=1,padx=5,pady=5)
mainFrame.pack()
```

Solution to Practice Problem 6.3

```python
note = tkinter.Text(mainFrame, width=20,height=3)
note.pack()
```

Solution to Practice Problem 6.4

```
def pressedIt():
    print("Oh, now you've done it!")

tkinter.Button(mainFrame,text="Now!", \
    command=pressedIt).pack()
```

Solution to Practice Problem 6.5

```
titleLabel = tkinter.Label(mainFrame, \
    text="What do you want?")
titleLabel.pack()
```

Solution to Practice Problem 6.6

```
bottomFrame = tkinter.Frame(root,borderwidth=1, \
    padx=5,pady=5)
bottomFrame.pack()

titleLabel = tkinter.Label(bottomFrame, \
    text="What do you want?")
titleLabel.grid(column=1,row=1)

tkinter.Button(bottomFrame,text="Now!", \
    command=pressedIt).grid(column=2,row=1)
```

Solution to Practice Problem 6.7

```
import tkinter.messagebox

    def pressedIt():
        print("Oh, now you've done it!")
        tkinter.messagebox.showinfo("Okey dokey", \
            "Well let me get "+note.get("1.0",tkinter.END)+ \
            "for you!")
```

Defining Classes

7

Python is an object-oriented language. This means, not only can we use objects, but we can define our own classes of objects. A class is just another name for a type in Python. We have been working with types (i.e. classes) since the first chapter of the text. Examples of classes are *int*, *str*, *bool*, *float* and *list*. While these classes are all built in to Python so we can solve problems involving these types, sometimes it is nice if we can solve a problem where a different type or class would be helpful.

Classes provide us with a powerful tool for abstraction. Abstraction is when we forget about details of how something works and just concentrate on using it. This idea makes programming possible. There are many abstractions that are used in this text without worrying about exactly how they are implemented. For example, a file is an A programs. Instead of worrying about how a line gets drawn in a window, we can just move the turtle along the line with its pen down to draw the line. How is this done? It's not important to us when we are using a Turtle. We just know it works.

So, classes are a great tool for programmers because when a programmer uses a class they don't have to worry about the details. But, sometimes we might be able to save time and implement a class that could be useful to us and maybe to someone else as well. When we use a class we don't worry about the details of how an object works. When we implement a class we must first decide what the abstraction is going to look like to the user of it and then we must think about how to provide the right methods to implement the abstraction. When defining or implementing a class, the *user* is either yourself or another programmer that is going to use the class when they create some objects of the class you defined.

Classes provide the definitions for objects. The *int* class defines what integers look like and how they behave in Python. The *Turtle* class defines what a turtle looks like and all the methods that control its behavior. In general, a class defines what objects of its type look like and how they behave. We all know what an integer looks like. Its behavior is the operations we can perform on it. For instance we might want to be able to add two integers together, print an integer, and so on. When we define our own classes we do two things.

- A Class defines one or more data items to be included in the objects or instances of the class. These data items are sometimes called the *member data* of the class. Each instance, or object, will contain the data defined by the class.

K.D. Lee, *Python Programming Fundamentals,* Undergraduate Topics in Computer Science, DOI 10.1007/978-1-84996-537-8_7, © Springer-Verlag London Limited 2011

- A Class defines the methods that operate on the data items or member data in objects of the class. The methods are functions which are given an object. A method defines a particular behavior for an object.

To understand how objects are created we can look at an example. In Chap. 4 we learned how to create Turtle objects and use them to do write some interesting programs.

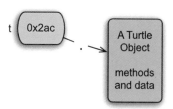

Fig. 7.1 A Turtle object

Example 7.1 When we execute the code below, Python creates a Turtle object pointed to by the reference *t* as shown in Fig. 7.1.

```
t = Turtle()
```

We have already learned that we could make the turtle go forward 50 units by writing *turtle.forward*(50). The *forward* function is a method on a Turtle. It is part of the turtle object's behavior. As another example, consider a Circle class. A circle must be drawn on the screen at a particular location. It must be given a radius. It might have a fill color and it might have a width and color for its outline.

7.1
Creating an Object

When an object is created there are two things that must happen: the space or memory of the object must be reserved, and the space must be initialized by storing some values within the object that make sense for a newly created object. Python takes care of reserving the appropriate amount of space for us when we create an object. We must write some code to initialize the space within the object with reasonable values. What are reasonable values? This depends on the program we are writing.

Example 7.2 To create a circle we might write something like this.

```
x = 10
y = 30
radius = 40
shape = Circle(x,y,radius,edgeWidth=3, \
          color="red",outline="gray")
```

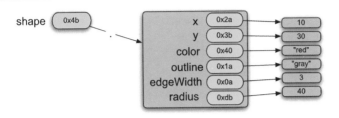

Fig. 7.2 A Circle object

Creating a circle called *shape* creates an object that contains the data that we give the *constructor* when the circle is created. The constructor is called when we write the class name, followed by the arguments to pass to the constructor. In this case, the call to the constructor is *Circle(x,y,radius,width=3,color="red",outline="gray")*. The constructor takes care of putting the given information in the object. Figure 7.2 shows what the data looks like in the object after calling the constructor.

The data in an object doesn't get filled in by magic. We must write some code to do this. When programming in an object-oriented language like Python we can write a *class* definition once and it can be used to create as many objects of that class as we want. To help us do this, Python creates a special reference called *self* that always points to the object we are currently working with. In this way, inside the class, instead of writing the reference *shape* we can write the reference *self*. By using the reference *self* when writing the code for the class, the code will work with any object we create, not just the one that *shape* refers to. We are not stuck just creating one circle object because Python creates the special *self* reference for us. We can create a *shape* and any other circle we care to create by writing just one Circle class.

Example 7.3 The first method of a class definition is called the *constructor* and is named _ _*init*_ _. It takes care of filling in the member data inside the object. The *self* reference is the extra reference, provided by Python, that points to the current object. This method gets called in response to creating an object as occurs in the code in Example 7.2.

```
class Circle:
    def __init__(self,x=0,y=0,radius=50,color="transparent", \
                 outline="black",edgeWidth=1):
        self.x = x
        self.y = y
        self.color = color
        self.outline = outline
        self.edgeWidth = edgeWidth
        self.radius = radius
```

In Example 7.3 notice that the formal parameters nearly match the arguments provided when the circle object is created in Example 7.2. The one additional parameter is the extra *self* parameter provided by Python. When the constructor is called, Python makes a new *self* local variable for the _ _ *init* _ _ function call. This *self* variable points at the

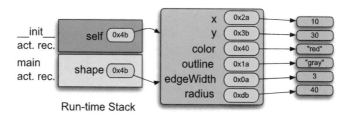

Run-time Stack

Fig. 7.3 A Circle object

newly created space for the object. Figure 7.3 shows the run-time stack with the *self* variable pointing at the newly created object. The picture shows what memory looks like just before returning from the _ _*init*_ _ constructor method. There are two activation records on the run-time stack. The first is the activation record for the function that creates the shape by executing the code in Example 7.2. The second activation record is for the _ _*init*_ _ function call (i.e. the call to the constructor). When the program returns from the constructor the top activation record will be popped and the *self* reference will go away.

To implement a class we must write the word *class*, the name of the class, and then the methods that will operate on the objects of that class. By convention, the first method is always the constructor. Generally other methods follow and must be indented under the class definition. The class definition ends when the indentation under it ends.

> **Practice 7.1** Decide what information you would need to implement a Rational class. Rational numbers are numbers that can be expressed as a fraction with an integer numerator and denominator. Then write a class definition for it including a constructor so you can create Rational objects.

> **Practice 7.2** Assume we want to implement a class for rectangles. A rectangle is created at a particular (x, y) location specifying the lower left corner of the rectangle. A rectangle has a width and height. Write a class definition for the Rectangle class so that a rectangle can be created by writing $box = Rectangle(100, 100, 50, 30)$ to create a rectangle at $(100, 100)$ with a width of 50 and a height of 30.

If we have a circle object, it would be nice to draw it on a turtle graphics screen. In addition, we may want to change its color, width, or outline color at some point. These are all actions that we want to perform on a circle object and because they change the object in some way they will become mutator methods when implemented. In addition, we may want to access the x, y, and radius values. These are implemented with accessor methods. The mutator and accessor methods must be defined in the class definition.

Example 7.4 Here is the complete code for the Circle class.

```python
class Circle:
    # This is the constructor for the class. It
    # takes the data provided as arguments
    # and stores the data in the object.
    def __init__(self,x=0,y=0,radius=50,color="transparent", \
                outline="black",edgeWidth=1):
        self.x = x
        self.y = y
        self.color = color
        self.outline = outline
        self.edgeWidth = edgeWidth
        self.radius = radius

    # The draw method is a mutator method, too. It does
    # not store anything in the object, but it uses the turtle
    # and therefore mutates the turtle object.
    def draw(self,turtle):
        turtle.penup()
        turtle.goto(self.x,self.y)
        turtle.width(self.edgeWidth)
        if self.color != "transparent":
            turtle.fillcolor(self.color)
        turtle.color(self.outline)
        turtle.fillcolor(self.color)
        turtle.setheading(0)
        turtle.forward(self.radius)
        if self.color != "transparent":
            turtle.begin_fill()
        turtle.pendown()
        for k in range(500):
            radians = (2*math.pi)*(k/500.0)
            turtle.goto(math.cos(radians)*self.radius+self.x, \
                        math.sin(radians)*self.radius+self.y)
        if self.color != "transparent":
            turtle.end_fill()
        turtle.penup()
        turtle.goto(self.x,self.y)

    # The following three methods are mutator methods.
    # They each take a single value passed to the
    # method and store it in the object.
    def setEdgeWidth(self,width):
        self.edgeWidth = width
```

```
def setFill(self,color):
    self.color = color

def setOutline(self,color):
    self.outline = color

# The last three methods are accessor methods.
# They return three of the fields of the object.
def getX(self):
    return self.x

def getY(self):
    return self.y

def getRadius(self):
    return self.radius
```

When a method is called on an object the variable is written first, followed by a dot (i.e. period), followed by the method name. So, for instance, to call the *getX* method on the *shape* you would write *shape.getX()*. When you look at the definition of *getX* there is one parameter, the self *parameter*. When you call *getX* it looks like there are no parameters. Python sets *self* to point to the same object that appears on the left side of the dot. So, in this example, the *self* parameter points at the *shape* object because *shape* was written on the left hand side of the dot. The picture in Fig. 7.3 applies to calling the *getX* method as well. When *getX* is called, an activation record is added to the stack with the *self* variable pointing at the object. This is true of all classes in Python. When implementing a class the first parameter to all the methods is always *self* and the object that is on the left hand side of the dot when the method is called is the object that becomes self while executing the method.

Practice 7.3 Complete the Rectangle class by writing a *draw* method that draws the rectangle on the screen. When drawing a rectangle allow the color of the border and the color of the background to be specified. Specify these parameters with default values of black and transparent respectively. Make these parameters keyword parameters with the names *outline* and *color* (for background color).

7.2
Inheritance

A class is an abstraction that helps programmers reuse code. Code reuse is important because it frees us to solve interesting problems while allowing us to forget the details of the classes we use to solve a problem. Code reuse can be achieved between classes as well. When objects are similar in most respects but one is a special case of another the relationship between the classes can be modeled using inheritance. A *subclass* inherits from a *superclass*. A When using inheritance, the subclass gets everything that's in the superclass. All data and methods that were a part of the superclass are available in the subclass. The subclass can then add additional data or methods and it can redefine existing methods in the superclass.

Inheritance in Computer Science is like inheritance in genetics. We inherit certain physical characteristics of our birth parents. We may look different from them but typically there are some similarities in hair color, eye color, height and so on. We probably also inherit behaviors from our parents, although this may come from social contact with our parents and isn't necessarily genetic. Inheritance when applied to Computer Science means that we don't have to rewrite all the code of the superclass. We can just use it in the subclass.

Inheritance comes up all over the place in OOP. For instance, the Turtle class inherits from the RawTurtle class. The Turtle class is essentially a RawTurtle except that a Turtle creates a TurtleScreen object if one has not already been created.

Example 7.5 Here is the entire Turtle class.

```
class Turtle(RawTurtle):
    """RawTurtle auto-creating (scrolled) canvas.

    When a Turtle object is created or a function derived
    from some Turtle method is called a TurtleScreen
    object is automatically created.
    """
    _pen = None
    _screen = None

    def __init__(self,
                 shape=_CFG["shape"],
                 undobuffersize=_CFG["undobuffersize"],
                 visible=_CFG["visible"]):
        if Turtle._screen is None:
            Turtle._screen = Screen()
        RawTurtle.__init__(self, Turtle._screen,
                           shape=shape,
                           undobuffersize=undobuffersize,
                           visible=visible)
```

While the code in Example 7.5 is difficult to completely understand out of context, the Turtle class only consists of a constructor, the minimum amount that can be provided in a derived class. The constructor creates the screen if needed and then calls the RawTurtle's constructor. Every class, whether a derived class or a base class, *must* provide its own constructor. When Python creates an object of a certain class, it needs the constructor to determine how the object is initialized. So, the class Turtle in Example 7.5 truly contains the minimal amount of methods possible for a derived class.

Essentially a Turtle and a RawTurtle are identical. It also turns out that Turtles (and RawTurtles) are based on Tkinter. A TurtleScreen contains a ScolledCanvas widget from Tkinter. To create a RawTurtle object we must provide a ScrolledCanvas for the Turtle to draw on.

Example 7.6 Here is the constructor definition for a RawTurtle.

```
class RawTurtle(TPen, TNavigator):
    """Animation part of the RawTurtle.
    Puts RawTurtle upon a TurtleScreen and provides tools for
    its animation.
    """
    screens = []

    def __init__(self, canvas=None,
                 shape=_CFG["shape"],
                 undobuffersize=_CFG["undobuffersize"],
                 visible=_CFG["visible"]):
```

Because turtle graphics is based on Tkinter, we can write a program that contains widgets including a canvas on which we can draw with turtle graphics! The constructor in Example 7.6 shows us that if we provide a canvas the RawTurtle object will use it. So, we could write a little drawing program that draws circles and rectangles on the screen and integrates other Tk widgets, like buttons for instance.

To begin building a draw application we'll put a ScrolledCanvas on the left side of a window and some buttons to control drawing on the right side. Since we've been looking at a Circle class, we'll start by drawing circles on the screen. It would be nice to provide the radius for the circle. We can do that with an entry field and a StringVar object as was seen in the last chapter.

Example 7.7 Here is some code that creates a ScrolledCanvas widget, a RawTurtle that draws on the canvas, and a Tkinter application that incorporates both. Figure 7.4 shows what the application window looks like when it is run.

```
from turtle import *
from tkinter import *
import math

noselection = 0
circle = 1

def main():
    global shapeSelection
    shapeSelection = noselection
    root = Tk()
    root.title("Draw!")
    cv = ScrolledCanvas(root,600,600,600,600)
    cv.pack(side = LEFT)
```

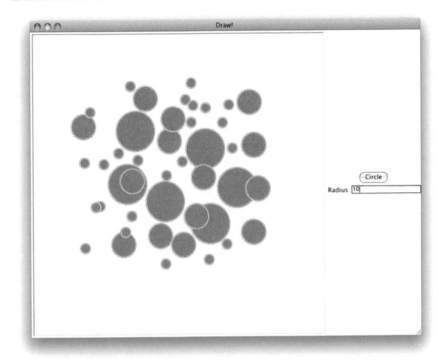

Fig. 7.4   A drawing application

```
aTurtle = RawTurtle(cv)
screen = aTurtle.getscreen()
aTurtle.ht()
screen.tracer(1000)
fram = Frame(root)
fram.pack(side = RIGHT,fill=BOTH)

def circCommand():
    global shapeSelection
    print("in circCommand")
    shapeSelection = circle

radiusEnt = StringVar()
radiusLabel = Label(fram,text="Radius:")
radiusLabel.grid(row=2,column=1,sticky=E)
radiusEntry = Entry(fram,textvariable=radiusEnt)
radiusEntry.grid(row=2,column=2,sticky=E+W)
circleButton = Button(fram, text = "Circle", \
      command=circCommand)
circleButton.grid(row=1,column=1,columnspan=2)
```

```
def clickHandler(x,y):
    print("In clickHandler")
    if shapeSelection == circle:
        print("shape selection was circle")
        radius = radiusEnt.get()
        if radius.strip() == "":
            radius = 50
        else:
            radius = float(radius)
        shape = Circle(x,y,radius,edgeWidth=3,color="red", \
            outline="gray")
        shape.draw(aTurtle)

screen.onclick(clickHandler)
mainloop()

if __name__ == "__main__":
    main()
```

The program in Example 7.7 is missing the *Circle* class which was defined in Example 7.4. The program waits for the *Circle* button to be pressed once. Then, after each mouse click, a circle is drawn on the ScrolledCanvas on the left side of the window.

Both a Circle and a Rectangle share a lot of common code. It makes sense for that common code to be in one base class that both classes inherit from. If a Shape class were defined that contained the shared code, then it would only have to be written once, which is a requirement of elegant code.

Example 7.8 Here is a Shape class that defines the code that is common to both Circles and Rectangles.

```
class Shape:
    def __init__(self,x=0,y=0,color="transparent", \
                outline="black",width=1):
        self.x = x
        self.y = y
        self.color = color
        self.outline = outline
        self.width = width

    def setWidth(self,width):
        self.width = width

    def setFill(self,color):
        self.color = color

    def setOutline(self,color):
        self.outline = color
```

```
    def getX(self):
        return self.x

    def getY(self):
        return self.y
```

With the Shape base class defined in Example 7.8 the definition of Circle can be simplified.

Example 7.9 Here is the code for the derived Circle class.

```
class Circle(Shape):
    def __init__(self,x=0,y=0,radius=50,color="transparent", \
                  outline="black",width=1):
        Shape.__init__(self,x,y,color,outline,width)
        self.radius = radius

    def draw(self,turtle):
        Shape.draw(self,turtle)
        turtle.penup()
        turtle.goto(self.x,self.y)
        turtle.width(self.width)
        if self.color != "transparent":
            turtle.fillcolor(self.color)
        turtle.color(self.outline)
        turtle.fillcolor(self.color)
        turtle.setheading(0)
        turtle.forward(self.radius)
        if self.color != "transparent":
            turtle.begin_fill()
        turtle.pendown()
        for k in range(500):
            radians = (2*math.pi)*(k/500.0)
            turtle.goto(math.cos(radians)*self.radius+self.x, \
                         math.sin(radians)*self.radius+self.y)
        if self.color != "transparent":
            turtle.end_fill()
        turtle.penup()
        turtle.goto(self.x,self.y)

    def getRadius(self):
        return self.radius
```

The Circle class still is the only class that will know how to draw a circle. And, of
course, shapes don't have a radius in general. All the other code that isn't circle specific is
now moved out of the Circle class.

Practice 7.4 Rewrite the Rectangle class so it inherits from the Shape class and use it in the draw program downloaded from the text's website.

7.3
A Bouncing Ball Example

A RawTurtle can move around the screen either with its pen up or its pen down. With its pen up, if we can imagine the turtle as something other than a little sprite, it can be essentially any object that we want it to be in a two dimensional world. The creators of the turtle graphics for Python realized this and added code so that we could change the turtle's picture to anything we would like. For instance, we might want to animate a bouncing ball. We can replace the turtle's sprite with an image of a ball.

Turtle graphics can do animation because it can be told to perform an action after an interval of time. A timer can be set in turtle graphics. When the timer goes off, the program can move the ball a little bit. If the interval between timer going off and moving the ball can be small enough that it happens several times a second, then to the human eye it will appear as if the ball is flying through the air.

A ball is a turtle. However, a turtle doesn't remember in which direction it is moving. It would be nice to have the ball remember the direction it is moving. At least somewhere in the program the ball's direction must be remembered and it makes sense for the ball to remember its own direction in an object-oriented design of the problem. Figure 7.5 depicts what a ball object should look like. A ball is turtle, but it is a little more than just a turtle. Again, this is an example of inheritance.

With the ball inheriting from the RawTurtle class we'll automatically get all the functionality of a turtle. We can tell a ball to *goto* a location on the screen. We can access the *x* and *y* coordinate of the ball by calling the *xcor* and *ycor* methods. We can even change its shape so it looks like a ball. As we've seen, for the Ball class to inherit from the RawTurtle

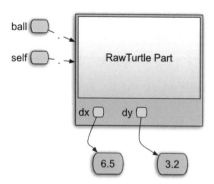

Fig. 7.5 A Ball object

class, the derived Ball class must implement its own constructor and call the constructor of the base class.

Example 7.10 In Appendix I the Ball class inherits from the RawTurtle class. To create a Ball object we could write

```
ball = Ball(6.5,3.2)
```

This creates a ball object as shown in Fig. 7.5. Here is the Ball class code.

```
class Ball(RawTurtle):
    def __init__(self,cv,dx,dy):
        RawTurtle.__init__(self,cv)

        self.penup()
        self.shape("soccerball.gif")
        self.dx = dx
        self.dy = dy

    def move(self):
        newx = self.xcor() + self.dx
        newy = self.ycor() + self.dy

        # some code goes here to make it bounce
        # off the walls.

        self.goto(newx,newy)
```

When we are using the ball object in Fig. 7.5 we refer to it using the *ball* reference. When we are in the Ball class we refer to the object using the *self* reference as described earlier in this chapter. In Fig. 7.5 the Turtle part of the object is greyed out. This is because the insides of the RawTurtle are available to us, but generally it is a bad idea to access the RawTurtle part of the object directly. Instead, we can use methods to access the RawTurtle part of the object when needed.

The constructor needs to initialize the RawTurtle part of the object as well as the Ball part of the object. To create a RawTurtle we could write *turtle = RawTurtle(cv)*. However, writing this won't work to initialize the RawTurtle part of the object. A line of code like this would create a new RawTurtle object. Remember, a Ball is a RawTurtle so we don't want to create a new RawTurtle object. Instead, we want to initialize the RawTurtle part of the Ball object. To do this, we explicitly call the RawTurtle constructor by writing *RawTurtle.__init__(self,cv)*. This calls the RawTurtle's constructor. In this case we call the constructor by writing the class name followed by a dot followed by the constructor's name *__init__*. Since self is a Ball *and* a RawTurtle, we pass self as the parameter to Raw-Turtle's constructor. This line of code initializes the RawTurtle part of the object. Then the Ball specific initialization occurs next.

The Ball class contains one more method, the move method. This is a new method not defined in the RawTurtle class. A Ball can move on the screen while a RawTurtle can not. A Ball moves by (*dx*, *dy*) each time the move method is called. The bouncing balls are animated by repeatedly calling the move method on each of the balls in the *ballList* defined in the main function of the program. Appendix I contains the complete code for the bouncing ball example.

7.4
Polymorphism

Polymorphism is a term used in object-oriented programming that means "many versions" or more than one version. When a subclass defines its own version of a method then the right version, either the subclass version or the base class version of the method, will be called depending on the type of object you have created. To best understand this it helps to look at an example.

Let's assume we wanted to modify the bouncing ball example so some balls bounce according to a simulated gravity instead of simply bouncing in space forever. It turns out this is very easy to do. We can have Ball objects bounce in space forever and GravityBall objects bounce according to a simulated gravity. Since GravityBalls are nearly the same as Balls we'll use inheritance to define the GravityBall class. The only real difference will be in the way the GravityBall moves when it is told to move.

Example 7.11 This code uses the Ball class and relies on polymorphism to get GravityBalls to bounce the right way.

```
class GravityBall(Ball):
    def __init__(self,cv,dx,dy):
        Ball.__init__(self,cv,dx,dy)

    def move(self):
        # Gravity's effect is -1/2 g t^2. Time is
        # estimated at 1/100 of a second for each
        # call to move.

        if abs(self.dy) < 0.2 and self.ycor() < 5:
            self.dy = 0
        else:
            self.dy = self.dy - 0.195

        if abs(self.dx) < 0.2:
            self.dx = 0
        else:
            # Friction reduces dx by a little bit
            self.dx = 0.999 * self.dx

        Ball.move(self)
```

> **Practice 7.5** Take the bouncing ball example and add the GravityBall class to it. Then, modify the program to create some GravityBalls and watch them bounce. The original Ball objects continue to bounce around as if they were in space. The GravityBall objects behave differently. Polymorphism makes this work. What is it about polymorphism that makes this work the way we want it to?

7.5
Getting Hooked on Python

A *hook* is a means by which one program allows another program to modify its behavior. The Python interpreter is a program that allows its behavior to be altered by means of certain hooks it makes available to programmers. Consider the Rational class described earlier in this chapter. With the definition you came up with (or the provided solution in practice problem 7.1) we can create Rational numbers. However, we can't do much more than create them at the moment. Without some more code, our rational implementation doesn't really do us much good.

Example 7.12 Here is some code that creates a Rational number and prints it to the screen. When run, this program prints something like *<__main__.Rational object at 0x113bc70>*. It prints the name of the module and the class and the value of the reference when printed to the screen.

```
class Rational:
  def __init__(self,num=0,den=1):
    self.num = num
    self.den = den

def main():
  x = Rational(4,5)
  print(x)

if __name__ == "__main__":
  main()
```

If we needed rational numbers in a program, it would be nice if they printed nicely when they were printed to the screen. This can be done using a hook in Python for string conversion. When an object is converted to a string, Python looks for the existence of the __str__ method in the class. If this method exists, Python will use it to convert the object to a string representation. If this method exists in the class, then it must return a string representation of the object. The method must also have only one parameter, the self parameter.

Example 7.13 If this method is added to the Rational class definition in Example 7.12, then when the Rational 4/5 is printed, it prints as 4/5.

```
def __str__(self):
  return str(self.num)+"/"+str(self.den)
```

The addition of the _ _*str*_ _ to the Rational class makes using rational numbers a bit easier because we can quickly convert it to a string when we want a nice representation of it. You can force the _ _*str*_ _ method to be called by calling the *str* built-in function in Python. So, writing *str(x)* will force a string version of *x* to be constructed using the _ _*str*_ _ method. The presence of the _ _*str*_ _ method doesn't mean that rational numbers will *always* be converted to a string when printed. Sometimes, the Python interpreter isn't interested in producing a strictly human-readable presentation of an object. Sometimes a Python readable representation is more appropriate.

Example 7.14 Consider the following code. When Rational objects are in a list they do not print using the _ _*str*_ _ method. Running this code prints [<_ _*main*_ _.Rational object at 0x113bcd0>, <_ _*main*_ _.Rational object at 0x113bc70>] to the screen.

```
def main():
  x = Rational(4,5)
  y = Rational(9,12)

  lst = [x,y]
  print(lst)
```

In Example 7.13 the _ _*str*_ _ was added and rational numbers printed nicely, but Example 7.14 shows that the Python interpreter does not use _ _*str*_ _ when printing a list of rationals. When printing a list, Python is producing a string representation of the list that would be suitable for Python to evaluate later to rebuild the list. If Python tried to read a number like 4/5 in the list, it would not know what to do with it. However, there is another hook that allows the programmer to determine the best representation of an object for Python's purposes.

Example 7.15 The _ _*repr*_ _ method is a Python hook for producing a Python representation of an object. With the addition of the method below to the Rational class started in Example 7.12, Python will print [*Rational*(4, 5), *Rational*(9, 12)] when the code in Example 7.14 is executed.

```
def __repr__(self):
  return "Rational("+str(self.num)+","+str(self.den)+")"
```

So, what is the difference between converting to a string and converting to a Python representation? A string version of an object can be in whatever format the programmer determines is best. But, a Python representation should be in a format so that if the built-in Python function *eval* is called on it, it will evaluate to its original value. The *eval* function is given an expression contained in a string and evaluates the expression to produce the Python value contained in the string. The appropriate representation for most programmer-defined classes is to use the same form that is required to construct the object in the first place. To construct the rational number 4/5 we had to write *Rational*(4, 5). For the *eval* function to correctly evaluate a string containing a Rational, the eval function should be given a rational in the *Rational(numerator,denominator)* form, not the *numerator/denominator* form.

There is another Python hook that controls how sorting is performed in Python. For any type of object in Python, if there is a natural ordering to those objects, Python can sort a list of them.

Example 7.16 Here is some code that sorts a list of names, alphabetically. This code, when run, prints the list [*'Freeman'*, *'Gorman'*, *'Lee'*, *'Lie'*, *'Morgan'*] to the screen.

```
nameList = ["Lee", "Lie", "Gorman", "Freeman", "Morgan"]
nameList.sort()
print(nameList)
```

If we attempt to sort the list *lst* from Example 7.14, Python will complain with the following error message: *builtins.TypeError: unorderable types: Rational() < Rational()*. While we have an understanding of rational numbers, Python has no way of understanding that the class of Rational numbers represents an ordered collection of values. To tell Python that it is an ordered collection, we have to implement the _ _*lt*_ _ method. To compare any two rational numbers, we must first make sure they have a common denominator. Once we have a common denominator, the numerator of the two rational numbers must be converted to units for the common denominator. It turns out we don't really need the common denominator at all. We just need the converted numerators. The _ _*lt*_ _ method must return True if the object *self* references is less than the object that *other* references and it must return False otherwise.

Example 7.17 The following _ _*lt*_ _ method, when added to the class in Example 7.12 converts the two numerators to their common denominator form so they can be compared.

```
def __lt__(self,other):
    #commonDenominator = self.den * other.den
    selfNum = self.numerator * other.den
    otherNum = other.numerator * self.den
    return selfNum < otherNum
```

Once the _ _lt_ _ method of Example 7.17 is added to the Rational class, Python understands how to sort them. The sort function sorts a list in place as shown in Example 7.16. If *sort* is called on the list *lst* from Example 7.14, Python reorders the list so it contains [*Rational*(9, 12), *Rational*(4, 5)].

7.6
Review Questions

1. What is another name for a class in Python?
2. What is the relationship between classes and objects?
3. What is the purpose of the _ _init_ _ method in a class definition?
4. Computer scientists say that objects have both *state* and *behavior*. What do *state* and *behavior* refer to in a class definition?
5. How do you create an object in Python?
6. In a class definition, when you see the word *self*, what does *self* refer to?
7. What is a superclass? Explain what the term means and give an example.
8. What is the benefit of inheritance in Python?
9. What does it mean for polymorphism to exist in a program? Why would you want this?
10. How do the _ _str_ _ and the _ _repr_ _ methods differ? Why are they both needed?
11. To be able to sort an ordered collection of your favorite type of objects, what method must be implemented on the objects?

7.7
Exercises

1. Go back to the original Reminder! program and redo it so that the Reminder! program contains a class called Reminder that replaces the parallel lists of reminders and notes with one list of reminders. This list should be a list of Reminder objects. A Reminder object keeps track of its *x*, *y* location on the screen. It also has some text that is provided when it is created. A Reminder must take care of creating the Text and Toplevel objects so a note can be displayed. Finally, the methods defined on a Reminder include *undraw* (to withdraw the window), *getX* to return the *X* value of the window location, *getY* similarly gets the *Y* value of the window location. The *getText* method should return the text field. Finally, the *setDeleteHandler* should set the handler to be called when a reminder is deleted. Write this class and modify the Reminder! application to use this new class.

   Here is an outline of the Reminder class definition. You need to finish defining it and alter the program to use it.

```
class Reminder:
    def __init__(self,x,y,text):
        ...

    def undraw(self):
        ...

    def getX(self):
        ...

    def getY(self):
        ...

    def getText(self):
        ...

    def setDeleteHandler(self,command):
        ...
```

Your job is to fill in the function definitions and then use the class in the Reminder! application.

2. Modify your address book program to use a class for address book cards. Call the new class AddressCard. An address card contains all the information for an address book entry including last and first name, street, city, state, zip, phone, and mobile phone number. To use the AddressCard class you need to modify the program so it stores all AddressCards in a list. The program should read all the addresses when it starts and make one AddressCard object for each address in the file. You will also write all the cards in the list to a file when the program terminates. Look at the code in Appendix H to see how this can be done.

   You will want to include three hook methods in your AddressCard class. The __str__ method should be included to convert an AddressCard to a string. To do this you will want to return a string representation of the object as discussed in the chapter. The AddressCard entry should convert to a string as follows:

```
Sophus Lie
Abel Avenue
Lavanger, Norway 554433
555-555-5555
444-444-4444
```

Your __str__ method should return a string that looks just like this. When you print your addresses to the file when the application closes, you can use the *str* function to convert each AddressCard object to a string. Don't forget the newline characters at the end of each line.

   The second special method is the __lt__ method. This method compares two AddressCard objects as described for Rationals in the chapter. Your __lt__ method should return True if the last name, first name of self is less than the last name, first name of the other AddressCard.

A third special method is the *__eq__* method. This method compares two Address-Card objects and is used by the *index* method on lists. If *self* is equal to *other* then *True* should be returned. If *self* is not equal to *other* then *False* should be returned. Here is how you might write this function.

```
class AddressCard:

    . . . .

    # This method provides a means of comparing
    # the current object (i.e. self) with another
    # object. It is used by the index method on lists
    # to discover if an object in a list "equals" the
    # object being searched for by the index method.

    def __eq__(self,other):
        if type(other) != type(self):
            raise "Invalid Comparison"

        if self.last+","+self.first == \
            other.last+","+other.first:

            return True

        return False
```

Each of the event handlers must be rewritten to use the new list of addresses. For instance, here is how the *Find* event handler might be written to use the index method on lists that is now possible with the definition of the *__eq__* method.

```
def findAddress():
    print("Find")

    card = AddressCard(lname.get().strip(), \
        fname.get().strip(),street.get().strip(), \
        city.get().strip(),state.get().strip(), \
        zip.get().strip(), phone.get().strip(), \
        mobile.get().strip())

    try:
        j = addresses.index(card)
        card = addresses[j]

        street.set(card.getStreet())
        city.set(card.getCity())
        state.set(card.getState())
        zip.set(card.getZip())
        phone.set(card.getPhone())
        mobile.set(card.getMobile())
        return
```

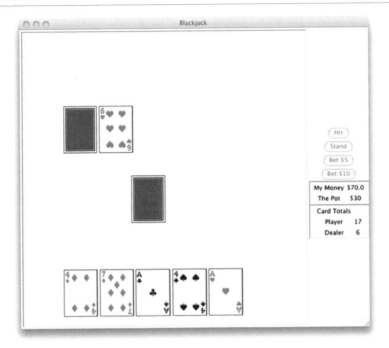

Fig. 7.6 A Blackjack Hand

```
except:
    True

messagebox.showwarning("Not Found", \
    "The entry was not found!")
```

Finally, you should use the *list* sort method to keep the address book sorted at all times.

3. In this exercise you are to implement a game of Blackjack using the turtle package. Blackjack is a simple game with simple rules. In this exercise you get practice using Object-Oriented Programming to implement a fairly complex program.

Rules of the Game

Blackjack is played by dealing two cards to each player and the dealer. The player's cards are face up. The dealer's first card is face down and the second is face up.

The goal is to get to 21 points. Each face card is worth 10 points. The Ace is worth 1 or 11 points depending on which is better for your hand. All other cards are worth their face value.

The player bets first. Then he/she asks for cards (hits) until they are satisfied with their score or they go over. If they have not gone over, the dealer then draws cards until the dealer hand is 17 or over. If the dealer goes over 21, the player wins. Otherwise, the player wins if his/her score is greater than the dealer's score.

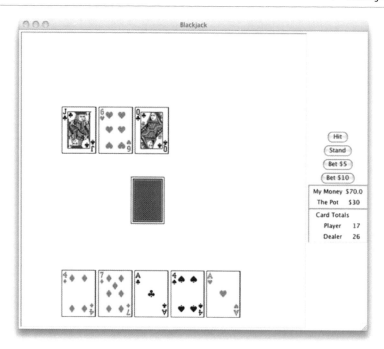

Fig. 7.7 The end of a Blackjack Hand

If the player gets a blackjack (21 with only two cards) then the player gets paid at a 3:2 ratio. Otherwise it is a 1:1 ratio payback.

Writing the Game

You should write this game incrementally. That means, write a little bit and test that little bit before going on. You don't want to debug this whole program after writing all the code.

You will need to implement a Card class. A Card object can inherit from RawTurtle. When you create a Card object you will want to give it an image for the front and back. The images can be downloaded from the text website. Download the cards.zip file, and then unzip it in the same folder where you will write your program. The cards folder should be a subfolder of the folder where you write your program.

The card images are named 1.gif, 2.gif, and so on. The back image is labeled back.gif. Images 1, 2, 3, 4 are the Aces. Images 5, 6, 7, 8 are the Kings and so on. To get the correct rank for a card you can use the formula $14 - val/4$ where val is the value of the card name. If the formula determines the rank is 14 it should be changed to 11. Ranks from 10–13 should be changed to 10.

The Card class will have at least four methods. You may want to define more. Here is a suggestion for the methods you should write.

- isFaceDown—This method returns true if the card is face down. It returns false if the card is face up.

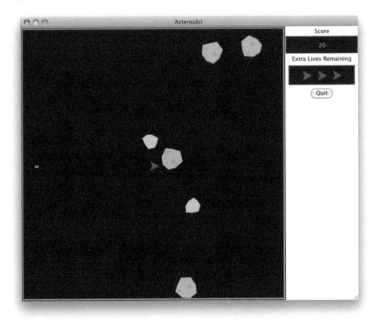

Fig. 7.8 Asteroids!

- setFaceDown—This method sets the Turtle shape to be the back of the card and remembers that it is now face down.
- setFaceUp—This method sets the Turtle shape to be the face of the card and remembers that the card is now face up.
- getBlackJackRank—This method returns the Blackjack rank of the card.

The main part of the program is placing buttons on the screen and handling the different button presses. Figure 7.6 shows what the application might look like during the playing of a hand. Figure 7.7 shows what the application might display at the end of that hand. Message boxes can be used to display the outcome of a hand.

4. Complete the Asteroids game available on the text web site as shown in Fig. 7.8. The Asteroids video game was originally designed and written by Atari. It was released to the public in 1979. In the game the player controls a spaceship that navigates space and blows up asteroids by shooting at them.

  When an asteroid is hit, the player scores points and the asteroid splits into two smaller asteroids. The largest asteroids are worth 20 points. Each medium asteroid is worth 50 points. The smallest asteroids are worth 100 points each. When the spaceship hits a small asteroid it is obliterated into dust and it disappears completely from the game.

  If an asteroid collides with the spaceship, the spaceship is destroyed, the asteroid that collided with it is destroyed (resulting in no points) and the player gets a new spaceship. The game starts with four spaceships total (the original game started with only three).

Code is available on the text's web site. The downloadable code makes the ship turn left when 4 is pressed. The ship will also move forward when 5 is pressed. Complete the program by implementing the game as described above. Some lessons are available on the text's web site that will guide you through many of the additions to the program described here. To make the game a little more interesting you should add one new level to this program. The second level should have 7 asteroids instead of 5 and you should get one more life if you have less than 4 when level 2 starts.

7.8
Solutions to Practice Problems

These are solutions to the practice problems in this chapter. You should only consult these answers after you have tried each of them for yourself first. Practice problems are meant to help reinforce the material you have just read so make use of them.

Solution to Practice Problem 7.1

A numerator and denominator are needed.

```
class Rational:
    def __init__(self,num=0,den=1):
        self.num = num
        self.den = den
```

Solution to Practice Problem 7.2

```
class Rectangle(Shape):
    def __init__(self,x,y,width,height,color="transparent", \
                 outline="black",edgeWidth=1):
        self.x = x
        self.y = y
        self.color = color
        self.outline = outline
        self.edgeWidth = edgeWidth
        self.width = width
        self.height = height
```

Solution to Practice Problem 7.3

```
def draw(self,turtle):
    turtle.penup()
    turtle.goto(self.x,self.y)
    turtle.setheading(0)
    turtle.pendown()
    turtle.width(self.edgeWidth)
    turtle.color(self.outline)
    turtle.fillcolor(self.color)
    if self.color != "transparent":
        turtle.begin_fill()
    turtle.pendown()
    turtle.forward(self.width)
    turtle.left(90)
    turtle.forward(self.height)
    turtle.left(90)
    turtle.forward(self.width)
    turtle.left(90)
    turtle.forward(self.height)
    turtle.left(90)
    if self.color != "transparent":
        turtle.end_fill()
    turtle.penup()
```

Solution to Practice Problem 7.4

Download code and try it out. Here is the Rectangle class in case you had trouble with defining it.

```
class Rectangle(Shape):
    def __init__(self,x,y,width,height,color="transparent", \
                 outline="black",edgeWidth=1):
        Shape.__init__(self,x,y,color,outline,edgeWidth)

        self.width = width
        self.height = height

    def draw(self,turtle):
        turtle.penup()
        turtle.goto(self.x,self.y)
        turtle.setheading(0)
        turtle.pendown()
        turtle.width(self.edgeWidth)
        turtle.color(self.outline)
        turtle.fillcolor(self.color)
        if self.color != "transparent":
```

```
        turtle.begin_fill()
    turtle.pendown()
    turtle.forward(self.width)
    turtle.left(90)
    turtle.forward(self.height)
    turtle.left(90)
    turtle.forward(self.width)
    turtle.left(90)
    turtle.forward(self.height)
    turtle.left(90)
    if self.color != "transparent":
        turtle.end_fill()
    turtle.penup()
```

Solution to Practice Problem 7.5

Create some GravityBall objects and add them to the ballList. That's all that needs to be done to have gravity balls and regular balls bouncing around with each other. The object on the left hand side of the dot in the ball *ball.move* is where polymorphism is at work. If *ball* is pointing to a Ball object, it behaves as a Ball would. If *ball* is pointing to a GravityBall object, then *ball.move* is the GravityBall move method. It's not the name on the left hand side of the dot, its the object that the name refers to that controls which methods are called.

Integer Operators

A

This documentation was generated from the Python documentation available by typing *help(int)* in the Python shell. In this documentation the variables *x*, *y*, and *z* refer to integers.

Operator	Returns	Comments
x+y	int	Returns the sum of x and y.
x-y	int	Returns the difference of x and y.
x*y	int	Returns the product of x and y.
x/y	float	Returns the quotient of x divided by y.
x//y	int	Returns the integer quotient of x divided by y.
x%y	int	Returns x modulo y. This is the remainder of dividing x by y.
-x	int	Returns the negation of x.
x&y	int	Returns the bit-wise *and* of x and y.
x | y	int	Returns the bit-wise *or* of x and y.
x^y	int	Returns the bit-wise *exclusive or* of x and y.
x<<y	int	Returns a bit-wise shift left of x by y bits. Shifting left by 1 bit multiplies x by 2.
x>>y	int	Returns a bit-wise right shift of x by y bits.
~x	int	Returns an integer where each bit in the x has been inverted. $x + x = -1$ for all x.
abs(x)	int	Returns the absolute value of x.
divmod(x, y)	(q,r)	Returns the quotient q and the remainder r as a tuple.
float(x)	float	Returns the float representation of x.
hex(x)	str	Returns a hexadecimal representation of x as a string.
int(x)	int	Returns x.
oct(x)	str	Return an octal representation of x as a string.
pow(x, y[, z])	int	Returns x to the y power modulo z. If z is not specified then it returns x to the y power.
repr(x)	str	Returns a string representation of x.
str(x)	str	Returns a string representation of x.

K.D. Lee, *Python Programming Fundamentals,* Undergraduate Topics in Computer Science, **193**
DOI 10.1007/978-1-84996-537-8, © Springer-Verlag London Limited 2011

Float Operators

B

This documentation was generated from the Python documentation available by typing *help(float)* in the Python shell. In this documentation at least one of the variables *x* and *y* refer to floats.

Operator	Returns	Comments
x+y	float	Returns the sum of x and y.
x-y	float	Returns the difference of x and y.
x*y	float	Returns the product of x and y.
x/y	float	Returns the quotient of x divided by y.
x//y	float	Returns the quotient of integer division of x divided by y. However, the result is still a float.
x%y	float	Returns x modulo y. This is the remainder of dividing x by y.
abs(x)	int	Returns the absolute value of x.
divmod(x, y)	(q,r)	Returns the quotient q and the remainder r as a tuple. Both q and r are floats, but integer division is performed. The value r is the whole and fractional part of any remainder. The value q is a whole number.
float(x)	float	Returns the float representation of x.
int(x)	int	Returns the floor of x as an integer.
pow(x, y)	float	Returns x to the y power.
repr(x)	str	Returns a string representation of x.
str(x)	str	Returns a string representation of x.

K.D. Lee, *Python Programming Fundamentals,* Undergraduate Topics in Computer Science, **195**
DOI 10.1007/978-1-84996-537-8, © Springer-Verlag London Limited 2011

String Operators and Methods

C

This documentation was generated from the Python documentation available by typing *help*(str) in the Python shell. In the documentation found here the variables *s* and *t* are references to strings.

Operator	Returns	Comments
s+t	str	Return a new string which is the concatenation of s and t.
s in t	bool	Returns True if s is a substring of t and False otherwise.
s==t	bool	Returns True if s and t refer to strings with the same sequence of characters.
s>=t	bool	Returns True if s is lexicographically greater than or equal to t.
s<=t	bool	Returns True if s is lexicographically less than or equal to t.
s>t	bool	Returns True if s is lexicographically greater than t.
s<t	bool	Returns True if s is lexicographically less than t.
s!=t	bool	Returns True if s is lexicographically not equal to t.
s[i]	str	Returns the character at index i in the string. If i is negative then it returns the character at index len(s)-i.
s[[i]:[j]]	str	Returns the slice of characters starting at index i and extending to index j-1 in the string. If i is omitted then the slice begins at index 0. If j is omitted then the slice extends to the end of the list. If i is negative then it returns the slice starting at index len(s)+i (and likewise for the slice ending at j).
s * i	str	Returns a new string with s repeated i times.
i * s	str	Returns a new string with s repeated i times.
chr(i)	str	Return the ASCII character equivalent of the integer i.
float(s)	float	Returns the float contained in the string s.
int(s)	int	Returns the integer contained in the string s.
len(s)	int	Returns the number of characters in s.
ord(s)	int	Returns the ASCII decimal equivalent of the single character string s.
repr(s)		Returns a string representation of s. This adds an extra pair of quotes to s.
str(s)	str	Returns a string representation of s. In this case you get just the string s.

K.D. Lee, *Python Programming Fundamentals,* Undergraduate Topics in Computer Science, **197**
DOI 10.1007/978-1-84996-537-8, © Springer-Verlag London Limited 2011

Method	Returns	Comments
s.capitalize()	str	Returns a copy of the string s with the first character upper case.
s.center(width[, fillchar])	str	Returns s centered in a string of length width. Padding is done using the specified fill character (default is a space)
s.count(sub[, start[, end]])	int	Returns the number of non-overlapping occurrences of substring sub in string s[start:end]. Optional arguments start and end are interpreted as in slice notation.
s.encode([encoding[, errors]])	bytes	Encodes s using the codec registered for encoding. encoding defaults to the default encoding. errors may be given to set a different error handling scheme. Default is 'strict' meaning that encoding errors raise a UnicodeEncodeError. Other possible values are 'ignore', 'replace' and 'xmlcharrefreplace' as well as any other name registered with codecs.register_error that can handle UnicodeEncodeErrors.
s.endswith(suffix[, start[, end]])	bool	Returns True if s ends with the specified suffix, False otherwise. With optional start, test s beginning at that position. With optional end, stop comparing s at that position. suffix can also be a tuple of strings to try.
s.expandtabs([tabsize])	str	Returns a copy of s where all tab characters are expanded using spaces. If tabsize is not given, a tab size of 8 characters is assumed.
s.find(sub[, start[, end]])	int	Returns the lowest index in s where substring sub is found, such that sub is contained within s[start:end]. Optional arguments start and end are interpreted as in slice notation. Return -1 on failure.
s.format(*args, **kwargs)	str	
s.index(sub[, start[, end]])	int	Like s.find() but raise ValueError when the substring is not found.
s.isalnum()	bool	Returns True if all characters in s are alphanumeric and there is at least one character in s, False otherwise.
s.isalpha()	bool	Returns True if all characters in s are alphabetic and there is at least one character in s, False otherwise.
s.isdecimal()	bool	Returns True if there are only decimal characters in s, False otherwise.
s.isdigit()	bool	Returns True if all characters in s are digits and there is at least one character in s, False otherwise.
s.isidentifier()	bool	Returns True if s is a valid identifier according to the language definition.

Method	Returns	Comments
s.islower()	bool	Returns True if all cased characters in s are lowercase and there is at least one cased character in s, False otherwise.
s.isnumeric()	bool	Returns True if there are only numeric characters in s, False otherwise.
s.isprintable()	bool	Returns True if all characters in s are considered printable in repr() or s is empty, False otherwise.
s.isspace()	bool	Returns True if all characters in s are whitespace and there is at least one character in s, False otherwise.
s.istitle()	bool	Returns True if s is a titlecased string and there is at least one character in s, i.e. upper- and titlecase characters may only follow uncased characters and lowercase characters only cased ones. Return False otherwise.
s.isupper()	bool	Returns True if all cased characters in s are uppercase and there is at least one cased character in s, False otherwise.
s.join(sequence)	str	Returns a string which is the concatenation of the strings in the sequence. The separator between elements is s.
s.ljust(width[, fillchar])	str	Returns s left-justified in a Unicode string of length width. Padding is done using the specified fill character (default is a space).
s.lower()	str	Returns a copy of the string s converted to lowercase.
s.lstrip([chars])	str	Returns a copy of the string s with leading whitespace removed. If chars is given and not None, remove characters in chars instead.
s.partition(sep)	(h,sep,t)	Searches for the separator sep in s, and returns the part before it, the separator itself, and the part after it. If the separator is not found, returns s and two empty strings.
s.replace (old, new[, count])	str	Returns a copy of s with all occurrences of substring old replaced by new. If the optional argument count is given, only the first count occurrences are replaced.
s.rfind(sub[, start[, end]])	int	Returns the highest index in s where substring sub is found, such that sub is contained within s[start:end]. Optional arguments start and end are interpreted as in slice notation. Returns -1 on failure.
s.rindex(sub[, start[, end]])	int	Like s.rfind() but raise ValueError when the substring is not found.
s.rjust(width[, fillchar])	str	Returns s right-justified in a string of length width. Padding is done using the specified fill character (default is a space).

Method	Returns	Comments
s.rpartition(sep)	(t,sep,h)	Searches for the separator sep in s, starting at the end of s, and returns the part before it, the separator itself, and the part after it. If the separator is not found, returns two empty strings and s.
s.rsplit([sep[, maxsplit]])	string list	Returns a list of the words in s, using sep as the delimiter string, starting at the end of the string and working to the front. If maxsplit is given, at most maxsplit splits are done. If sep is not specified, any whitespace string is a separator.
s.rstrip([chars])	str	Returns a copy of the string s with trailing whitespace removed. If chars is given and not None, removes characters in chars instead.
s.split([sep[, maxsplit]])	string list	Returns a list of the words in s, using sep as the delimiter string. If maxsplit is given, at most maxsplit splits are done. If sep is not specified or is None, any whitespace string is a separator and empty strings are removed from the result.
s.splitlines([keepends])	string list	Returns a list of the lines in s, breaking at line boundaries. Line breaks are not included in the resulting list unless keepends is given and true.
s.startswith(prefix[, start[, end]])	bool	Returns True if s starts with the specified prefix, False otherwise. With optional start, test s beginning at that position. With optional end, stop comparing s at that position. prefix can also be a tuple of strings to try.
s.strip([chars])	str	Returns a copy of the string s with leading and trailing whitespace removed. If chars is given and not None, removes characters in chars instead.
s.swapcase()	str	Returns a copy of s with uppercase characters converted to lowercase and vice versa.
s.title()	str	Returns a titlecased version of s, i.e. words start with title case characters, all remaining cased characters have lower case.
s.translate(table)	str	Returns a copy of the string s, where all characters have been mapped through the given translation table, which must be a mapping of Unicode ordinals to Unicode ordinals, strings, or None. Unmapped characters are left untouched. Characters mapped to None are deleted.
s.upper()	str	Returns a copy of s converted to uppercase.
s.zfill(width)	str	Pad a numeric string s with zeros on the left, to fill a field of the specified width. The string s is never truncated.

List Operators and Methods

This documentation was generated from the Python documentation available by typing *help(list)* in the Python shell. In the documentation found here the variables *x* and *y* are references to lists.

Method	Returns	Comments
list()	list	Returns a new empty list. You can also use [ ] to initialize a new empty list.
list(sequence)	list	Returns new list initialized from sequence's items.
[item [,item]+]	list	Writing a number of comma-separated items in square brackets constructs a new list of those items.
x+y	list	Returns a new list containing the concatenation of the items in x and y.
e in x	bool	Returns True if the item e is in x and False otherwise.
del x[i]		Deletes the item at index i in x. This is not an expression and does not return a value.
x==y	bool	Returns True if x and y contain the same number of items and each of those corresponding items are pairwise equal.
x>=y	bool	Returns True if x is greater than or equal to y according to a lexicographical ordering of the elements in x and y. If x and y have different lengths their items are == up to the shortest length, then this returns True if x is longer than y.
x<=y	bool	Returns True if x is lexicographically before y or equal to y and False otherwise.
x>y	bool	Returns True if x is lexicographically after y and False otherwise.
x<y	bool	Returns True if x is lexicographically before y and False otherwise.
x !=y	bool	Returns True if x and y are of different length or if some item of x is not == to some item of y. Otherwise it returns False.
x[i]	item	Returns the item at index i of x.

K.D. Lee, *Python Programming Fundamentals,* Undergraduate Topics in Computer Science, **201**
DOI 10.1007/978-1-84996-537-8, © Springer-Verlag London Limited 2011

Method	Returns	Comments
x[[i]:[j]]	list	Returns the slice of items starting at index i and extending to index j-1 in the string. If i is omitted then the slice begins at index 0. If j is omitted then the slice extends to the end of the list. If i is negative then it returns the slice starting at index len(x)+i (and likewise for the slice ending at j).
x[i]=e		Assigns the position at index i the value of e in x. The list x must already have an item at index i before this assignment occurs. In other words, assigning an item to a list in this way will not extend the length of the list to accommodate it.
x+=y		This mutates the list x to append the items in y.
x*=i		This mutates the list x to be i copies of the original x.
iter(x)	iterator	Returns an iterator over x.
len(x)	int	Returns the number of items in x.
x*i	list	Returns a new list with the items of x repeated i times.
i*x	list	Returns a new list with the items of x repeated i times.
repr(x)	str	Returns a string representation of x.
x.append(e)	None	This mutates the value of x to add e as its last element. The function returns None, but the return value is irrelevant since it mutates x.
x.count(e)	int	Returns the number of occurrences of e in x by using == equality.
x.extend(iter)	None	Mutates x by appending elements from the iterable, iter.
x.index(e,[i,[j]])	int	Returns the first index of an element that == e between the start index, i, and the stop index, j-1. It raises ValueError if the value is not present in the specified sequence. If j is omitted then it searches to the end of the list. If i is omitted then it searches from the beginning of the list.
x.insert(i, e)	None	Insert e before index i in x, mutating x.
x.pop([index])	item	Remove and return the item at index. If index is omitted then the item at len(x)-1 is removed. The pop method returns the item and mutates x. It raises IndexError if list is empty or index is out of range.
x.remove(e)	None	remove first occurrence of e in x, mutating x. It raises ValueError if the value is not present.
x.reverse()	None	Reverses all the items in x, mutating x.
x.sort()	None	Sorts all the items of x according to their natural ordering as determined by the item's __cmp__ method, mutating x. Two keyword parameters are possible: key and reverse. If reverse=True is specified, then the result of sorting will have the list in reverse of the natural ordering. If key=f is specified then f must be a function that takes an item of x and returns the value of that item that should be used as the key when sorting.

Dictionary Operators and Methods

E

This documentation was generated from the Python documentation available by typing *help(dict)* in the Python shell. In the documentation found here the variable *D* is a reference to a dictionary. A few methods were omitted here for brevity.

Method	Returns	Comments
dict()	dict	new empty dictionary.
dict(mapping)	dict	new dictionary initialized from a mapping object's (key, value) pairs.
dict(seq)	dict	new dictionary initialized as if via: D = {} for k, v in seq: D[k] = v
dict(**kwargs)	dict	new dictionary initialized with the name=value pairs in the keyword arg list. For example: dict(one=1, two=2)
k in D	bool	True if D has key k, else False
del D[k]		Deletes key k from dictionary D.
D1==D2	bool	Returns True if dictionaries D1 and D2 have same keys mapped to same values.
D[k]	value type	Returns value k maps to in D. If k is not mapped, it raises a KeyError exception.
iter(D)	iterator	Returns an iterator over D.
len(D)	int	Returns the number of keys in D.
D1!=D2	bool	Returns True if D1 and D2 have any different keys or keys map to different values.
repr(D)	str	Returns a string representation of D.
D[k]=e		Stores the key,value pair k,e in D.
D.clear()	None	Remove all items from D.
D.copy()	dict	a shallow copy of D
D.get(k[,e])	value type	D[k] if k in D, else e. e defaults to None.
D.items()	items	a set-like object providing a view on D's items

K.D. Lee, *Python Programming Fundamentals,* Undergraduate Topics in Computer Science, **203**
DOI 10.1007/978-1-84996-537-8, © Springer-Verlag London Limited 2011

Method	Returns	Comments
D.keys()	keys	a set-like object providing a view on D's keys
D.pop(k[,e])	v	remove specified key and return the corresponding value. If key is not found, e is returned if given, otherwise KeyError is raised
D.popitem()	(k, v)	remove and return some (key, value) pair as a 2-tuple; but raise KeyError if D is empty.
D.setdefault(k[,e])	D.get(k,e)	Returns D.get(k,e) and also sets d[k]=e if k not in D
D.update(E, **F)	None	Update D from dict/iterable E and F. If E has a .keys() method, does: for k in E: D[k] = E[k] If E lacks .keys() method, does: for (k, v) in E: D[k] = v In either case, this is followed by: for k in F: D[k] = F[k]
D.values()	values	an object providing a view on D's values

Turtle Methods

F

This documentation was generated from the Python documentation available by typing

```
from turtle import *
help(Turtle)
```

in the Python shell. In the documentation found here the variable *turtle* is a reference to a Turtle object. This is a subset of that documentation. To see complete documentation use the Python help system as described above.

Method Description

turtle.back(distance)
Aliases: backward bk
 	
Argument:
distance – a number
 	
Move the turtle backward by distance, opposite to the direction the turtle is headed. Do not change the turtle's heading.
 	
Example (for a Turtle instance named turtle):
>>> turtle.position()
(0.00, 0.00)
>>> turtle.backward(30)
>>> turtle.position()
(-30.00, 0.00)

turtle.begin_fill()
Called just before drawing a shape to be filled.
 	
Example (for a Turtle instance named turtle):
>>> turtle.color("black", "red")
>>> turtle.begin_fill()
>>> turtle.circle(60)
>>> turtle.end_fill()

K.D. Lee, *Python Programming Fundamentals,* Undergraduate Topics in Computer Science, **205**
DOI 10.1007/978-1-84996-537-8, © Springer-Verlag London Limited 2011

Method Description
turtle.begin_poly()   Start recording the vertices of a polygon. Current turtle position   is first point of polygon.   Example (for a Turtle instance named turtle):   >>> turtle.begin_poly()

turtle.circle(radius, extent=None, steps=None)
 Arguments:
 radius—a number
 extent (optional)—a number
 steps (optional)—an integer
 	
 Draw a circle with given radius. The center is radius units left
 of the turtle; extent—an angle—determines which part of the
 circle is drawn. If extent is not given, draw the entire circle.
 If extent is not a full circle, one endpoint of the arc is the
 current pen position. Draw the arc in counterclockwise direction
 if radius is positive, otherwise in clockwise direction. Finally
 the direction of the turtle is changed by the amount of extent.
 	
 As the circle is approximated by an inscribed regular polygon,
 steps determines the number of steps to use. If not given,
 it will be calculated automatically. Maybe used to draw regular
 polygons.
 	
 call: circle(radius) # full circle
 –or: circle(radius, extent) # arc
 –or: circle(radius, extent, steps)
 –or: circle(radius, steps=6) # 6-sided polygon
 	
 Example (for a Turtle instance named turtle):
 >>> turtle.circle(50)
 >>> turtle.circle(120, 180) # semicircle

turtle.clear()   Delete the turtle's drawings from the screen. Do not move turtle.   State and position of the turtle as well as drawings of other   turtles are not affected.   Examples (for a Turtle instance named turtle):   >>> turtle.clear()
turtle.color(*args)   Arguments: Several input formats are allowed.   They use 0, 1, 2, or 3 arguments as follows: color()   Return the current pencolor and the current fillcolor   as a pair of color specification strings as are returned   by pencolor and fillcolor.

Method	Description

	color(colorstring), color((r,g,b)), color(r,g,b) inputs as in pencolor, set both, fillcolor and pencolor, to the given value. color(colorstring1, colorstring2), color((r1,g1,b1), (r2,g2,b2)) equivalent to pencolor(colorstring1) and fillcolor(colorstring2) and analogously, if the other input format is used. If turtleshape is a polygon, outline and interior of that polygon is drawn with the newly set colors. For mor info see: pencolor, fillcolor
	
	Example (for a Turtle instance named turtle):
	>>> turtle.color('red', 'green')
	>>> turtle.color()
	('red', 'green')
	>>> colormode(255)
	>>> color((40, 80, 120), (160, 200, 240))
	>>> color()
	('#285078', '#a0c8f0')

turtle.degrees()	Set the angle measurement units to degrees.
	
	Example (for a Turtle instance named turtle):
	>>> turtle.heading()
	1.5707963267948966
	>>> turtle.degrees()
	>>> turtle.heading()
	90.0

turtle.dot(size=None, *color)	Optional arguments:
	size—an integer >= 1 (if given)
	color—a colorstring or a numeric color tuple
	
	Draw a circular dot with diameter size, using color.
	If size is not given, the maximum of pensize+4 and 2*pensize is used.
	
	Example (for a Turtle instance named turtle):
	>>> turtle.dot()
	>>> turtle.fd(50); turtle.dot(20, "blue"); turtle.fd(50)

turtle.end_fill()	Fill the shape drawn after the call begin_fill().
	
	Example (for a Turtle instance named turtle):
	>>> turtle.color("black", "red")
	>>> turtle.begin_fill()
	>>> turtle.circle(60)
	>>> turtle.end_fill()

Method Description

turtle.end_poly()

    Stop recording the vertices of a polygon. Current turtle position is
    last point of polygon. This will be connected with the first point.

    Example (for a Turtle instance named turtle):
    >>> turtle.end_poly()

turtle.filling()

    Return fillstate (True if filling, False else).

    Example (for a Turtle instance named turtle):
    >>> turtle.begin_fill()
    >>> if turtle.filling():
        turtle.pensize(5)
        else:
        turtle.pensize(3)

turtle.fillcolor(*args)

    Return or set the fillcolor.

    Arguments:
    Four input formats are allowed:
    – fillcolor()
    Return the current fillcolor as color specification string,
    possibly in hex-number format (see example).
    May be used as input to another color/pencolor/fillcolor call.
    – fillcolor(colorstring)
    s is a Tk color specification string, such as "red" or "yellow"
    – fillcolor((r, g, b))
    a tuple of r, g, and b, which represent, an RGB color,
    and each of r, g, and b are in the range 0..colormode,
    where colormode is either 1.0 or 255
    – fillcolor(r, g, b)
    r, g, and b represent an RGB color, and each of r, g, and b
    are in the range 0..colormode

    If turtleshape is a polygon, the interior of that polygon is drawn
    with the newly set fillcolor.

    Example (for a Turtle instance named turtle):
    >>> turtle.fillcolor('violet')
    >>> col = turtle.pencolor()
    >>> turtle.fillcolor(col)
    >>> turtle.fillcolor(0, .5, 0)

turtle.forward(distance)

    Aliases: fd

    Argument:
    distance—a number (integer or float)

    Move the turtle forward by the specified distance, in the direction
    the turtle is headed.

Method Description

Example (for a Turtle instance named turtle):
>>> turtle.position()
(0.00, 0.00)
>>> turtle.forward(25)
>>> turtle.position()
(25.00,0.00)
>>> turtle.forward(-75)
>>> turtle.position()
(-50.00,0.00)

turtle.get_poly()
Return the lastly recorded polygon.
 	
Example (for a Turtle instance named turtle):
>>> p = turtle.get_poly()
>>> turtle.register_shape("myFavouriteShape", p)

turtle.get_shapepoly()
Return the current shape polygon as tuple of coordinate pairs.
 	
Examples (for a Turtle instance named turtle):
>>> turtle.shape("square")
>>> turtle.shapetransform(4, -1, 0, 2)
>>> turtle.get_shapepoly()
((50, -20), (30, 20), (-50, 20), (-30, -20))

turtle.getscreen()
Return the TurtleScreen object, the turtle is drawing on.
So TurtleScreen-methods can be called for that object.
 	
Example (for a Turtle instance named turtle):
>>> ts = turtle.getscreen()
>>> ts
<turtle.TurtleScreen object at 0x0106B770>
>>> ts.bgcolor("pink")

turtle.goto(x, y=None)
Aliases: setpos setposition
 	
Arguments:
x—a number or a pair/vector of numbers
y—a number None
 	
call: goto(x, y) # two coordinates
– or: goto((x, y)) # a pair (tuple) of coordinates
– or: goto(vec) # e.g. as returned by pos()
 	
Move turtle to an absolute position. If the pen is down,
a line will be drawn. The turtle's orientation does not change.
 	
Example (for a Turtle instance named turtle):
>>> tp = turtle.pos()
>>> tp

Method Description

(0.00, 0.00)
>>> turtle.setpos(60,30)
>>> turtle.pos()
(60.00,30.00)
>>> turtle.setpos((20,80))
>>> turtle.pos()
(20.00,80.00)
>>> turtle.setpos(tp)
>>> turtle.pos()
(0.00,0.00)

turtle.heading()
Return the turtle's current heading.
 	
Example (for a Turtle instance named turtle):
>>> turtle.left(67)
>>> turtle.heading()
67.0

turtle.hideturtle() Makes the turtle invisible. Aliases: ht It's a good idea to do this while you're in the middle of a complicated drawing, because hiding the turtle speeds up the drawing observably. Example (for a Turtle instance named turtle): >>> turtle.hideturtle()

turtle.isdown()
Return True if pen is down, False if it's up.
 	
Example (for a Turtle instance named turtle):
>>> turtle.penup()
>>> turtle.isdown()
False
>>> turtle.pendown()
>>> turtle.isdown()
True

turtle.isvisible()
Return True if the Turtle is shown, False if it's hidden.
 	
Example (for a Turtle instance named turtle):
>>> turtle.hideturtle()
>>> print(turtle.isvisible())
False

turtle.left(angle) Aliases: lt Argument: angle—a number (integer or float)

Method Description

Turn turtle left by angle units. (Units are by default degrees, but can be set via the degrees() and radians() functions.) Angle orientation depends on mode. (See this.)
 	
Example (for a Turtle instance named turtle):
>>> turtle.heading()
22.0
>>> turtle.left(45)
>>> turtle.heading()
67.0

turtle.onclick(fun, btn=1, add=None)
Bind fun to mouse-click event on this turtle on canvas.
 	
Arguments:
fun—a function with two arguments, to which will be assigned the coordinates of the clicked point on the canvas.
num—number of the mouse-button defaults to 1 (left mouse button).
add—True or False. If True, new binding will be added, otherwise it will replace a former binding.
 	
Example for the anonymous turtle, i.e. the procedural way:
 	
>>> def turn(x, y):
     turtle.left(360)
 	
>>> onclick(turn) # Now clicking into the turtle will turn it.
>>> onclick(None) # event-binding will be removed

turtle.ondrag(fun, btn=1, add=None) Bind fun to mouse-move event on this turtle on canvas. Arguments: fun—a function with two arguments, to which will be assigned the coordinates of the clicked point on the canvas. num—number of the mouse-button defaults to 1 (left mouse button). Every sequence of mouse-move-events on a turtle is preceded by a mouse-click event on that turtle. Example (for a Turtle instance named turtle): >>> turtle.ondrag(turtle.goto) ### Subsequently clicking and dragging a Turtle will ### move it across the screen thereby producing handdrawings ### (if pen is down).
turtle.onrelease(fun, btn=1, add=None) Bind fun to mouse-button-release event on this turtle on canvas. Arguments: fun—a function with two arguments, to which will be assigned the coordinates of the clicked point on the canvas. num— number of the mouse-button defaults to 1 (left mouse button).

Method Description
turtle.pencolor(*args)
Return or set the pencolor.
Arguments:
Four input formats are allowed:
– pencolor()
Return the current pencolor as color specification string,
possibly in hex-number format (see example).
May be used as input to another color/pencolor/fillcolor call.
– pencolor(colorstring)
s is a Tk color specification string, such as "red" or "yellow"
– pencolor((r, g, b))
a tuple of r, g, and b, which represent, an RGB color,
and each of r, g, and b are in the range 0..colormode,
where colormode is either 1.0 or 255
– pencolor(r, g, b)
r, g, and b represent an RGB color, and each of r, g, and b
are in the range 0..colormode
If turtleshape is a polygon, the outline of that polygon is drawn
with the newly set pencolor.
Example (for a Turtle instance named turtle):
>>> turtle.pencolor('brown')
>>> tup = (0.2, 0.8, 0.55)
>>> turtle.pencolor(tup)
>>> turtle.pencolor()
'#33cc8c'
turtle.pendown()
Pull the pen down—drawing when moving.
Aliases: pd down
Example (for a Turtle instance named turtle):
>>> turtle.pendown()
turtle.pensize(width=None)
Set or return the line thickness.
Aliases: width
Argument:
width—positive number
Set the line thickness to width or return it. If resizemode is set
to "auto" and turtleshape is a polygon, that polygon is drawn with
the same line thickness. If no argument is given, current pensize
is returned.
Example (for a Turtle instance named turtle):
>>> turtle.pensize()
1
turtle.pensize(10) # from here on lines of width 10 are drawn

Method Description

turtle.penup()
 	
    Pull the pen up—no drawing when moving.
 	
    Aliases: pu up
 	
    Example (for a Turtle instance named turtle):
    >>> turtle.penup()

turtle.radians()
 	
    Set the angle measurement units to radians.
 	
    Example (for a Turtle instance named turtle):
    >>> turtle.heading()
    90
    >>> turtle.radians()
    >>> turtle.heading()
    1.5707963267948966

turtle.reset()
 	
    Delete the turtle's drawings from the screen, re-center the turtle
    and set variables to the default values.
 	
    Example (for a Turtle instance named turtle):
    >>> turtle.position()
    (0.00,-22.00)
    >>> turtle.heading()
    100.0
    >>> turtle.reset()
    >>> turtle.position()
    (0.00,0.00)
    >>> turtle.heading()
    0.0

turtle.setheading(to_angle)
 	
    Set the orientation of the turtle to to_angle.
 	
    Aliases: seth
 	
    Argument:
    to_angle—a number (integer or float)
 	
    Set the orientation of the turtle to to_angle.
    Here are some common directions in degrees:
 	
    standard—mode: logo-mode:
    ————————————————
 	
    0 - east 0 - north
    90 - north 90 - east
    180 - west 180 - south
    270 - south 270 - west
 	
    Example (for a Turtle instance named turtle):
    >>> turtle.setheading(90)
    >>> turtle.heading()
    90

Method Description
turtle.shape(name=None)

Set turtle shape to shape with given name / return current shapename.

Optional argument:
name—a string, which is a valid shapename

Set turtle shape to shape with given name or, if name is not given,
return name of current shape.
Shape with name must exist in the TurtleScreen's shape dictionary.
Initially there are the following polygon shapes:
'arrow', 'turtle', 'circle', 'square', 'triangle', 'classic'.
To learn about how to deal with shapes see Screen-method register_shape.

Example (for a Turtle instance named turtle):
>>> turtle.shape()
'arrow'
>>> turtle.shape("turtle")
>>> turtle.shape()
'turtle'

turtle.showturtle()

Makes the turtle visible.

Aliases: st

Example (for a Turtle instance named turtle):
>>> turtle.hideturtle()
>>> turtle.showturtle()

turtle.speed(speed=None)

Return or set the turtle's speed.

Optional argument:
speed—an integer in the range 0..10 or a speedstring (see below)

Set the turtle's speed to an integer value in the range 0 .. 10.
If no argument is given: return current speed.

If input is a number greater than 10 or smaller than 0.5,
speed is set to 0.
Speedstrings are mapped to speedvalues in the following way:
'fastest' : 0
'fast' : 10
'normal' : 6
'slow' : 3
'slowest' : 1
speeds from 1 to 10 enforce increasingly faster animation of
line drawing and turtle turning.

Attention:
speed = 0 : *no* animation takes place. forward/back makes turtle jump
and likewise left/right make the turtle turn instantly.

Example (for a Turtle instance named turtle):
>>> turtle.speed(3)

Method Description
turtle.undo()
Undo (repeatedly) the last turtle action.
Number of available undo actions is determined by the size of
the undobuffer.
Example (for a Turtle instance named turtle):
>>> for i in range(4):
turtle.fd(50); turtle.lt(80)
>>> for i in range(8):
turtle.undo()
turtle.write(arg, move=False, align='left', font=('Arial', 8, 'normal'))
Write text at the current turtle position.
Arguments:
arg—info, which is to be written to the TurtleScreen
move (optional)—True/False
align (optional)—one of the strings "left", "center" or "right"
font (optional)—a triple (fontname, fontsize, fonttype)
Write text—the string representation of arg—at the current
turtle position according to align ("left", "center" or "right")
and with the given font.
If move is True, the pen is moved to the bottom-right corner
of the text. By default, move is False.
Example (for a Turtle instance named turtle):
>>> turtle.write('Home = ', True, align="center")
>>> turtle.write((0,0), True)
turtle.xcor()
Return the turtle's x coordinate.
Example (for a Turtle instance named turtle):
>>> reset()
>>> turtle.left(60)
>>> turtle.forward(100)
>>> print(turtle.xcor())
50.0
turtle.ycor()
Return the turtle's y coordinate
Example (for a Turtle instance named turtle):
>>> reset()
>>> turtle.left(60)
>>> turtle.forward(100)
>>> print(turtle.ycor())
86.6025403784

This documentation was generated from the Python documentation available by typing

from turtle **import** *
help(TurtleScreen)

in the Python shell. In the documentation found here the variable *turtle* is a reference to a Turtle object and *screen* is a reference to the *TurtleScreen* object. This is a subset of that documentation. To see complete documentation use the Python help system as described above.

Method Description
screen.addshape(name)   Same thing as screen.register_shape(name)

screen.bgcolor(*args)
  Set or return backgroundcolor of the TurtleScreen.
 	
  Arguments (if given): a color string or three numbers
  in the range 0..colormode or a 3-tuple of such numbers.
 	
  Example (for a TurtleScreen instance named screen):
  >>> screen.bgcolor("orange")
  >>> screen.bgcolor()
  'orange'
  >>> screen.bgcolor(0.5,0,0.5)
  >>> screen.bgcolor()
  '#800080'

screen.bgpic(picname=None)
  Set background image or return name of current backgroundimage.
 	
  Optional argument:
  picname—a string, name of a gif-file or "nopic".

K.D. Lee, *Python Programming Fundamentals,* Undergraduate Topics in Computer Science, DOI 10.1007/978-1-84996-537-8, © Springer-Verlag London Limited 2011

Method Description

If picname is a filename, set the corresponding image as background. If picname is "nopic", delete backgroundimage, if present. If picname is None, return the filename of the current backgroundimage.
 	
Example (for a TurtleScreen instance named screen):
>>> screen.bgpic()
'nopic'
>>> screen.bgpic("landscape.gif")
>>> screen.bgpic()
'landscape.gif'

screen.clear()

Delete all drawings and all turtles from the TurtleScreen.

Reset empty TurtleScreen to its initial state: white background, no backgroundimage, no eventbindings and tracing on.

Example (for a TurtleScreen instance named screen):
screen.clear()

Note: this method is not available as function.

screen.colormode(cmode=None)

Return the colormode or set it to 1.0 or 255.

Optional argument:
cmode—one of the values 1.0 or 255

r, g, b values of colortriples have to be in range 0..cmode.

Example (for a TurtleScreen instance named screen):
>>> screen.colormode()
1.0
>>> screen.colormode(255)
>>> turtle.pencolor(240,160,80)

screen.delay(delay=None)

Return or set the drawing delay in milliseconds.

Optional argument:
delay—positive integer

Example (for a TurtleScreen instance named screen):
>>> screen.delay(15)
>>> screen.delay()
15

screen.getcanvas()

Return the Canvas of this TurtleScreen.

Example (for a Screen instance named screen):
>>> cv = screen.getcanvas()
>>> cv
<turtle.ScrolledCanvas instance at 0x010742D8>

Method Description
screen.getshapes() Return a list of names of all currently available turtle shapes. Example (for a TurtleScreen instance named screen): >>> screen.getshapes() ['arrow', 'blank', 'circle', ..., 'turtle']
screen.listen(xdummy=None, ydummy=None) Set focus on TurtleScreen (in order to collect key-events) Dummy arguments are provided in order to be able to pass listen to the onclick method. Example (for a TurtleScreen instance named screen): >>> screen.listen()

screen.mode(mode=None)
Set turtle-mode ('standard', 'logo' or 'world') and perform reset.
 	
Optional argument:
mode—on of the strings 'standard', 'logo' or 'world'
 	
Mode 'standard' is compatible with turtle.py.
Mode 'logo' is compatible with most Logo-Turtle-Graphics.
Mode 'world' uses userdefined 'worldcoordinates'. *Attention*: in
this mode angles appear distorted if x/y unit-ratio doesn't equal 1.
If mode is not given, return the current mode.
 	
Mode Initial turtle heading positive angles
 	
'standard' to the right (east) counterclockwise
'logo' upward (north) clockwise
 	
Examples:
>>> mode('logo') # resets turtle heading to north
>>> mode()
'logo'

screen.onclick(fun, btn=1, add=None)
Bind fun to mouse-click event on canvas.
 	
Arguments:
fun—a function with two arguments, the coordinates of the
clicked point on the canvas.
num—the number of the mouse-button, defaults to 1
 	
Example (for a TurtleScreen instance named screen
and a Turtle instance named turtle):
 	
>>> screen.onclick(turtle.goto)
 	
### Subsequently clicking into the TurtleScreen will 	
### make the turtle move to the clicked point. 	
>>> screen.onclick(None)
 	
### event-binding will be removed 	

Method Description

screen.onkey(fun, key)
>   Bind fun to key-release event of key.
>
>   Arguments:
>   fun—a function with no arguments
>   key—a string: key (e.g. "a") or key-symbol (e.g. "space")
>
>   In order to be able to register key-events, TurtleScreen
>   must have focus. (See method listen.)
>
>   Example (for a TurtleScreen instance named screen
>   and a Turtle instance named turtle):
>
>   >>> def f():
>   turtle.fd(50)
>   turtle.lt(60)
>
>
>   >>> screen.onkey(f, "Up")
>   >>> screen.listen()
>
>   ### Subsequently the turtle can be moved by
>   ### repeatedly pressing the up-arrow key,
>   ### consequently drawing a hexagon

screen.onkeypress(fun, key=None)
>   Bind fun to key-press event of key if key is given,
>   or to any key-press-event if no key is given.
>
>   Arguments:
>   fun—a function with no arguments
>   key—a string: key (e.g. "a") or key-symbol (e.g. "space")
>
>   In order to be able to register key-events, TurtleScreen
>   must have focus. (See method listen.)
>
>   Example (for a TurtleScreen instance named screen
>   and a Turtle instance named turtle):
>
>   >>> def f():
>   turtle.fd(50)
>
>
>   >>> screen.onkey(f, "Up")
>   >>> screen.listen()
>
>   ### Subsequently the turtle can be moved by
>   ### repeatedly pressing the up-arrow key,
>   ### or by keeping pressed the up-arrow key.
>   ### consequently drawing a hexagon.

Method Description

screen.ontimer(fun, t=0)
 Install a timer, which calls fun after t milliseconds.
 	
 Arguments:
 fun—a function with no arguments.
 t—a number >= 0
 	
 Example (for a TurtleScreen instance named screen):
 	
 >>> running = True
 >>> def f():
 if running:
       turtle.fd(50)
       turtle.lt(60)
       screen.ontimer(f, 250)
 	
 >>> f() ### makes the turtle marching around
 >>> running = False

screen.register_shape(name, shape=None)   Adds a turtle shape to TurtleScreen's shapelist.   Arguments: (1) name is the name of a gif-file and shape is None.   Installs the corresponding image shape.   !! Image-shapes DO NOT rotate when turning the turtle,   !! so they do not display the heading of the turtle!   (2) name is an arbitrary string and shape is a tuple   of pairs of coordinates. Installs the corresponding   polygon shape   (3) name is an arbitrary string and shape is a   (compound) Shape object. Installs the corresponding   compound shape.   To use a shape, you have to issue the command shape(shapename).   call: register_shape("turtle.gif")   –or: register_shape("tri", ((0,0), (10,10), (-10,10)))   Example (for a TurtleScreen instance named screen):   >>> screen.register_shape("triangle", ((5,-3),(0,5),(-5,-3)))
screen.reset()   Reset all Turtles on the Screen to their initial state.   Example (for a TurtleScreen instance named screen):   >>> screen.reset()

Method Description
screen.screensize(canvwidth=None, canvheight=None, bg=None) Resize the canvas the turtles are drawing on. Optional arguments: canvwidth—positive integer, new width of canvas in pixels canvheight— positive integer, new height of canvas in pixels bg—colorstring or color-tupel, new backgroundcolor If no arguments are given, return current (canvaswidth, canvasheight) Do not alter the drawing window. To observe hidden parts of the canvas use the scrollbars. (Can make visible those parts of a drawing, which were outside the canvas before!) Example (for a Turtle instance named turtle): >>> turtle.screensize(2000,1500) ### e.g. to search for an erroneously escaped turtle ;-)

screen.setworldcoordinates(llx, lly, urx, ury)
Set up a user defined coordinate-system.
 	
Arguments:
llx—a number, x-coordinate of lower left corner of canvas
lly—a number, y-coordinate of lower left corner of canvas
urx—a number, x-coordinate of upper right corner of canvas
ury—a number, y-coordinate of upper right corner of canvas
 	
Set up user coodinat-system and switch to mode 'world' if necessary.
This performs a screen.reset. If mode 'world' is already active,
all drawings are redrawn according to the new coordinates.
 	
But ATTENTION: in user-defined coordinatesystems angles may appear
distorted. (see Screen.mode())
 	
Example (for a TurtleScreen instance named screen):
>>> screen.setworldcoordinates(-10,-0.5,50,1.5)
>>> for _ in range(36):
    turtle.left(10)
    turtle.forward(0.5)

screen.title(titlestr) Set the title of the Turtle Graphics screen. The title appears in the title bar of the window.

Method Description

screen.tracer(n=None, delay=None)

Turns turtle animation on/off and set delay for update drawings.

Optional arguments:
n—nonnegative integer
delay—nonnegative integer

If n is given, only each n-th regular screen update is really performed.
(Can be used to accelerate the drawing of complex graphics.)
Second arguments sets delay value (see RawTurtle.delay())

Example (for a TurtleScreen instance named screen):
```
>>> screen.tracer(8, 25)
>>> dist = 2
>>> for i in range(200):
        turtle.fd(dist)
        turtle.rt(90)
        dist += 2
```

screen.turtles()

Return the list of turtles on the screen.

Example (for a TurtleScreen instance named screen):
```
>>> screen.turtles()
[<turtle.Turtle object at 0x00E11FB0>]
```

screen.update()

Perform a TurtleScreen update.

screen.window_height()

Return the height of the turtle window.

Example (for a TurtleScreen instance named screen):
```
>>> screen.window_height()
480
```

screen.window_width()

Return the width of the turtle window.

Example (for a TurtleScreen instance named screen):
```
>>> screen.window_width()
640
```

screen.mainloop()

Starts event loop—calling Tkinter's mainloop function.

Must be last statement in a turtle graphics program.
Must NOT be used if a script is run from within IDLE in -n mode
(No subprocess)—for interactive use of turtle graphics.

Example (for a TurtleScreen instance named screen):
```
>>> screen.mainloop()
```

Method Description

screen.numinput(title, prompt, default=None, minval=None, maxval=None)
Pop up a dialog window for input of a number.

Arguments: title is the title of the dialog window,
prompt is a text mostly describing what numerical information to input.
default: default value
minval: minimum value for imput
maxval: maximum value for input

The number input must be in the range minval .. maxval if these are
given. If not, a hint is issued and the dialog remains open for
correction. Return the number input.
If the dialog is canceled, return None.

Example (for a TurtleScreen instance named screen):
>>> screen.numinput("Poker", "Your stakes:", 1000, minval=10, maxval=10000)

screen.textinput(title, prompt)
Pop up a dialog window for input of a string.

Arguments: title is the title of the dialog window,
prompt is a text mostly describing what information to input.

Return the string input
If the dialog is canceled, return None.

Example (for a TurtleScreen instance named screen):
>>> screen.textinput("NIM", "Name of first player:")

```
1   import sys
2   import tkinter
3   import tkinter.messagebox
4   import os
5
6   def addReminder(text,x,y,notes,reminders):
7       notewin = tkinter.Toplevel()
8       notewin.resizable(width=False,height=False)
9       notewin.geometry("+"+str(x)+"+"+str(y))
10
11      reminder = tkinter.Text(notewin,bg=``yellow'', width=30,height=15)
12
13      reminder.insert(tkinter.END,text)
14
15      reminder.pack()
16
17      notes.append(notewin)
18      reminders.append(reminder)
19
20
21      def deleteWindowHandler():
22          print("Window Deleted")
23          notewin.withdraw()
24          notes.remove(notewin)
25              reminders.remove(reminder)
26
27      notewin.protocol("WM_DELETE_WINDOW", deleteWindowHandler)
28
29
30  def main():
31
32      def post():
33              print("Post")
34          addReminder(note.get("1.0",tkinter.END), \
35                  root.winfo_rootx()+5,root.winfo_rooty()+5,notes,reminders)
36          note.delete("1.0",tkinter.END)
37
38      root = tkinter.Tk()
39
40      root.title("Reminder!")
41      root.resizable(width=False,height=False)
42
43      notes = []
44      reminders = []
45
46      bar = tkinter.Menu(root)
47
```

K.D. Lee, *Python Programming Fundamentals*, Undergraduate Topics in Computer Science, **225**
DOI 10.1007/978-1-84996-537-8, © Springer-Verlag London Limited 2011

```
48      fileMenu = tkinter.Menu(bar,tearoff=0)
49      fileMenu.add_command(label="Exit",command=root.quit)
50      bar.add_cascade(label="File",menu=fileMenu)
51      root.config(menu=bar)
52
53      mainFrame = tkinter.Frame(root,borderwidth=1,padx=5,pady=5)
54      mainFrame.pack()
55
56      note = tkinter.Text(mainFrame,bg=``yellow'', width=30,height=15)
57      note.pack()
58
59      tkinter.Button(mainFrame,text="New Reminder!", command=post).pack()
60
61      try:
62          print("reading reminders.txt file")
63          file = open("reminders.txt","r")
64          x = int(file.readline())
65          y = int(file.readline())
66          root.geometry("+"+str(x)+"+"+str(y))
67
68          line = file.readline()
69          while line.strip() != "":
70              x = int(line)
71              y = int(file.readline())
72              text = ""
73              line = file.readline()
74              while line.strip() != "____.…._____._._._":
75                  text = text + line
76                  line = file.readline()
77
78              text = text.strip()
79
80              addReminder(text,x,y,notes,reminders)
81
82              line = file.readline()
83      except:
84          print("reminders.txt not found")
85
86
87
88      def appClosing():
89          print("Application Closing")
90          file = open("reminders.txt","w")
91
92          file.write(str(root.winfo_x())+"\n")
93          file.write(str(root.winfo_y())+"\n")
94
95          for i in range(len(notes)):
96              print(notes[i].winfo_rootx())
97              print(notes[i].winfo_rooty())
98              print(reminders[i].get("1.0",tkinter.END))
99
100             file.write(str(notes[i].winfo_rootx())+"\n")
101             file.write(str(notes[i].winfo_rooty())+"\n")
102             file.write(reminders[i].get("1.0",tkinter.END)+"\n")
103             file.write("____.…._____._._._\n")
104
105         file.close()
106         root.destroy()
107         root.quit()
108         sys.exit()
109
110
111     root.protocol("WM_DELETE_WINDOW", appClosing)
112
113
114     tkinter.mainloop()
115
116  if __name__ == "__main__":
117      main()
```

```
1   from turtle import *
2   import tkinter
3   import random
4
5   screenMaxX = 300
6   screenMaxY = 300
7   screenMinX = -300
8   screenMinY = -300
9
10  # This is a example of a class that uses inheritance.
11  # The Ball class inherits from the RawTurtle class.
12  # This is indicated to Python by writing
13  # class Ball(RawTurtle):
14  # That says, class Ball inherits from RawTurtle, which
15  # means that a Ball is also a RawTurtle, but it is a
16  # little more than just a RawTurtle. The Ball class also
17  # maintains a dx and dy value that is the amount
18  # to move as it is animated.
19  class Ball(RawTurtle):
20      # The __init__ is the CONSTRUCTOR. Its purpose is to
21      # initialize the object by storing data in the object. Anytime
22      # self.variable = value is written a value is being stored in
23      # the object referred to by self. self always points to the
24      # current object.
25      def __init__(self,cv,dx,dy):
26          # Because the Ball class inherits from the RawTurtle class
27          # the Ball class constructor must call the RawTurtle class
28          # constructor to initialize the RawTurtle part of the object.
29          # The RawTurtle class is called the BASE class. The Ball class
30          # is called the DERIVED class. The call to initialize the
31          # base class part of the object is always the first thing
32          # you do in the derived class's constructor.
33          RawTurtle.__init__(self,cv)
34
35          # Then the rest of the object can be initialized.
36          self.penup()
37          self.shape("soccerball.gif")
38          self.dx = dx
39          self.dy = dy
40
41      # The move method is a mutator method. It changes the data
42      # of the object by adding something to the Ball's x and y
43      # position.
44      def move(self):
```

```
45                    newx = self.xcor() + self.dx
46                    newy = self.ycor() + self.dy
47
48                    # The if statements below make the ball
49                    # bounce off the walls.
50                    if newx < screenMinX:
51                        newx = 2 * screenMinX - newx
52                        self.dx = -self.dx
53                    if newy < screenMinY:
54                        newy = 2 * screenMinY - newy
55                        self.dy = - self.dy
56                    if newx > screenMaxX:
57                        newx = 2 * screenMaxX - newx
58                        self.dx = - self.dx
59                    if newy > screenMaxY:
60                        newy = 2 * screenMaxY - newy
61                        self.dy = -self.dy
62
63                    # Then we call a method on the RawTurtle
64                    # to move to the new x and y position.
65                    self.goto(newx,newy)
66
67    # Once the classes and functions have been defined we'll put our
68    # main function at the bottom of the file. Main isn't necessarily
69    # written last. It's simply put at the bottom of the file. Main
70    # is not a method. It is a plain function because it is not
71    # defined inside any class.
72    def main():
73
74        # Start by creating a RawTurtle object for the window.
75        root = tkinter.Tk()
76        root.title("Bouncing Balls!")
77        cv = ScrolledCanvas(root,600,600,600,600)
78        cv.pack(side = tkinter.LEFT)
79        t = RawTurtle(cv)
80        fram = tkinter.Frame(root)
81        fram.pack(side = tkinter.RIGHT,fill=tkinter.BOTH)
82
83        screen = t.getscreen()
84        screen.setworldcoordinates(screenMinX,screenMinY,screenMaxX,
85                                    screenMaxY)
86        t.ht()
87        screen.tracer(20)
88        screen.register_shape("soccerball.gif")
89
90        # The ballList is a list of all the ball objects. This
91        # list is needed so the balls can be animated by the
92        # program.
93        ballList = []
94
95        # Here is the animation handler. It is called at
96        # every timer event.
97        def animate():
98            # Tell all the balls to move
99            for ball in ballList:
100               ball.move()
101
102           # Set the timer to go off again
103           screen.ontimer(animate)
104
105       # This code creates 10 balls heading
106       # in random directions
107       for k in range(10):
108           dx = random.random() * 3 + 1
109           dy = random.random() * 3 + 1
110           # Here is how a ball object is created. We
```

```
111          # write ball = Ball(5,4)
112          # to create an instance of the Ball class
113          # and point the ball reference at that object.
114          # That way we can refer to the object by writing
115          # ball.
116          ball = Ball(cv,dx,dy)
117          # Each new ball is added to the Ball list so
118          # it can be accessed by the animation handler.
119          ballList.append(ball)
120
121      # This is the code for the quit Button handling. This
122      # function will be passed to the quitButton so it can
123      # be called by the quitButton when it wasPressed.
124      def quitHandler():
125          # close the window and quit
126          print("Good Bye")
127          root.destroy()
128          root.quit()
129
130      # Here is where the quitButton is created. To create
131      # an object we write
132      # objectReference = Class(<Parameters to Constructor>)
133      quitButton = tkinter.Button(fram, text = "Quit", command=quitHandler)
134      quitButton.pack()
135
136      # This is another example of a method call. We've been doing
137      # this all semester. It is an ontimer method call to the
138      # TurtleScreen object referred to by screen.
139      screen.ontimer(animate)
140
141      tkinter.mainloop()
142
143  if __name__ == "__main__":
144      main()
```

Glossary

API An abbreviation for Application Programming Interface An API is a collection of functions that provide some service or services to an application

ASCII Abbreviation for the American Standard Code for Information Interchange

American Standard Code for Information Interchange A widely accepted standard for the representation of characters within a computer

CPU The abbreviation of Central Processing Unit

GUI An abbreviation for Graphical User Interface

I/O device An Input/Output device. The device is capable of both storing and retrieving information

IDE An abbreviation for Integrated Development Environment

Linux A freely available open source operating system originated by Linus Torvalds

Mac OS X An operating system developed and supported by Apple, Inc.

Microsoft Windows An operating system developed and supported by Microsoft Corporation

None A special value which is the only value of its type, the NoneType

Python An interpreted programming language

Tk A windowing toolkit or API available for a variety of operating systems

Wing IDE 101 A freely available IDE for educational purposes available from www. wingware.com

XML A meta-language for describing hierarchically organized data. XML stands for eXtensible Markup Language

XML element One node in an XML file that is delimited by start and end tags

accessor method A method that accesses the data of an object (and returns some of it) but does not change the object

accumulator A variable that is used to count something in a program

accumulator pattern An idiom for counting in a program

activation record An area of memory that holds a copy of each variable that is defined in the local scope of an actively executing function

address The name of a byte within memory Addresses are sequentially assigned starting at 0 and continuing to the limit of the CPU's addressable space

arguments Values passed to a method that affect the action that the method performs

K.D. Lee, *Python Programming Fundamentals,* Undergraduate Topics in Computer Science, 231
DOI 10.1007/978-1-84996-537-8, © Springer-Verlag London Limited 2011

assignment statement A fundamental operation of storing a value in a named location in a program

binary A counting system composed of 0's and 1's, the only numbers a computer can store

bit A memory location that can hold a 0 or 1

bool The name of the type for True and False representation in Python

bottom-up design A design process where smaller tasks are implemented first and then the solutions, usually in the form of functions or classes, to these smaller tasks are integrated into a solution for a bigger problem

byte Eight bits grouped together. A byte is the smallest unit of addressable memory in a computer

central processing unit The brain of a computer. Often abbreviated CPU

class A collection of methods that all work with the data of a particular type of object. A class and a type are synonymous in Python

computer An electronic device that can be programmed to complete a variety of data processing tasks

constructor A part of a class that is responsible for initializing the data of an object

debugger A program that lets a programmer set breakpoints, look at variables, and trace the execution of a programmer the programmer is developing

delimiter A special character or characters, usually occurring in pairs that sets some text off from surrounding text

dict A type of value that stores key/value pairs in Python

dictionary A mapping from keys to values. The key can be any hashable object. The value can be any object. Keys within the dictionary must be unique. Values do not have to be unique

event An abstraction used to describe the availability of some input to a program that became available while the program was executing. Event-driven programs are written so they can respond to events when the occur

exception A mechanism for handling abnormal conditions during the execution of a program

file A grouping of related data that can be read by a computer program. It is usually stored on a hard drive, but may be stored on a network or any other I/O device

float The name of the type for real number representation in Python

formal parameter A name given to an argument when it is passed to a function

function A sequence of code that is given a name and may be called when appropriate in a program. A Function is passed arguments so it can perform an appropriate action for the current state of the program

garbage collector A part of the Python interpreter that periodically looks for objects in memory that no longer have any references pointing to them. When such an object is found the garbage collector returns the storage for the object to the available memory for creating new objects

gigabyte $1024 = 2^{10}$ megabytes. Abbreviated GB

guess and check A pattern or idiom that can be used to discover a property of the data a program is working with

hard drive An Input/Output device containing non-volatile storage. The contents of the hard drive are not erased when the power is turned off

hashable A technical term that means that the object can be quickly converted to an integer through some encoding of the data within the object

hexadecimal A counting system where each digit has sixteen different values including 0–9 and A–F

hook A means by which a program allows another program to modify its behavior. The Python interpreter has several hooks that allow a programmer

idiom When used in the context of computer programming, an idiom is a short sequence of code that can be used in certain recurring situations

if-then statement A statement where the evaluation of a condition determines which code will executed

immutable A object that cannot be changed once it is created is said to be immutable. Strings, ints, floats, and bools are examples of immutable types. Lists are not immutable

index An integer used to select an item from a sequence. Indices start at 0 for the first item in a sequence

inheritance The reuse of code in object-oriented programming. The reuse makes sense when there is an is-a relationship between two class. For instance, a Circle is-a Shape

instruction A simple command understood by the CPU. For instance, two numbers can be added together by an instruction

int The name of the integer type in Python

integrated development environment A program that includes an editor and debugger for editing and debugging computer programs

interpreter A program that reads another program and executes the statements found there

iteration Repeating the execution of several statements of a program, more than once. The statement are written once, but a loop construct repeats the execution of the statements when the program executes

kilobyte $1024 = 2^{10}$ bytes. Abbreviated KB

list The name of the type for list representation in Python

loop See iteration

megabyte $1024 = 2^{10}$ kilobytes. Abbreviated MB

memory A random access device that stores a program and data while the program is executing. Frequently memory is called RAM, which stands for Random Access Memory

method A sequence of code that accesses or updates the data of an object. A method is an action we take on an object

module A file containing code in Python. Files or modules may be imported into other modules using an *import* statement. Modules must end in *.py* to be imported

mutator method A method that changes or mutates the data of an object

object A grouping of data and the valid operations on that data

octal A counting system where each digit has eight possibilities including 0–7

operator A method that is not called using the *reference.method(arguments)* format

parallel lists A set of two or more lists where corresponding locations within the multiple lists contiain related information. Using parallel lists is a programming technique for maintaining lists of information when there are many values that correspond to one record

polymorphism Literally meaning many forms, polymorphism in computer science refers to the right version of a method being called when the same method occurs in more than one type of object. Python supports polymorphism by dynamically looking up the correct method each time it is called in the object it is called on

predicate A function that returns True or False

python shell An interactive session with the Python interpreter

record A grouping of data in a file (for example several lines in a file) that are related to one entity in some way

recursion When a function calls itself it is said to be recursive. Recursion occurs when the function is executing and either directly or indirectly calls itself

reference A pointer that points to an object. A reference is the address of an object in memory

run-time error An error in a program discovered while the interpreter is executing the program

run-time stack A data structure that is used by Python to execute programs. It is a stack of activation records

scope The area in a program where a variable is defined. Scope becomes a factor when writing functions which define a new local scope. The LEGB rule [3] helps us remember there is local, enclosing, global, and built-in scopes in Python

self A reference that points at the current object when a method is executing. Python makes self point to the object that the method was called on

sequence A grouping of like data that can be iterated over. Lists and strings are sequences

set A container type in Python

short-circuit logic An evaluation strategy where a boolean expression is evaluated from left to right only until the truth or falsity of the expression is determined. Any error condition that may have occurred by evaluating further to the right will not be found if the expression's value is known before the offending part is encountered. For instance $5 > 6$ and $6/0 == 1$ would evaluate to False, and would not raise an exception using short-circuit logic

stack See run-time stack

statement The smallest executable unit in the Python programming language

step into The term used when the debugger stops during the execution of the next instruction at any intermediate computation that is performed

step over The term used when a debugger stops after the next statement is executed. Stepping over does not stop at any intermediate computations

str The name of the type for string representation in Python

subclass A class that inherits from another class called the superclass. A subclass is also called a derived class

superclass A class that was inherited from to make a subclass. A superclass is also called a base class

syntactic sugar The ability to write the same thing in at least two ways in a language, one of which is preferable to the other

syntax error An error in the format of a program. Syntax errors are found by the interpreter before actually running a program

tag A delimiter in an XML file

terabyte $1024 = 2^{10}$ gigabytes. Abbreviated TB

top-down design A design process where details are left until later and the main part of the program is written first calling functions that will eventually take care of the details

tuple An aggregate type in Python

turtle A module in Python that provides an abstraction for drawing pictures

type An interpretation of a group of bytes in memory. Certain operations are valid only for certain types of values

volatile store Refers to the properties of a device. Volatile store loses its contents when the power is turned off

while loop A statement used for indefinite iteration. Indefinite means there is no sequence being iterated over in a while loop. Instead the iteration continues until a condition becomes False

widget An element of a GUI application

word Usually four bytes group together. Typically a word is used to store integers in a computer

References

1. James H. Cross, II, T. Dean Hendrix, and Larry A. Barowski. Using the debugger as an integral part of teaching cs1, 2002.
2. David Flanagan and Yukihiro Matsumoto. *The ruby programming language.* O'Reilly, Sebastopol, CA, 2008.
3. Mark Lutz. *Learning Python.* O'Reilly & Associates, Inc., Sebastopol, CA, USA, 2003.
4. Money Magazine. Best jobs in america, 2006. [Online; accessed 1/29/2010; http://money.cnn.com/popups/2006/moneymag/bestjobs/frameset.exclude.html].
5. Alex Martelli. *Python in a Nutshell. A Desktop Quick Reference; 2nd ed.* Nutshell handbook. O'Reilly, Sebastopol, CA, 2006.
6. Robin Milner. A theory of type polymorphism in programming. *Journal of Computer and System Sciences,* 17:348–375, 1978.
7. The U.S. Consitution Online. Steve mount, 2010. [Online; accessed 1/29/2010; http://www.usconstitution.net/const.html#A2Sec1].
8. Mark Pilgrim. Porting code to python 3 with 2to3, 2010. [Online; accessed 1/29/2010; http://diveintopython3.org/porting-code-to-python-3-with-2to3.html].
9. Arild Stubhaug. *The Mathematician Sophus Lie.* Springer, Berlin, Germany, 2002.
10. Guido van Rossum. Guido's personal home page, 2010. [Online; accessed 1/29/2010; http://www.python.org/~guido/].
11. Brent B. Welch. *Practical programming in Tcl and Tk (3rd ed.).* Prentice Hall PTR, Upper Saddle River, NJ, USA, 2000.
12. Wikipedia. Ascii, 2010. [Online; accessed 1/29/2010; http://en.wikipedia.org/wiki/ASCII].
13. Wikipedia. George boole, 2010. [Online; accessed 1/29/2010; http://en.wikipedia.org/wiki/George_Boole].
14. Wikipedia. Logo (programming language), 2010. [Online; accessed 1/29/2010; http://en.wikipedia.org/wiki/Logo_(programming_language)].
15. Wikipedia. W. edwards deming, 2010. [Online; accessed 1/29/2010; http://en.wikipedia.org/wiki/William_Deming].

Index

Made in the USA
Lexington, KY
27 February 2012